THE PENGUIN GOOD NEW ZEALAND WINE GUIDE

Vic Williams was born in Rawene and educated at St Paul's College, Auckland. As a teenager he developed a keen interest in food and wine, and numerous trips to Europe and Asia have broadened his knowledge of other cuisines. His enthusiasm for the food and wine of New Zealand has led to his present career as a writer and broadcaster.

For three years he was the food and wine presenter for Television One's *Weekend* programme and in 1990 he wrote *Summer Cooking With Vic Williams* to accompany that television programme. His writing appears in several magazines and newspapers throughout New Zealand, he is a consultant to The New Zealand Wine Society, and he broadcasts regularly on a number of local radio stations. He has delivered presentations on New Zealand wine in Seattle, New York, California and Hong Kong.

Vic lives in Auckland with his wife Shirley and enjoys entertaining friends at their home in Freemans Bay.

PENGUIN BOOKS

Penguin Books (NZ) Ltd, 182–190 Wairau Road, Auckland 10, New Zealand
Penguin Books Ltd, 27 Wrights Lane, London W8 5TZ, England
Penguin USA, 375 Hudson Street, New York, NY 10014, United States
Penguin Books Australia Ltd, 487 Maroondah Highway, Ringwood, Australia 3134
Penguin Books Canada Ltd, 10 Alcorn Avenue, Toronto, Ontario, Canada M4V 3B2

Penguin Books Ltd, Registered Offices: Harmondsworth, Middlesex, England
First published 1993
10 9 8 7 6 5 4 3 2 1
Copyright © Vic Williams, 1993
All rights reserved

Designed by Jonathan King
Printed in New Zealand by G.P. Print Limited

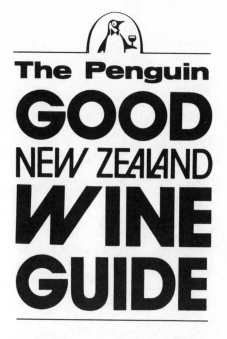

The Penguin
GOOD
NEW ZEALAND
WINE
GUIDE

1993 EDITION

Vic Williams

PENGUIN BOOKS

Contents

Introduction

Welcome to the 1993 edition of *The Penguin Good New Zealand Wine Guide*, a book written as much for people still feeling their way into the wonderful world of wine as for long-time enthusiasts who want an unbiased opinion before committing themselves to a previously untried bottle.

The *1992 Guide* was designed to take the mystique out of wine buying. Wine is made to be enjoyed; and if you're nervous about buying or serving the 'wrong' bottle, that enjoyment can be ruined.

Yet wine appreciation is purely subjective, so if you enjoy a wine that people you know have dismissed as rubbish, don't be put off. If you think it's good, it *is* good — pure and simple.

The assessments of quality and value in this book are solely mine, and you are welcome to disagree — in fact, it would be a boring old world if you *didn't* disagree with some of them. Nevertheless, I hope my comments will at least form the basis for a stimulating discussion.

Most of the wines were tasted blind (so I was not influenced by the labels) and alongside others of similar style. The descriptions are designed to be simple and direct, but occasionally the use of technical terms was the only way to get the message across. An explanation of such terms will be found in the glossary at the back of the book.

Of all beverages, wine is the only one designed specifically to accompany food, so I have suggested a dish as a partner for most of the wines. I hope you enjoy these ideas, but I emphasise that working out your own wine and food matches is a very important part of wine appreciation.

In the first *Guide*, nearly all the wines listed were quite widely available. For the 1993 edition, I have stretched the net a little further to include wines that are harder to find, but are well worth the search. As in the first edition, a list of New Zealand wineries at the back of the book will help you track down the real rarities.

Wines made exclusively for mail-order clubs and societies have not been included. They are often very good, but they are not available in retail outlets. In any case, they are usually reviewed in promotional literature sent out by the organisers. Many of the commercial wines sent out by the clubs will, however, also be found in this guide.

Nor are cask wines reviewed. The same wines are often available in bottle, and from my experience these are more reliable. If you do buy wine in casks, check the 'use-by' date on the bottom. I have tried cask wine that was still all right after a year, but three months is a more realistic keeping time.

I haven't reviewed fortified wines, simply because I had to draw the line somewhere.

The wines are divided into sections according to grape variety, and within each section alphabetically *according to the way they are labelled*. This means you will find Stoneleigh wines, for example, under 'S', even though they are made by Corbans.

The price you pay for the same bottle of wine in different outlets can vary greatly, and for this reason winemakers are cautious about quoting recommended retail prices. That's why there is a low and a high figure listed for each wine. If you find one priced lower, well done. If it is more expensive, I apologise — but I suggest you shop around.

Where there is a large discrepancy between the two prices listed, beware. The low figure is the recommended retail price given to me by the winemaker; the high figure is what I've seen it for on a shelf. This situation often applies to hard-to-get wines, and it is a rip-off that annoys the winemaker as much as the consumer. In such cases, I suggest you write to the maker and ask about buying the wine direct.

The practice also makes it hard to determine a value rating. In such cases, I have based it mostly on the winery's recommended figure, but with a realistic eye kept on the high level, if that seems to be the commonly available price.

Finally, let me emphasise once again that wine is designed to be enjoyed in the company of fine food and good friends. I hope the first guide was able to help that enjoyment, and that this second edition will prove equally helpful.

Vic Williams

Vic Williams
May 1993

The Rating System

The rating system used in this book is designed to give an easily followed picture of the wine's quality and value for money. The five-glass and five-star method is as simple as we could make it — the more of each, the better the wine.

QUALITY

🍷🍷🍷🍷🍷 A wonderful product that encapsulates all that is good about the winemaker's art. A benchmark for which other companies should aim.

🍷🍷🍷🍷🍷 Excellent wine that will taste every bit as good as a five-star model except in the most analytical of circumstances.

🍷🍷🍷🍷 Very good wine, only a couple of shades away from a top rating.

🍷🍷🍷🍷 Good, eminently drinkable wine with no faults and just a touch of class.

🍷🍷🍷 A wine that doesn't make the earth move, but one I would be happy to drink in any situation.

🍷🍷🍷 An honestly made wine that is enjoyable enough with food, but could be improved upon.

🍷🍷 An unremarkable wine that needs to be extremely well priced to merit consideration.

🍷 and 🍷 Anything below 🍷🍷 I didn't bother writing about. This is, after all, a *good* wine guide.

VALUE

★★★★★ Grab as much as you can afford — at this price, it won't last.

★★★★+ A bargain by anybody's standards, well worth stocking up on.

★★★★ Still great value, but the company isn't quite as generous as some of its competitors.

★★★+ Good -value wine, selling for a fraction less than its quality justifies.

★★★ A fairly priced wine. You're getting what you pay for.

★★+ The company is being a bit hopeful. Worth buying only if no better-priced examples are available.

★★ Cheekily priced wine. The company needs to be jolted back to commercial reality.

★+ At this level, the asking price far exceeds the quality.

★ Forget it. Keep your wallet firmly shut.

One point to keep in mind: a wine that merits ♟♟♟♟ for quality but costs $30 will often be better value than one which costs under $10 but scores only ♟♟.

CELLAR

▍ Enjoy without delay. This wine's either so good right now it seems a waste to cellar it, or it's on the way downhill and won't benefit from being put away.

▍2 Good to drink now, but this wine will keep, change a little and perhaps improve if cellared up to the number of years indicated.

▬ 2–5 Should be cellared for the minimum and maximum number of years indicated.

▬ 5 Put it away in a quiet spot for the number of years indicated.

The cellaring estimations should be taken from May 1993.

PREVIOUS OUTSTANDING VINTAGES

Previous outstanding vintages are listed for some wines. If only one year is mentioned, it usually means the wine is a relative newcomer.

A NOTE ON CELLARING

The joy of sharing good wine with friends and family is all the more keen if the wine comes from your own 'cellar', but just what does the term mean?

A 'cellar' doesn't need to be under the house, although that cool, quiet environment is ideally suited for the purpose. Wine hates light, sudden temperature changes and vibration, so choose a cupboard on the cool side of the house in a room where there is a minimum amount of movement. If you have stairs, the space under them can serve well, but to minimise vibration leave the shelves free-standing rather than attached to the underside of the steps.

Store the wine on its side to keep the cork moist and swollen; air is another of wine's natural enemies. Use proprietary shelving, wooden planks strewn with straw to stop the bottles rolling around (it looks nicely rustic as well), field tiles or, least expensively, wooden beer crates.

Two more rules: don't become a hoarder — wine is made to be enjoyed, not collected. Conversely, no matter how convivial the company, don't be tempted to open something you have sworn to put away for a set period of time. You'll be sorry when you see the empty bottle next morning — I know from sad experience.

Regions and the Quality Factor

It has taken little more than a couple of decades to go from the days when every New Zealand winery produced every type of wine, plus often a blackberry nip or something similar, to today's more enlightened climate when few companies produce more than a dozen or so wines, and some are happy to search for perfection in just one style.

Yet the struggle to establish the best growing regions for specific grape types continues in the '90s. Broad guidelines have been established, but most varieties are still being grown all over New Zealand. Compare this with France, where the varieties from which the wines of particular regions can be made are specified by law.

Guidelines as to which grapes suit particular areas are broad and riddled with exceptions. Prevailing wisdom has it, for example, that good reds can't be made in Marlborough, but Vavasour, Te Whare Ra and Grove Mill are just three of several companies who regularly disprove the argument.

So beware of regional generalisations. They are useful as guidelines, but it is just as important to watch the performance of individual vineyards. As you travel round the wineries, ask plenty of questions. Is the emphasis more on achieving big crops than smaller ones of higher quality? Does the soil drain well? Does the viticulturalist pluck leaves to allow more sun onto the grapes? Factors like these can often play as big a part as regional climate in determining whether a wine is mediocre or exceptional.

Look, too, for where the vineyard is situated. Early New Zealand plantings were commonly made in the most fertile soil the horticulturally minded growers could find. These vines grew like weeds and produced large amounts of grapes, but the quality was often mediocre.

Nowadays, most viticulturalists believe the best wine comes from vines that are stressed to some degree, and New Zealand wines are becoming better and more regionally distinctive because of it. As with all aspects of wine-making, it comes down to balance. The vines must, of course, be healthy, but the grower must be willing to lessen the size of his crop in the interests of getting more flavour concentration into the remaining grapes.

Wine and Food

'White wine with fish and white meat, red wine with red meat.'

That's the common rule, but in today's culinarily enlightened society, do this and other potential restrictions really matter?

In a word, no. Wine appreciation is a totally subjective matter, and the same applies to wine and food combinations — if it works for you, that's fine.

Nevertheless, there are combinations that work particularly well for most people and you should certainly try them out.

Oysters and chardonnay, smoked salmon and sauvignon blanc, and roast lamb and pinot noir, for example, are all generally agreeable partners that few people will find offensive.

Most of the wines in this book carry a recommended food companion. They are there as suggestions — try them out, but don't hesitate to swap one of the partners for your own particular favourite.

It is more important to match the comparative strengths of the wine and food than the colour. A gentle riesling, for example, would be completely overpowered by a chilli-spiked beef casserole, but a meaty, wood-aged chardonnay would perform as well as a cabernet sauvignon. Conversely, that same chardonnay would be too much for quietly poached scallops; the riesling would be much better.

And while we're on about wine and food, don't serve your whites too cold or your reds too warm. Overchilling kills the flavour, so put your still whites in the refrigerator for only half an hour or so, and sparkling wines for an hour.

If your 'cellar' is as cool as it should be, your red wines may well be too cold to serve immediately. Bring them to room temperature by placing them on the kitchen table for an hour or so or, if you're in a hurry, put them in the hot-water cupboard for twenty minutes. Never employ more drastic measures such as running them under a hot tap or standing them in front of the heater. I've seen both done, and mentally kicked myself for being too polite to say anything when asked to drink the obviously startled wine.

And speaking of red wine, if you are serving both cheese and sweets at a dinner party serve the cheese first. That way, your guests have something with which to enjoy the last of their red (or dry white) wine before moving on to the dessert course.

Good wine deserves nice glassware. That means it should ideally be clear, so the wine's colour can be admired, and the rim should be narrower than the waist. This tulip shape concentrates the flavour and helps pick up the nuances in the bouquet.

One last rule: never cook with a wine you wouldn't drink. That's not to say you have to use your last bottle of 1987 Stonyridge Larose for the casserole, but neither should you pour in that half-empty bottle of dry red that's been standing on top of the refrigerator for a month.

Vintage Report

As I write this, it is a couple of weeks before the first grapes are picked for the 1993 harvest, but barring typhoons, hurricanes or torrential downpours, it is possible to make a guesstimate of what sort of vintage it will be.

Generally, the last twelve months have been similar to the twelve before that. The combined effects of the El Niño weather pattern and the haze of ash from the Mt Pinutabo eruption meant there was less direct sunlight to ripen the grapes, so the harvest in most parts of the country is a week or two late.

Colder regions will, once again, produce crisp, high-acid whites and soft reds. Even in some warmer areas the grapes have had a hard time of it getting ripe.

As in 1992, there will still be some excellent wines produced, but they will need a little more attention from the grape grower and guidance from the winemaker — and there is no doubt that the very best wines are those that virtually make themselves.

Following are my assessments for the major grape-growing regions in the country. Use them as a rough guide — weather that adversely affected one vineyard may have left another a few kilometres away unscathed. There are always good wines produced in bad years and vice versa — your own palate is the best judge.

AUCKLAND
1993 The harvest is about ten days later than average, but both quality and quantity look good. Expect big-flavoured whites and better-than-average reds.
1992 The late harvest delayed ripening and accentuated flavours, but high acids made things difficult. Whites are austere in their youth, and reds lack that final touch of warmth.
1991 A good year for white wine, particularly chardonnay. Not quite so good for red varieties, although some pretty classy cabernet sauvignon was produced.
1990 The reverse situation. Some good red wines were produced, but whites were generally less successful.

WAIKATO

1993 Picking was due to start about two weeks after last year's date, mainly because the red grapes weren't ripe enough. Whites will be crisp and flavoursome, reds a little lighter than average with a danger of herbaceousness. The quantities are better than last year.

1992 The season was cool but dry, resulting in some very good whites and better than average reds.

1991 A great year for white wines, and almost as good for reds. Chardonnay, particularly, revelled in the conditions.

1990 Better for red wine than white, but most growers were happy with both types.

GISBORNE/POVERTY BAY

1993 Excessive rain, with its potential to rot the grapes, dampened the hopes of most Gisborne growers. The vintage looks below average for both whites and reds, although as we go to press, a fortnight of fine days would improve things dramatically.

1992 Growers were happy with all white varieties but particularly thrilled with chardonnay. Reds were comparatively lean.

1991 Tough for reds, better for whites — that's the summation of the 1991 vintage on the East Coast. Once again, chardonnay did better than other varieties.

1990 The reverse situation — 1990 produced better reds than whites, but it was not a classic year for either.

HAWKE'S BAY

1993 Conditions have been pretty similar to those along the coast in Gisborne. Good wines will be made by those growers willing to spend time exposing grapes to the sun, but generally speaking it won't be a great vintage.

1992 Low yields, but very good whites and average reds were the result of the cold weather for months before harvest.

1991 A classic year for whites and pretty good too for reds. Riesling and chardonnay both performed well, and cabernet sauvignon, merlot, cabernet franc and malbec all ripened well.

1990 A very good year for reds; generally good but a bit patchy for whites. Some excellent cabernet sauvignons were produced, both on their own and blended with merlot and cabernet franc.

WAIRARAPA/MARTINBOROUGH

1993 As we went to press, one grower described the vintage as a 'knife-edge' one. The harvest was about two weeks late, but the quality for both white and red grapes was fine, provided there were no early April frosts. The crop size is bigger than 1992.

1992 A year most winemakers would rather forget. Several vineyards were partly or wholly wiped out by frost, so wines were made by buying in fruit from other regions. Some of the results of this vinous cross-pollination, however, were exceptional.

1991 A great year for whites and a very good one for reds. Look for some top-class chardonnay and light but flavoursome pinot noir.

1990 A good year for all varieties, with reds just having the edge over whites. Chardonnay did well, but cabernet sauvignon liked the conditions better than did pinot noir.

MARLBOROUGH

1993 Chardonnay should be heavier than the 1992 models, and sauvignon blanc will be a little better, but not as good as the classic '91s. Reds will have a hard time of it getting ripe, but they have fared better in the Awatere Valley than the Wairau Valley.

1992 Not as good a year as the classic '91, but most wineries did okay despite the unseasonal cold. Crisp whites and lean reds are the order of the day, but there are plenty of exceptions.

1991 A great year for sauvignon blanc and chardonnay — some say the best ever — and good too for reds. Cabernet sauvignon did as well as it ever does in the area, and merlot performed exceptionally well.

1990 Things were looking good for grape growers until a frost right at harvest time knocked some varieties for a six. Most sauvignon blanc from 1990 is pleasant enough, but a mere shadow of the 1991 versions. Chardonnay fared better, but it was not a classic year for any variety.

NELSON

1993 The harvest is later than 1992, but the quantity is way up. The quality of both whites and reds should be very good, particularly from those vineyards whose owners spent a bit of time plucking leaves away from the ripening grapes.

1992 Cool, clear days for a week or so before harvest saved a crop battered by rain. Whites are crisp and well flavoured; pinot noir did well, but cabernet was harder to get ripe, so many of the wines are lean.

1991 Better for white wines than red, but pretty good for both. Sauvignon blanc was generally less herbaceous than Marlborough versions from the same year, and chardonnay was a little lighter.

1990 Hotter than 1991, which meant riper grapes and richer flavours. Nelson was unaffected by the frosts that did considerable damage to some varieties in neighbouring Marlborough.

CANTERBURY

1993 Frosts were the major concern for growers in this region. Those who were able to avoid their worst ravages report good crops of both white and red grapes, but for others both quantity and quality have been affected.

1992 Crop levels were down, but quality levels were average or a bit above. Pinot noir and riesling did best in the conditions, with other varieties faring reasonably well.

1991 There was plenty of warm weather, but an excess of autumn rain had growers worried about quality. As things turned out, the fruit arrived at the wineries in quite reasonable condition, but whites fared better than reds.

1990 A hot growing season was good news for both white and red varieties. Look for some classic pinot noir and riesling, and flavoursome chardonnay.

CENTRAL OTAGO

1993 This was the place to grow grapes this year. While the harvest was late everywhere else, Central growers were getting ready to pick their grapes a week or two early. Both whites and reds should be richly flavoured and good cellaring prospects.

1992 Getting the fruit ripe was a major problem down here, so the whites had high acids, which meant they were unapproachable in their youth, but should age well. Some flavoursome but light pinot noir was produced, and a few crisp chardonnays.

1991 A difficult year, yet good wines were produced despite cold conditions prior to harvest. Better for whites than reds.

1990 The pick of the three most recent vintages, good for both white and red varieties.

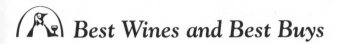 Best Wines and Best Buys

Last year, I selected only three 'best' wines — a white, a red and a sparkling. This year, I decided that was too restrictive, so I have picked a top wine in all the major categories. They have been selected purely according to their quality, which means they may be expensive. Greatness seldom comes cheap.

The top wines should be reasonably readily available, but you may have to search around for some. If you can't find them anywhere, try contacting the winery direct, using the list at the back of the book.

Another innovation this year is the listing of 'Best Buys' under each category. You should find each of these wines for less than $15 at your local retailer. Their quality ratings range from good to very good, and they all offer above-average value for money.

BEST CHARDONNAY
Kumeu River 1992
The Americans simply call it 'the great New Zealand white'. I can't argue. It has strength of character and wonderful elegance.

Best Buys
Corbans White Label Gisborne 1992
Forest Flower Collection 1992
Lincoln East Coast 1992
Mission Hawke's Bay 1992
Seifried Estate 1992

BEST CHENIN BLANC
Collards 1992
The Collard family consistently makes the best chenin blanc in New Zealand. This one is no exception.

Best Buys
Collards Dry 1992
Corbans White Label 1992

Totara 1990
West Brook Hawke's Bay 1991

BEST GEWÜRZTRAMINER
Dry River (Dry River Estate) 1992
Dry River's Dr Neil McCallum says he loves this variety's outspokenness. His devotion shows in this splendid wine.

Best Buys
Babich 1992
Phoenix 1991
Seifried Estate (Reserve Dry) 1991

BEST MÜLLER-THURGAU
Martinborough Vineyards 1992
Sadly, this is the last of this wine we will see — the vines have been pulled out to make room for pinot gris.

Best Buys
Seifried Estate 1992

BEST PINOT GRIS
Gibbston Vineyard Reserve 1992
Another reason why we should keep an eye on our newest grape-growing region, Central Otago.

Best Buys
Mission 1992

BEST RIESLING
Neudorf Moutere 1992
A wine that reflects the sunny personality of its makers, Tim and Judy Finn.

Best Buys
Babich 1992
Collards Marlborough Rhine Riesling 1992
Collards Rhine Riesling 1991
Corbans White Label Marlborough 1992
Mission 1992
Alan Scott Marlborough 1992
Seifried Estate 1992
Seifried Estate (Reserve Dry) 1991
Yelas Estate 1992

BEST SAUVIGNON BLANC/SEMILLON
Cloudy Bay 1992
Kevin Judd demonstrates that he can make great wine even in difficult years.

Best Buys
Babich Hawke's Bay 1992
Babich Marlborough 1991
Collards Marlborough 1992
Coopers Creek Marlborough 1992
Nobilo Marlborough 1992
Penfolds Cottle Bush 1992
Robard & Butler Fumé Blanc 1991
West Brook Hawke's Bay 1992

Non-specific 'Best Buy' White:
Babich Chablis 1992
Collards White Burgundy 1992
St Jerome Chablis 1992

BEST CABERNET SAUVIGNON/MERLOT AND BLENDS
Te Mata Coleraine 1991
Seen by many as the benchmark, and right at the top of the pole for 1991, this
wine combines power with velvet-smooth elegance.

Best Buys
Babich Cabernet Sauvignon 1991
Mission Cabernet/Merlot 1992
Seibel Cabernet Franc/Merlot/Cabernet Sauvignon 1989
Soljans Cabernet/Merlot 1991
West Brook Henderson Merlot 1991

BEST PINOT NOIR
Martinborough Vineyards 1991
Chunky, earthy and moreish, this controversial pinot noir takes the variety
in new directions for this country.

Non-specific 'Best Buy' Red:
Soljans Pinotage 1991

BEST SPARKLING WINE
Daniel Le Brun Blanc de Blancs 1990
Frenchman Daniel Le Brun shows how to make a world-class sparkler with
only one of the three grapes he uses for other versions.

BEST ROSÉ or BLUSH
Seibel Henderson Cabernet Sauvignon Blanc de Noir 1990
Most rosés are best enjoyed young and fresh, but this one has developed into something pretty special.

BEST DESSERT WINE
Ngatarawa Penny Noble Harvest Riesling 1992
Alwyn Corban names a wine for his partner's daughter, and creates one of the great New Zealand sweet wines.

Best Buys
Collards Late Harvest Semillon 1990
Coopers Creek Riesling Late Harvest 1990
Martinborough Vineyards Müller-Thurgau Late Harvest 1992
Seibel Hawke's Bay White Reisling Late Harvest 1990
Selaks Ice Wine 1992

White Wines

Chardonnay

It has been said that if a hundred winemakers were each given a tonne of chardonnay grapes from the same vineyard, they would produce a hundred distinctly different wines. More attention in the form of winery techniques like barrel fermentation, wood ageing and malolactic fermentation (see *Glossary*) is lavished on this grape than any other white variety. But despite the wide variance of styles, New Zealand chardonnay can be broadly divided into two types — fresh, crisp and citric in one corner, and buttery, mealy and mouth-fillingly rich in the other. Given an example of each style at a tasting a couple of years ago, a high-flying Californian winemaker summed things up well when she said, 'They're both very good, but one speaks of the vineyard, and the other of the winemaker.'

Ararimu Chardonnay

Not a new winery, but a new label for Matua Valley Wines of Waimauku, in West Auckland. This and the companion cabernet sauvignon are packaged in tall, elegant bottles with a very stylish label.

CURRENT RELEASE 1991 There are some lovely toast characters and evidence of sweet, ripe grapes on the nose, and the same characters are carried onto the palate. The wine's fruit and oak tastes are beautifully balanced and it has a deliciously long finish. Enjoy it with a pan-fried chicken breast lightly dusted with Cajun spices.

STYLE dry
QUALITY ▾▾▾▾▾
VALUE ★★★
GRAPES chardonnay
REGION Gisborne
CELLAR ▪▬ 3-4
PRICE $27-29

Ata Rangi Chardonnay

Clive Paton and Phyll Pattie's Martinborough vineyard has established a solid reputation for crisp chardonnays and flavoursome reds. The vineyard was hit hard by frost in 1992, with the result that this chardonnay was made from fruit grown in Hawke's Bay.

Previous outstanding vintages: '89, '91

CURRENT RELEASE 1992 There's a lovely toasty, vanilla nose on this stylish wine, with a hint of figs in there somewhere as well. Good, sweet fruit is obvious on the palate, and it boasts a long, classy finish.

STYLE dry
QUALITY �♛♛♛
VALUE ★★★+
GRAPES chardonnay
REGION Hawke's Bay
CELLAR ▦— 3-4
PRICE $18-$20

Babich East Coast Chardonnay

In wine-label language, East Coast usually means Gisborne, but this wine has some Hawke's Bay fruit added to the blend.

Previous outstanding vintages: '89

CURRENT RELEASE 1991 There's a faintly leathery character about the nose of this inexpensive Babich offering, along with a whiff of grapefruit. The taste is spicy and reasonably mouth-filling, and there is enough crisp acid to guarantee a refreshing finish. Try it with kina (sea-egg) spread on hot buttered toast, if you're brave enough.

STYLE dry
QUALITY ♛♛♛♛
VALUE ★★★+
GRAPES chardonnay
REGION Gisborne and Hawke's Bay
CELLAR ▌ 2
PRICE $12-14

Babich Irongate Chardonnay

The Irongate vineyard is situated on an old shingle bed once covered in water from the Ngaruroro River in Hawke's Bay. The name is reserved for Babich's top-of-the-line wines.

Previous outstanding vintages: '86, '87, '89

CURRENT RELEASE 1991 Peaches and lemons are the dominant characters in the bouquet of this stylish wine. The taste is all about rich, sweet fruit — the sort of thing you find in a ripe pawpaw — and the finish is delightfully rich. Enjoy it with a pan-fried turkey breast.

STYLE dry
QUALITY ♛♛♛♛♛
VALUE ★★★+
GRAPES chardonnay
REGION Hawke's Bay
CELLAR ▦— 4-5
PRICE $19-24

Babich Stopbank Chardonnay

The name comes from a stopbank in the Hawke's Bay vineyard where these grapes are grown. Vineyard manager Jim Hamilton says the bank provides shelter for the vines.

CURRENT RELEASE 1991 Butterscotch, peaches and nectarines are the pleasant flavour keys on the nose, and the sweet, ripe fruit sensations continue in the mouth. The wine is quite round, but good acids give it a crisp, refreshing finish. Try it with a fillet of snapper, simply cooked with a little butter and parsley.

STYLE dry
QUALITY ♥♥♥♥
VALUE ★★★★
GRAPES chardonnay
REGION Hawke's Bay
CELLAR ▬ 1-3
PRICE $16-18

Black Ridge Chardonnay

The Black Ridge winery at Earnscleugh, Central Otago, is close to the Clyde Dam, and it boasts one of the most ruggedly rocky sites in the country.

CURRENT RELEASE 1992 Winemaker Michael Wolter had an even longer ripening period to contend with than the rest of the country, but he has made a good job of this chardonnay. It is toasty and rich on the nose, and fills the mouth most satisfactorily. Try it with a Thai chicken curry.

STYLE dry
QUALITY ♥♥♥♥
VALUE ★★★
GRAPES chardonnay
REGION Central Otago
CELLAR ▬ 2-4
PRICE $17-25

Blue Rock Chardonnay

This relatively new winery on the Martinborough scene has enough grapes planted to become a major player in the future.

CURRENT RELEASE 1991 Quite a refreshing style, with mealiness and citric characters in pretty good balance on the nose and on the palate. Partner it with crumbed chicken drumsticks.

STYLE dry
QUALITY ♥♥♥
VALUE ★★+
GRAPES chardonnay
REGION Martinborough
CELLAR ▮ 3
PRICE $18-22

Brajkovich Chardonnay

Brajkovich is the second label for the Kumeu River winery, but this chardonnay is treated in exactly the same way as the much-praised version that wears the Kumeu River label. The only difference, winemaker Michael Brajkovich, MW, assures us, is that the grapes come from a higher-yielding vineyard (low-yielding vines produce better wine).
CURRENT RELEASE 1992 There's some nice toast on the nose, along with a bit of nuttiness and something that reminds me of Marmite. The taste is more conventionally citric and is quite mouth-filling. Try it with a whole pan-fried flounder.

STYLE dry
QUALITY 🍷🍷🍷🍷
VALUE ★★★
GRAPES chardonnay
REGION West and South Auckland
CELLAR 🍷 2
PRICE $16-20

Brookfields Estate Chardonnay

The Estate label is used for a series Brookfields owner/winemaker Peter Robertson calls his 'baby' wines, and prices accordingly.
CURRENT RELEASE 1992 Grapefruit and the spicy characters of American oak are in evidence in the bouquet of this nicely structured chardonnay. The wine is quite mouth-filling, and the finish is apple-like and long-lasting. Peter designs it for easy drinking, but it has more than a touch of class. Try it alongside lightly-crumbed chicken Maryland legs.

STYLE dry
QUALITY 🍷🍷🍷
VALUE ★★★+
GRAPES chardonnay
REGION Hawke's Bay
CELLAR 🍷 3
PRICE $13-15

Brookfields Reserve Chardonnay

This top-of-the-line chardonnay from Brookfield isn't as well known as other Hawke's Bay high-fliers, but those in the know buy a case or three each year.
Previous outstanding vintages: '87, '89
CURRENT RELEASE 1992 Apples, pears, oranges — they're all there on the nose of this delightful chardonnay. The wine is fermented in French oak barrels, and about a quarter of it undergoes a malolactic fermentation. The result is a bevy of mealy characters that act as a pleasant foil to the citric tastes of the fruit. It's great with roast pork — and don't forget the crackling.

STYLE dry
QUALITY 🍷🍷🍷🍷
VALUE ★★★
GRAPES chardonnay
REGION Hawke's Bay
CELLAR ▬ 2-4
PRICE $22-26

Chard Farm Chardonnay

Situated on the edge of the Kawarau Gorge, twenty kilometres from Queenstown, Chard Farm is one of the most spectacularly sited vineyards in the country.
CURRENT RELEASE 1992 I love the nose! Brothers Rob and Greg Hay gave the wine only a short time in oak, but while it was there they stirred it pretty regularly to mix the yeast characters through the wine. The result is mealy, toasty and just plain appealing. On the palate it displays Central Otago's usual high acids and plenty of clean, firm fruit. Great with herb-sprinkled roast chicken.

STYLE dry
QUALITY ♟♟♟♟
VALUE ★★+
GRAPES chardonnay
REGION Central Otago
CELLAR ▬ 2-4
PRICE $22-28

Chard Farm Judge and Jury Chardonnay

This stylish chardonnay is named after a rock outcrop on the other side of the gorge, and is sold in the elegant imported bottle used by Central Otago winemakers for their top wines.
CURRENT RELEASE 1992 Although it had more oak than the 'standard' model, the nose is more fruit-led, with grapefruit leading the parade of citric flavours. The same character is evident on the palate. The wine has firm, crisp acids and a limey finish, and would be a fine companion to a piece of pan-fried blue cod.

STYLE dry
QUALITY ♟♟♟♟
VALUE ★★+
GRAPES chardonnay
REGION Central Otago
CELLAR ▬ 3-6
PRICE $28-34

Chifney Chardonnay

Winemaker Stan Chifney loves to play the violin when he's not working in his vineyard or winery. The orchestra for which he played during the recent Toast Martinborough festival was called the Academy of St Kuranui in the Paddock.
CURRENT RELEASE 1991 The nose is citric and clean, and there are some big, spicy tastes on the palate. Stan is better known for reds than whites, but this is a good 'un.

STYLE dry
QUALITY ♟♟♟♙
VALUE ★★★
GRAPES chardonnay
REGION Martinborough
CELLAR ▮ 2
PRICE $17-19

Church Road Chardonnay

The Montana-owned winery where this wine is made was established by industry doyen, the late Tom McDonald. One of the buildings has been restored as a wine museum.
CURRENT RELEASE 1992 There's a delightful belt of butterscotch on the nose, along with sweet vanilla and peachy fruit. The taste is citric but well rounded, and the finish has enough zing to be memorable. Enjoy it with Chinese-style steamed prawns.

STYLE dry
QUALITY ▼▼▼▼
VALUE ★★★+
GRAPES chardonnay
REGION Hawke's Bay
CELLAR ▬ 2-4
PRICE $17-19

Cloudy Bay Chardonnay

The name is synonymous with sauvignon blanc, but in most years this chardonnay is an equally impressive act. Previous outstanding vintages: '87, '88
CURRENT RELEASE 1991 Elegance is the keynote to this splendidly made chardonnay, both on the nose and in the taste. There's plenty of toast character in the bouquet, and in the mouth it is clean, spicy and frisky. I can think of no better partner for a whole baked Marlborough salmon.

STYLE dry
QUALITY ▼▼▼▼▼
VALUE ★★★
GRAPES chardonnay
REGION Marlborough
CELLAR ▬ 2-4
PRICE $28-32

Collards Gisborne Chardonnay

The Collards produce chardonnay wines from grapes grown in various parts of the country. The Gisborne version is the least expensive.
CURRENT RELEASE 1992 The nose has a touch of steel in with its lemon characteristics, and the taste is clean, soft and understated. Nice with a pan-fried flounder.

STYLE dry
QUALITY ▼▼▼▼
VALUE ★★★
GRAPES chardonnay
REGION Gisborne
CELLAR ▮ 3
PRICE $15-17

Collards Hawke's Bay Chardonnay

The mid-range wine in the Collards chardonnay line-up, made from grapes grown by Gisborne doctor David Yates.

CURRENT RELEASE 1991 The bouquet is toasty, nutty and invitingly rich, and there is some clean, spicy fruit on the palate. Partner it with a medallion of genuine white veal, if you can find one, or a pan-fried pork chop.

STYLE dry
QUALITY ♟♟♟♟
VALUE ★★★+
GRAPES chardonnay
REGION Hawke's Bay
CELLAR ▮ 3
PRICE $18-22

Collards Marlborough Chardonnay

This new label for the Collard family is a blend of juice from three different Marlborough vineyards.

CURRENT RELEASE 1991 Gentle spice from the wine's time in oak backs up the grapefruit and apricot aromas in the bouquet. The taste is clean and fresh, with crisp acids and a flinty finish. Good with sushi.

STYLE dry
QUALITY ♟♟♟♟
VALUE ★★★
GRAPES chardonnay
REGION Marlborough
CELLAR ▬▬ 3
PRICE $18-22

Collards Rothesay Vineyard Chardonnay

The top chardonnay for the Collard family, and the recipient of many awards in the last few years.

Previous outstanding vintages: '86, '87, '89

CURRENT RELEASE 1991 The nose is all toast and honey-suckle, followed by clean, rich fruit once you get the wine into your mouth. The oak is nicely integrated and the finish reasonably long. Enjoy it with chicken drumsticks, rolled in a little olive oil and grated parmesan before being grilled.

STYLE dry
QUALITY ♟♟♟♟
VALUE ★★★
GRAPES chardonnay
REGION West Auckland
CELLAR ▬▬ 2-4
PRICE $25-32

Conders Bend Chardonnay

Craig Gass made a name for himself at his previous vineyard, Korepo, in Nelson, with an extraordinarily good (and very expensive) dessert wine. Nowadays, Korepo has been renamed Ruby Bay and Craig is producing a range of wines across the hills in Marlborough. CURRENT RELEASE 1992 Oranges and pears are discernible in the bouquet, while the palate just announces good, ripe fruit underpinned by the sensible use of oak. Enjoy it with a flounder steamed with ginger in the Chinese manner.

STYLE dry
QUALITY ▼▼▼▼
VALUE ★★★
GRAPES chardonnay
REGION Marlborough
CELLAR ▬ 2-3
PRICE $18-20

Cooks Hawke's Bay Chardonnay Winemaker's Reserve

This top label for Cooks, part of the Corbans group, has won a heap of medals over the years. The 1989 vintage was the top white wine in the *1992 Penguin Guide*. Previous outstanding vintages: '86, '87, '89
CURRENT RELEASE 1990 The wine is more fruit-led than the bold, almost over-the-top 1989. There are grapefruit characters on the nose and evidence of ripe Hawke's Bay fruit. The wine combines fruit and spice on the palate with nicely balanced oak. Enjoy it with a perfectly roasted chicken with small whole beans, roast potatoes and kumara.

STYLE dry
QUALITY ▼▼▼▼▼
VALUE ★★★
GRAPES chardonnay
REGION Hawke's Bay
CELLAR ▬ 3-4
PRICE $22-25

Coopers Creek Gisborne Chardonnay

The Coopers Creek winery in West Auckland is a popular spot on the local wine trail. The company makes a range of chardonnays and has had considerable medal success with them over the years.
CURRENT RELEASE 1992 I can find apricots on the nose, but there's little sign of oak until you put the wine in your mouth — which is fair enough, I guess, because that's what drinking's all about. The wine is clean and fresh, with spice and limey flavours making a pleasant mouthful. Partner it with chicken satay.

STYLE dry
QUALITY ▼▼▼▼
VALUE ★★★+
GRAPES chardonnay
REGION Gisborne
CELLAR ▮ 2
PRICE $13-15

Coopers Creek Hawke's Bay Chardonnay

The top Coopers Creek chardonnay used to be called
Swamp Road, and this version was a second-tier wine.
At the 1992 Air New Zealand Wine Awards, however,
this was the one that took gold. The Swamp Reserve, as
its big brother is now known, managed only bronze.
CURRENT RELEASE 1992 Balance is what this wine is all
about. There are toast, vanilla and citrus notes in the
bouquet, but nothing dominates. On the palate it is
smooth, rich and very controlled. Enjoy it with focaccia
bread sprinkled with chopped sun-dried tomatoes.

STYLE dry
QUALITY ♟♟♟♟♟
VALUE ★★★★
GRAPES chardonnay
REGION Hawke's Bay
CELLAR ▬ 2-5
PRICE $16-19

Coopers Creek Swamp Reserve Chardonnay

When this wine was first released, the name attracted as
much attention as the flavour. Originally named after a
specific vineyard (in Swamp Road), it is now a blend of
the best Hawke's Bay chardonnay grapes the winery can
get its hands on.
Previous outstanding vintages: '86
CURRENT RELEASE 1991 The colour is burnished gold, and
that's a pretty good start. The bouquet has got toffee,
melon and peach flavours, and the taste is full, rich and
spicy. Enjoy it with a herb-laced chicken and mushroom pie.

STYLE dry
QUALITY ♟♟♟♟♟
VALUE ★★★
GRAPES chardonnay
REGION Hawke's Bay
CELLAR ▬ 2-4
PRICE $24-27

Corbans Private Bin Chardonnay

The Private Bin range from Corbans includes some
pretty serious wines in its ranks. This chardonnay has
had all sorts of techniques lavished upon it.
Previous outstanding vintages: '86, '89
CURRENT RELEASE 1990 There's mealiness from the barrel
fermentation, fresh-bread characters from long contact
with the yeast cells and butteriness from the malolactic
fermentation all on the nose. That sounds like break-
fast, but anybody who tackles this generously flavoured
chardonnay before the sun is high is brave indeed. The
palate boasts melon-skin and citric characters and plenty
of ripe-grape flavours. Great with roast pork.

STYLE dry
QUALITY ♟♟♟♟
VALUE ★★★+
GRAPES chardonnay
REGION Marlborough
CELLAR ▬ 2-3
PRICE $23-25

Corbans White Label Gisborne Chardonnay

The White Label trio from Corbans is good value. The
company has access to a huge amount of Gisborne
chardonnay, giving it the ability to tailor-make the
wine to a price.
CURRENT RELEASE 1992 Melon skins and tangelos share
the aroma honours. In the mouth the wine starts sweet,
goes spicy in the middle and finishes with a dose of
austerity. Not an earth-mover, but well made and very
well priced. Try it alongside a Spanish potato and onion
tortilla.

STYLE dry
QUALITY ▼▼▼
VALUE ★★★★+
GRAPES chardonnay
REGION Gisborne
CELLAR ▮ 3
PRICE $10-12

Crab Farm Hawke's Bay Chardonnay

The Crab Farm winery is situated about five minutes
from Napier Airport. It has an outside deck which is a
pleasant place to sit if you're running early for your flight
out of town.
CURRENT RELEASE 1992 There's a touch of flint on the
nose of this well-crafted wine, backed up by apple-skin
and rock melon characters. It is quite soft in the mouth
but cuts in with a crisp, acid finish. Try it with barbecued pork sausages.

STYLE dry
QUALITY ▼▼▼
VALUE ★★★+
GRAPES chardonnay
REGION Hawke's Bay
CELLAR ▮ 2
PRICE $14-18

Crab Farm Hawke's Bay Reserve Chardonnay

Crab farm owners James and Hamish Jardine have
enjoyed a good reputation in Hawke's Bay. Now their
wines are being recognised further afield.
CURRENT RELEASE 1992 Butterscotch and apricots are
much in evidence on the nose, while the palate speaks
of richly ripe fruit. The wine is dry, yet it finishes quite
sweet. Try it with grilled scallops.

STYLE dry
QUALITY ▼▼▼▼
VALUE ★★★
GRAPES chardonnay
REGION Hawke's Bay
CELLAR ▬ 2-4
PRICE $20-25

Cross Roads Chardonnay

Partner and winemaker Malcolm Reeves is known as an expert on fruit wines, but he's always had a keen interest in the product of the grape. Malcolm and partner Lester O'Brien have done well with this relatively new label on the Hawke's Bay wine scene.

CURRENT RELEASE 1991 A hint of vanilla backs up the lemony characters of clean chardonnay grapes on the nose of this gentle wine. The same citric characters dominate the palate, and contribute to a crisp, long-lasting finish.

STYLE dry
QUALITY ▼▼▼▼
VALUE ★★★
GRAPES chardonnay
REGION Hawke's Bay
CELLAR ▋ 2
PRICE $18-22

Cross Roads Chardonnay Reserve

A new label for the lads, reserved for the best fruit they can get their hands on. This means it may not be made every year.

CURRENT RELEASE 1991 The lemony characters of the 'standard' release are joined by tangelos and spice in the bouquet of its upmarket brother. The ripeness of the grapes is much in evidence in the mouth. The wine is mouth-fillingly delicious and boasts a lingering finish.

STYLE dry
QUALITY ▼▼▼▼
VALUE ★★★+
GRAPES chardonnay
REGION Hawke's Bay
CELLAR ▬▶ 2-4
PRICE $20-23

Daniel Le Brun Marlborough Terrace Chardonnay

Best known for their award-winning champagne-style sparklers, Daniel and Adele Le Brun also produce a handful of still wines.

CURRENT RELEASE 1991 Lemons and grapefruit are to be found in the bouquet, and on the palate the wine is uncomplicated and well rounded, with a wee bit of spice on the end. Good with chicken and chips.

STYLE dry
QUALITY ▼▼▼▼
VALUE ★★★
GRAPES chardonnay
REGION Marlborough
CELLAR ▋ 2
PRICE $17-20

Dashwood Chardonnay

Dashwood is a second label for the Vavasour winery, situated in the Awatere Valley forty minutes from Blenheim. Winemaker Glenn Thomas says he aims for a 'fruit-dominant' style with this wine, so he gives it minimal wood treatment.

CURRENT RELEASE 1992 Spicy lemons form a pleasant introduction to this middleweight wine. In the mouth it is fresh, citric and clean and would make a fine companion to a Chinese-style whole wok-fried snapper.

STYLE dry
QUALITY ▼▼▼▼
VALUE ★★★
GRAPES chardonnay
REGION Marlborough
CELLAR ▮ 2
PRICE $19-21

Delegat's Hawke's Bay Chardonnay

A good seller for this Auckland-based winery, one step below the Proprietor's Reserve bottling but consistently well made and priced.

CURRENT RELEASE 1991 Spicy peaches and lemons on the nose and lime juice and cinnamon in the mouth are okay with me. This is a fresh, appealing wine that goes well with freshly shucked oysters.

STYLE dry
QUALITY ▼▼▼▼
VALUE ★★★+
GRAPES chardonnay
REGION Hawke's Bay
CELLAR ▮ 2
PRICE $15-17

Delegat's Proprietor's Reserve Hawke's Bay Chardonnay

The Proprietor's Reserve label, usually referred to simply as P.R., is used for the top Delegat wines, but they are made in larger quantities than many similar products from other wineries. The chardonnay has been a regular medal winner over the years.

Previous outstanding vintages: '86, '89

CURRENT RELEASE 1991 Toast, mealiness and something like oranges are in good balance in the bouquet. The taste is a little shy, but the wine is nicely soft and mouth-filling. It goes well with barbecued vegetables such as eggplant and kumara.

STYLE dry
QUALITY ▼▼▼▼▼
VALUE ★★★
GRAPES chardonnay
REGION Hawke's Bay
CELLAR ▭— 2-5
PRICE $25-27

deRedcliffe Estates Mangatawhiri Chardonnay

The Japanese-owned de Redcliffe winery is situated at Mangatawhiri, forty-five minutes south of Auckland, but draws much of its fruit from other areas. This chardonnay, however, was made from home-vineyard grapes.

CURRENT RELEASE 1991 The nose is reserved, but there are some classic citric chardonnay characters in there when you search. The first impression in the mouth is of ripe, sweet fruit, followed by a nice touch of spice, which carries through onto the finish. It's good with a chicken and radish sandwich.

STYLE dry
QUALITY ♙♙♙♙
VALUE ★★★+
GRAPES chardonnay
REGION Mangatawhiri
CELLAR ▬ 1-3
PRICE $15-18

Duke of Marlborough Chardonnay

Te Whare Ra is best known for a range of lusciously sweet dessert wines, and the fruit in this full-flavoured chardonnay was so ripe when it was harvested that it, too, has an initial impression of sweetness.

CURRENT RELEASE 1992 The sweet introduction is ably assisted by a healthy dose of vanilla from the oak barrels in which the wine was aged. The palate reeks of ripe fruit, and there is a luxuriously long finish. If you're feeling flush, enjoy it alongside crayfish cut in half lengthwise and grilled with herb-laced butter.

STYLE dry
QUALITY ♙♙♙♙♙
VALUE ★★★★
GRAPES chardonnay
REGION Marlborough
CELLAR ▬ 3-5
PRICE $17-18

Esk Valley Private Bin Chardonnay

The long-established Esk Valley winery boasts a pleasant ocean view from its hillside location. Formerly owned by the Bird family, the company is now part of the Villa Maria group.

CURRENT RELEASE 1991 There's a spicy Weet-Bix nose with a touch of toast in this nicely made mid-range white. The palate speaks of ripe fruit, and there's a clean, reasonably long finish. Try it with cheese-topped pasta.

STYLE dry
QUALITY ♙♙♙♙
VALUE ★★★+
GRAPES chardonnay
REGION Hawke's Bay
CELLAR ▮ 3
PRICE $13-16

Esk Valley Reserve Chardonnay

The top chardonnay label for this Hawke's Bay winery is consistently well made and worth cellaring. Previous outstanding vintages: '89

CURRENT RELEASE 1991 Toasty, vanilla oak and grapefruit mix together in the bouquet. The wine is nicely balanced, citric but well rounded, and boasts lovely crisp acids that will ensure it keeps for a few years. Enjoy it with pan-fried chicken.

STYLE dry
QUALITY ♛♛♛♛
VALUE ★★+
GRAPES chardonnay
REGION Hawke's Bay
CELLAR ▬ 2-4
PRICE $22-28

Forest Flower Collection Chardonnay

This colourfully labelled series is part of the Villa Maria collection, and is aimed to fit somewhere between the St Aubyns and Private Bin wines.

CURRENT RELEASE 1992 The bouquet is properly lemony, and the taste is light but pleasant with a clean, crisp finish. Enjoy it with fish and chips.

STYLE dry
QUALITY ♛♛♛
VALUE ★★★★
GRAPES chardonnay
REGION Gisborne
CELLAR ▮ 1
PRICE $9-11

Gibbston Valley Southern Selection Chardonnay

Ex-TV reporter Alan Brady's Queenstown vineyard features one of the best casual restaurants in the area — and his wines are good too.

CURRENT RELEASE 1991 Grapefruit and lemons share the honours on the nose. In the mouth this wine's cold-climate origins are obvious from the crisp, austere acids that lead into a spicy, medium-long finish. This is one for the cellar.

STYLE dry
QUALITY ♛♛♛♛
VALUE ★★+
GRAPES chardonnay
REGION Queenstown
CELLAR ▬ 3-4
PRICE $21-25

Giesen Marlborough School Road Chardonnay

The words School Road on a Giesen label usually mean the grapes came from Burnham School Road in Canterbury, but not this time. The fruit for this wine came from Marlborough.

CURRENT RELEASE 1992 There's a good measure of oaky spice on the nose, which isn't really surprising — the wine spent ten months in a mixture of German, French and American barrels. The taste is rich and generous, and the finish pleasantly toasty. Good wine for plain roast chicken.

STYLE dry
QUALITY ✦✦✦✦✦
VALUE ★★★+
GRAPES chardonnay
REGION Marlborough
CELLAR ■– 2-4
PRICE $16-19

Goldwater Delamore Chardonnay

Waiheke vintners Kim and Jeanette Goldwater don't grow chardonnay grapes, so they name this wine after the neighbouring vineyard where they buy them. If you want to try a genuinely different chardonnay, this is the one to go for.

CURRENT RELEASE 1992 I get pawpaw and cloves on the nose of this full-flavoured wine. The taste is fresh, clean and spicy, and there is a nicely drawn-out finish. It's a great partner for barbecued prawns.

STYLE dry
QUALITY ✦✦✦✦
VALUE ★★★
GRAPES chardonnay
REGION Waiheke Island
CELLAR ■– 4
PRICE $22-25

Goldwater Marlborough Chardonnay

This is a new label for the Goldwaters, made according to their specifications by contract winemaker John Belsham at Marlborough's Vintech winery.

CURRENT RELEASE 1992 There's a touch of the barnyard about the nose of this wine, which you'll either love or hate. The same characteristic is found in many French burgundies. Once you get it into your mouth, however, the clean, frisky tastes of good Marlborough chardonnay take over and gather for a refreshingly citric finish. Try it with wiener schnitzel.

STYLE dry
QUALITY ✦✦✦✦
VALUE ★★+
GRAPES chardonnay
REGION Marlborough
CELLAR ■– 1-2
PRICE $22-25

Grape Republic Waterfall Bay Chardonnay

The Grape Republic Wine Company at Te Horo, north of Wellington, is the first winery in the Horowhenua region. Winemaker Alastair Pain also makes fruit wines under the Parsonage Hill label.

CURRENT RELEASE 1991 Alastair picked up a silver medal for this wine at the 1992 Air New Zealand Wine Awards. I get lemons, grapefruit and peaches on the nose, along with a wee hint of toastiness. The taste is zingy but viscous, and the finish is nicely crisp. Good with fish and chips.

STYLE dry
QUALITY ♟♟♟♟
VALUE ★★★
GRAPES chardonnay
REGION Horowhenua
CELLAR 🍾 2
PRICE $22-28

Grove Mill Marlborough Chardonnay

The Grove Mill winery in Marlborough is the only one situated right in the province's major town, Blenheim. It shares a converted granary with a pleasant restaurant.

CURRENT RELEASE 1992 Orange peel and cloves are the twin calling cards in the bouquet. Cloves are there in the taste as well, but they are surrounded by sweet fruit sensations. The finish is spicy and impressively long.

STYLE dry
QUALITY ♟♟♟♟♟
VALUE ★★★
GRAPES chardonnay
REGION Marlborough
CELLAR 🍾 4
PRICE $18-21

Highfield Estate Marlborough Chardonnay

Recently in receivership but now boasting both British and Japanese ownership, this company will be worth watching.

CURRENT RELEASE 1992 I get the distinctive aroma of Nashi pears in the nose of this well-made wine. The palate is big and mouth-filling, and the finish satisfyingly long. It's good with a poached Bratwurst sausage and Bavarian grain mustard.

STYLE dry
QUALITY ♟♟♟♟
VALUE ★★★+
GRAPES chardonnay
REGION Marlborough
CELLAR ▬ 2-4
PRICE $18-21

Hunter's Chardonnay

The tremendous overseas success achieved by various vintages of Hunter's sauvignon blanc has overshadowed the almost equally impressive performance of the company's chardonnay wines in both the UK and the US.

Previous outstanding vintages: '88

CURRENT RELEASE 1991 Nashi pears are in evidence on the nose of this refreshing wine as well — maybe it's a new Marlborough characteristic. On the palate it's spicy and vanilla-like from its sojourn in French oak barrels, and boasts a fruit-salad sort of finish. Try it alongside pipis, topped with garlic butter and grilled.

STYLE dry
QUALITY ♟♟♟♟
VALUE ★★★
GRAPES chardonnay
REGION Marlborough
CELLAR ▬ 3-4
PRICE $22-24

Jackson Estate Chardonnay

The first vintage of this wine, 1991, took a silver medal at the 1992 Liquorland Royal Easter Wine Awards.

CURRENT RELEASE 1992 Melon skins and yeast share the honours in the bouquet. The taste is quite peachy and well rounded, but there are enough acids to give it a dose of finishing zing. Enjoy it with a salad of mussels and tomatoes.

STYLE dry
QUALITY ♟♟♟♟
VALUE ★★★
GRAPES chardonnay
REGION Marlborough
CELLAR ▬ 2-4
PRICE $19-23

Kumeu River Chardonnay

This wine has won more praise overseas than it has in this country, partly because the company doesn't enter it in competitions. US wine guru Robert Parker simply calls it 'the great white wine of New Zealand'.

Previous outstanding vintages: '87, '89, '91

CURRENT RELEASE 1992 Peaches and spice (and all things nice) are much in evidence on the nose of this stylish wine. The taste is all about elegance — it starts with a zingy punch of acid and stays firm and beautifully balanced right to the lingering finish. Enjoy a glassful on its own, then partner it with almond-stuffed chicken breasts.

STYLE dry
QUALITY ♟♟♟♟♟
VALUE ★★★
GRAPES chardonnay
REGION West Auckland
CELLAR ▬ 2-5
PRICE $28-33

Landfall Chardonnay

Landfall is one of the names used for wines made at Gisborne solicitor Ross Revington's Gisborne vineyard. Others are labelled under his own name.
CURRENT RELEASE 1992 The nose reminded me of cornflakes and oranges, which wasn't all bad. The wine is well rounded on the palate, and there's a nice bit of oaky spice on the finish. Enjoy it with a white veal cutlet.

STYLE dry
QUALITY ♟♟♟♟
VALUE ★★★+
GRAPES chardonnay
REGION Gisborne
CELLAR ▮ 2
PRICE $16-18

Lansdowne Chardonnay

Not a company name but the label used for Grove Mill's top chardonnay, which has had great success on the show circuit.
Previous outstanding vintages: '89
CURRENT RELEASE 1991 There's a French-style earthiness about the nose, which some people may find off-putting, but it's worth hanging in there. The taste is of richly ripe fruit, and there's a big, long finish. Great wine for a butter-roasted chicken with kumara and roast potatoes.

STYLE dry
QUALITY ♟♟♟♟
VALUE ★★★
GRAPES chardonnay
REGION Marlborough
CELLAR ▬▶ 3-4
PRICE $25-27

Lawson's Dry Hills Marlborough Chardonnay

A new name for Marlborough, but one that should be worth keeping an eye on.
CURRENT RELEASE 1992 The nose is properly peachy, and there's a nice hint of spicy melons in the taste. It's good wine, but it finishes a bit short.

STYLE dry
QUALITY ♟♟♟
VALUE ★★+
GRAPES chardonnay
REGION Marlborough
CELLAR ▮ 2
PRICE $19-24

Lincoln East Coast Chardonnay

The Lincoln winery is one of the last half-dozen or so left in Lincoln Road, Henderson, which used to be full of vineyards until encroaching residential development and subsequent high rates made such extensive land use uneconomical. Winemaker Nick Chan makes a range of chardonnay wines in different styles; the East Coast version is relatively simple but pleasant drinking.

CURRENT RELEASE 1992 The nose is quite shy, but there are some peachy notes in there if you sniff hard enough. Things are more outspoken on the palate. The wine is smooth, pleasantly citric rather than oak-led, and it finishes cleanly. Goes well with fish and chips.

STYLE dry
QUALITY ♟♟♟♟
VALUE ★★★★
GRAPES chardonnay
REGION Gisborne and Hawke's Bay
CELLAR 🍾 2
PRICE $10-12

Lincoln Hawke's Bay Chardonnay

This label has done well for Lincoln after its release for the first time last year.

CURRENT RELEASE 1991 This wine has developed nicely since I assessed it last year. The bouquet is toasty and grainy with a nice touch of spice, and the palate has rounded out and boasts a delightfully sweet finish. Partner it with osso buco.

STYLE dry
QUALITY ♟♟♟♟
VALUE ★★★+
GRAPES chardonnay
REGION Hawke's Bay
CELLAR 🍾 2
PRICE $17-19

Lincoln Parklands Chardonnay

Another Gisborne wine, but one on which Nick lavishes more attention.

CURRENT RELEASE 1990 This wine has developed an earthy character on the nose since I reviewed it for last year's *Penguin Guide*, but there are plenty of grapefruit characters in there as well. The taste is peachy, full and well rounded, gently tannic and a little oily from its malolactic fermentation. The finish is pleasant but short.

STYLE dry
QUALITY ♟♟♟
VALUE ★★★
GRAPES chardonnay
REGION Gisborne
CELLAR 🍾 2
PRICE $16-18

Linden Hawke's Bay Chardonnay

Winery owner Win van der Linden has only twelve hectares of vines, so he buys in a lot of fruit from contract growers around the Bay.
CURRENT RELEASE 1992 There are some nice spiced grapefruit tones on the nose, and clean, citric tastes on the palate. This middleweight wine would suit simple food like grilled chicken wings.

STYLE dry
QUALITY ♟♟♟♟
VALUE ★★★+
GRAPES chardonnay
REGION Hawke's Bay
CELLAR ▮ 2
PRICE $16-19

Martinborough Vineyards Chardonnay

Winemaker Larry McKenna has made a name for himself with pinot noir, but he's also got a nice touch with chardonnay.
CURRENT RELEASE 1991 Balance is what this beautifully crafted wine is all about. It's got citric fruit, oaky spice and mealiness on the nose, but nothing dominates, and the taste is clean and peachy. Enjoy a bit on its own, then partner it with plain roast chicken.

STYLE dry
QUALITY ♟♟♟♟♟
VALUE ★★★
GRAPES chardonnay
REGION Martinborough
CELLAR ▮ 3
PRICE $25-30

Matua Chardonnay (Gisborne Estates)

Gisborne was once regarded as the home of bulk wine and little else, an image the grape growers and vintners of the area are determined to dispel. A current campaign is promoting Gisborne as the chardonnay capital of New Zealand, partly to publicise the fact that wines like this use Gisborne grapes but are made out of the area.
CURRENT RELEASE 1991 The nose is clean and lemony, and the taste is fresh, surprisingly fruity for a chardonnay but thoroughly refreshing. Serve it with a chicken-liver and bacon salad.

STYLE dry
QUALITY ♟♟♟
VALUE ★★★+
GRAPES chardonnay
REGION Gisborne
CELLAR ▮ 2
PRICE $13-17

Matua Chardonnay Judd Estate

Matua's top-priced chardonnay, and a regular medal-winner for the company over the years.
Previous outstanding vintages: '87
CURRENT RELEASE 1992 Winemaker Mark Robertson has achieved good balance between fruit and oak. There's a peachy note on the palate, backed up by a hint of oak spice and buttery qualities from the wine's partial malolactic fermentation. Enjoy it with pan-fried snapper topped with slivered almonds.

STYLE dry
QUALITY ♟♟♟♟
VALUE ★★★
GRAPES chardonnay
REGION Gisborne
CELLAR ▮ 3
PRICE $18-21

Mills Reef Chardonnay

The Mills Reef winery is in Tauranga, but Paddy Preston draws all his fruit from Hawke's Bay.
CURRENT RELEASE 1992 The nose is delightful — it's chock-full of butterscotch and faint chocolate characters. The wine tastes clean and moderately rich, and would suit a beaten-out and crumbed pan-fried chicken breast.

STYLE dry
QUALITY ♟♟♟♟
VALUE ★★★
GRAPES chardonnay
REGION Hawke's Bay
CELLAR ▮ 3
price $22-25

Mills Reef Elspeth Chardonnay

This new label for Mills Reef is made from only the finest chardonnay grapes Paddy can get his hands on, and they get all the best treatment.
CURRENT RELEASE 1991 And I thought the 'plain' version smelled of butterscotch! This one fairly reeks of it, along with cloves and cinnamon, and that's fine with me. The taste is smooth, rich and mouth-filling. I'd love to try it with half a crayfish, topped with herb butter and grilled, so I'm saving up.

STYLE dry
QUALITY ♟♟♟♟♟
VALUE ★★★
GRAPES chardonnay
REGION Hawke's Bay
CELLAR ▬ 2-5
PRICE $29-33

Millton Gisborne Chardonnay

Owner/winemakers James and Annie Millton have had a lot of fun with chardonnay grapes, making a range of different styles over the years. Like all their wines, this chardonnay is made from organically grown grapes.
CURRENT RELEASE 1991 Ripe lemons backed by a touch of mealiness from the wine's barrel fermentation form attractive aromas on the nose. They are supported by a well-rounded palate. The wine is smooth and eminently drinkable, but finishes a little short.

STYLE dry
QUALITY ♥♥♥♥
VALUE ★★★
GRAPES chardonnay
REGION Gisborne
CELLAR ▮ 2
PRICE $20-23

Mission Chanel Reserve Chardonnay

There are two Mission wines using the name Chanel. This is the mid-range model.
CURRENT RELEASE 1991 The bouquet carries hints of apricots and muesli, and the taste keys are toast and grapefruit. This is a nicely made wine, with a pleasantly lingering finish. Enjoy it with a Caesar salad, and be generous with the parmesan.

STYLE dry
QUALITY ♥♥♥♥
VALUE ★★★★+
GRAPES chardonnay
REGION Hawke's Bay
CELLAR ▮ 3
PRICE $15-17

Mission Hawke's Bay Chardonnay

Mission has been known for fairly simple chardonnays that emphasised the fruit rather than winery techniques, but recent vintages have been more complex.
CURRENT RELEASE 1992 I get grapefruit and Weet-Bix on the nose of this nicely structured wine, and good, ripe citrus fruit on the palate. The finish is spicy and quite long. Enjoy it with pan-fried flounder.

STYLE dry
QUALITY ♥♥♥♥
VALUE ★★★★
GRAPES chardonnay
REGION Hawke's Bay
CELLAR ▮ 2
PRICE $12-14

Mission St Peter Chanel Chardonnay

The Mission winery is run by an order of Catholic brothers, hence the religious connotations of many of its wine names.

CURRENT RELEASE 1991 This is a big, mouth-filling wine with an upfront bouquet, yet it manages to be elegant at the same time. It would make a fine companion for a piece of casseroled wild pork, but most of us will have to settle for the tame version.

STYLE dry
QUALITY ♥♥♥♥
VALUE ★★★+
GRAPES chardonnay
REGION Hawke's Bay
CELLAR ▬ 2-3
PRICE $18-23

Montana Estates Renwick Estate Chardonnay

Most people prefer the Ormond version (see *Overflow*), but I am happy to admit a preference for its more subdued relation.

CURRENT RELEASE 1990 The nose is limey and flinty, and the taste firm, fresh and very clean. It doesn't make anywhere near as strong a statement as the Ormond wine, but I like its finesse.

STYLE dry
QUALITY ♥♥♥♥♥
VALUE ★★+
GRAPES chardonnay
REGION Marlborough
CELLAR ▬ 2-5
PRICE $29-33

Montana Gisborne Chardonnay

Made with minimal oak treatment and therefore often touted as a wine to show what untrammelled chardonnay tastes like, this wine is a steady seller for Montana both in New Zealand and overseas.

CURRENT RELEASE 1991 The bouquet is shy, with gentle citrus characters and just a suggestion of vanilla. The taste is fairly plain, but pleasantly clean and crisp. Enjoy it with a tuna and olive salad.

STYLE dry
QUALITY ♥♥♥
VALUE ★★★½
GRAPES chardonnay
REGION Gisborne
CELLAR ▮ 3
PRICE $8-13

Montana Marlborough Chardonnay

Unlike its Gisborne cousin, the Marlborough version spends a year in French and American barrels and is usually given an extra year's bottle age before being released.

CURRENT RELEASE 1990 The mealy nose reminds me of cornflakes with a touch of ripe pawpaw, while the taste is appealingly round, reasonably rich and has enough acid to ensure a medium-long citric finish. Good with pork bangers and mash.

STYLE dry
QUALITY ▼▼▼▼
VALUE ★★★½
GRAPES chardonnay
REGION Marlborough
CELLAR 🍾 3
PRICE $12-13

Morton Estate Chardonnay (Yellow Label)

Morton Estate's Yellow Label wines are inexpensive and not designed for long-term cellaring. The chardonnay gets no wood treatment.

CURRENT RELEASE 1992 The wine doesn't give much away on the nose, but you can pick up limes and apple skin if you search. The tastes are rather more obvious and give evidence of sweet, ripe grapes. Unusually for the variety, it's quite refreshing on its own, but also does sterling service alongside a plate of grilled chicken wings.

STYLE dry
QUALITY ▼▼▼
VALUE ★★★+
GRAPES chardonnay
REGION Gisborne and Hawke's Bay
CELLAR 🍾 1
PRICE $11-13

Morton Estate Hawke's Bay Chardonnay (Black Label)

This big, complex wine has won all sorts of praise for the Morton label over the years, and looks set to continue to do so far into the future.

Previous outstanding vintages: '86

CURRENT RELEASE 1991 Spiced orange peel — that's what I find on the nose of this stylish wine. In the mouth it's rich and mealy, and the finish is reasonably long. Enjoy it with a fillet or two of pan-fried tarakihi.

STYLE dry
QUALITY ▼▼▼▼▼
VALUE ★★★
GRAPES chardonnay
REGION Hawke's Bay
CELLAR ▭▬ 2-4
PRICE $24-28

Morton Estate Hawke's Bay Chardonnay (White Label)

One step down from the near-legendary Black Label model, this reliable wine is often almost as good but costs around half as much.

CURRENT RELEASE 1991 Clean, citric characters on the nose form a pleasant introduction, and they are followed up by some refreshing lime-cordial-like flavours on the palate. Good wine for a plate of grilled scallops.

STYLE dry
QUALITY ♀♀♀♀
VALUE ★★★+
GRAPES chardonnay
REGION Hawke's Bay
CELLAR 🍾 3
PRICE $15-17

Nautilus Marlborough Chardonnay

Quite a few wineries make a Hawke's Bay chardonnay and a Marlborough sauvignon blanc. Australian-owned Nautilus reverses the trend.

CURRENT RELEASE 1992 The bouquet is quite nutty, and I fancy I can pick up some grapefruit character as well. The wine is softer than the '91 model, but still boasts nice, rich flavours. Good with a chicken casserole.

STYLE dry
QUALITY ♀♀♀♀
VALUE ★★★
GRAPES chardonnay
REGION Marlborough
CELLAR 🍾 3
PRICE $20-23

Neudorf Moutere Chardonnay

This wine delighted Nelson fans by taking a gold medal at last year's Air New Zealand National Wine Awards. Previous outstanding vintages: '89

CURRENT RELEASE 1991 Limes, lemons and all those other wonderful chardonnay characteristics make for a pleasant bouquet. The palate reeks of sweet, ripe grapes leading up to a clean, long-lasting finish. Enjoy it with — what else — freshly boiled Nelson crabs.

STYLE dry
QUALITY ♀♀♀♀♀
VALUE ★★★+
GRAPES chardonnay
REGION Nelson
CELLAR 🍾 3-4
PRICE $22-25

Ngatarawa Alwyn Chardonnay

Ngatarawa's top labels carry the name of an individual connected with the Corbans and Glazebrooks, who own the vineyard. Alwyn Chardonnay, named after winemaker Alwyn Corban, is made in an idiosyncratic style that has won many friends.

CURRENT RELEASE 1991 As always, this wine boasts a clean, crisp limey bouquet, with subtle oak following on behind. In the mouth good acids make it delightfully refreshing, but the overall impression is of elegance. It's a great companion for briny rock oysters.

STYLE dry
QUALITY 🍷🍷🍷🍷🍷
VALUE ★★★
GRAPES chardonnay
REGION Hawke's Bay
CELLAR ▬▬ 3-5
PRICE $25-27

Ngatarawa Stables Chardonnay

The Stables series is a second label for owner/winemaker Alwyn Corban's Hastings vineyard. The chardonnay is usually a fairly simple style, designed to be enjoyed while it is young, but the grapes were so good in 1991 that this model has something of big brother Alwyn's class.

CURRENT RELEASE 1991 The bouquet has hints of nectarine with a bit of sweet hay. The ripe, sweet palate is rich and appealing, and there's a definite 'pour another glass' sort of finish.

STYLE dry
QUALITY 🍷🍷🍷🍷
VALUE ★★★+
GRAPES chardonnay
REGION Hawke's Bay
CELLAR 🍾 2
PRICE $15-18

Nobilo Poverty Bay Chardonnay

If you want to check out the taste of pure chardonnay, undisguised by oak, yeast character or malolactic fermentation, this is the one to go for. It joins Montana's Gisborne model as one of the few unoaked chardonnays made in New Zealand.

CURRENT RELEASE 1992 The nose is predictably steely and limey, and the flavour is pure chardonnay. This is a simple, clean, crisp wine, and is all the more refreshing for that. It's great with Nelson Bay rock oysters.

STYLE dry
QUALITY 🍷🍷🍷
VALUE ★★★+
GRAPES chardonnay
REGION Gisborne
CELLAR 🍾 1
PRICE $12-14

Nobilo Reserve Chardonnay (Dixon Vineyard)

A famous line for the company, and one that has earned a fair share of awards.

Previous outstanding vintages: '87

CURRENT RELEASE 1991 The bouquet has got mealy characters from the wine's fermentation in barrels, along with toast and butterscotch. In the mouth it is well rounded, spicy and rich. It's great with roast chicken and kumara.

STYLE dry
QUALITY ▼▼▼▼▼
VALUE ★★★
GRAPES chardonnay
REGION Gisborne
CELLAR ▬ 2-4
PRICE $23-26

Nobilo Reserve Chardonnay (Marlborough)

The grapes for this stylish chardonnay came from the Rapaura district, where stony soil reflects the sun's warmth back onto the ripening bunches.

CURRENT RELEASE 1991 The nose is earthy, but also boasts toasty hints. On the palate the wine is a middleweight, has enough citric character to keep things interesting, and finishes cleanly. Try it with crayfish, if you should be so lucky.

STYLE dry
QUALITY ▼▼▼▼
VALUE ★★★
GRAPES chardonnay
REGION Marlborough
CELLAR ▮ 2
PRICE $20-23

Nobilo Reserve Chardonnay (Tietjen Vineyard)

Taste a wine like this and you realise the Gisbornites have got a point in claiming their region as the chardonnay capital of New Zealand.

CURRENT RELEASE 1991 The nose is steely and firm, with apricot characters wandering around at the back. In the mouth it is rich but controlled, buttery and smooth. Enjoy it with pan-fried snapper.

STYLE dry
QUALITY ▼▼▼▼▼
VALUE ★★★+
GRAPES chardonnay
REGION Gisborne
CELLAR ▬ 3-5
PRICE $18-22

Okahu Estate Clifton Chardonnay

Okahu Estate is the Far North's only commercial winery. Early wines were made from grapes brought in from other areas, but now the home vineyard is beginning to mature.

CURRENT RELEASE 1992 The nose speaks of orange peel, and the palate starts well, gets a little thin in the middle but finishes with a nice bit of spice. Partner it with a bowl of olives.

STYLE dry
QUALITY ▼▼▼
VALUE ★★+
GRAPES chardonnay
REGION Northland
CELLAR ▮ 2
PRICE $19-24

Oyster Bay Chardonnay

I'm not sure if I'm supposed to tell you this, because it's not mentioned on the label, but Oyster Bay is a mainly export line produced by Delegat's Wine Estate. Originally, Jim and Rosemari Delegat intended to export the lot, but the range has done so well it's in big demand at home. This chardonnay grabbed gold at the 1992 Air New Zealand Wine Awards.

CURRENT RELEASE 1992 Peaches, melons and a nice bit of oaky spice are all in perfect balance in the bouquet. The wine is rich but elegant, and very together. Enjoy it with seafood-topped fettucine.

STYLE dry
QUALITY ▼▼▼▼▼
VALUE ★★★+
GRAPES chardonnay
REGION Marlborough
CELLAR ▬▬ 2-4
PRICE $19-24

Palliser Chardonnay

One of the larger players on the Martinborough wine scene, Palliser enjoys a good reputation for both chardonnay and pinot noir.

Previous outstanding vintages: '89

CURRENT RELEASE 1992 A hint of mealiness behind the citric characters suggest barrel fermentation. The wine is smooth, clean and fresh, and suits simple food like pan-fried snapper.

STYLE dry
QUALITY ▼▼▼▼
VALUE ★★
GRAPES chardonnay
REGION Martinborough
CELLAR ▬▬ 2-3
PRICE $30-32

C. J. Pask Chardonnay

Former topdressing pilot Chris Pask owns some of the best vineyards in Hawke's Bay, and he's got one of the most talented winemakers in the country in Kate Radburnd — as Kate Marris, she won many medals and trophies for her former employer, Vidal Wines.

CURRENT RELEASE 1991 There's a hint of gunpowder on the nose, along with apricots and Weet-Bix. The palate is spicy and quite rich, and the finish is reminiscent of a ripe pawpaw. Partner it with a green salad topped with pink chicken livers.

STYLE dry
QUALITY ▼▼▼▼
VALUE ★★★+
GRAPES chardonnay
REGION Hawke's Bay
CELLAR ▮ 2
PRICE $17-19

Penfolds Winemaker's Reserve Chardonnay

This is part of a new Penfolds range replacing the oddly named Ne Plus Ultra series, and therefore designed to be near the top of the market.

CURRENT RELEASE 1991 There's a pleasant mealiness on the nose, and the vanilla characters of the oak barrels in which the wine was fermented and aged are also discernible. The palate is soft and peachy with a nice grapey finish. Enjoy it with a creamy chicken and baby onion casserole.

STYLE dry
QUALITY ▼▼▼▼
VALUE ★★★
GRAPES chardonnay
REGION Marlborough
CELLAR ▮ 3
PRICE $14-15

Revington Vineyard Chardonnay

The first chardonnay from Ross Revington's recently established Gisborne vineyard gave immediate notice that it was going to be a high-flyer by taking a fistful of gold medals and a trophy or two at various wine shows. Previous outstanding vintages: '89

CURRENT RELEASE 1991 Ross Revington seems to have gone for a more fruit-led wine with this vintage than he has in the past. The citric tones are quite upfront and help give the wine firm, clean flavours and a pleasant amount of richness. Partner it with a Salad Nicoise.

STYLE dry
QUALITY ▼▼▼▼
VALUE ★★★
GRAPES chardonnay
REGION Gisborne
CELLAR ▭ 2-4
PRICE $23-28

Robard & Butler Gisborne Chardonnay

A very successful label for this Corbans-owned company, and the good news is there's plenty of it made each year.

Previous outstanding vintages: '86, '88, '89

CURRENT RELEASE 1991 Toasty, Weet-Bix characters dominate the nose, while the palate is chock-full of rich, ripe fruit and vanilla. The finish is spicy and long-lasting. Partner it with hot baked ham.

STYLE dry
QUALITY ♟♟♟♟♟
VALUE ★★★+
GRAPES chardonnay
REGION Gisborne
CELLAR ▬▬ 4-5
PRICE $18-22

Rongopai Chardonnay

Rongopai owner Tom van Dam used to work as a research scientist at the Te Kauwhata viticultural research station near the winery. His chardonnays are a little different from the norm, and have found a loyal following.

CURRENT RELEASE 1992 I get spicy butterscotch on the nose of this chunky chardonnay. The taste is well rounded and biscuity, and there's not a lot wrong with that. Partner it with beef satay.

STYLE dry
QUALITY ♟♟♟♟
VALUE ★★★★
GRAPES chardonnay
REGION
Hawke's Bay 80%,
Te Kauwhata 20%
CELLAR ▮ 2
PRICE $14-17

Rongopai Te Kauwhata Chardonnay

Te Kauwhata isn't an area recognised as ideal for growing chardonnay, but the Rongopai team sells plenty of this well-made wine from their roadside shop.

CURRENT RELEASE 1991 I get toasted muesli and figs on the nose of this nicely presented wine. The palate is rich, soft and mouth-filling, characters that make the wine a great partner for a long-cooked chicken casserole.

STYLE dry
QUALITY ♟♟♟♟
VALUE ★★★
GRAPES chardonnay
REGION Te Kauwhata
CELLAR ▬▬ 2-3
PRICE $22-26

St George Estate Hawke's Bay Chardonnay

Winemaker Michael Bennett used to work for one of Hawke's Bay's most famous vineyards, Te Mata Estate. Nowadays much of his wine is sold in his own vineyard restaurant.

CURRENT RELEASE 1991 The wine was barrel-fermented and given a full malolactic fermentation, so it is a little different from the norm. There is plenty of spicy oak on the nose, and the taste is clean and fresh. Try it with a pork loin chop.

STYLE dry
QUALITY 🍷🍷🍷½
VALUE ★★★
GRAPES chardonnay
REGION Hawke's Bay
CELLAR 🍾 3
PRICE $18-20

St Helena Chardonnay

St Helena was one of the first wineries established in Canterbury. It was on the market for a while, but owners, the Mundy brothers, changed their minds and are now back running it with their old enthusiasm.

CURRENT RELEASE 1991 There's a touch of mealiness in with the aroma of grapefruit on the nose. In the mouth there is evidence of good, sweet fruit and an attractive softness, presumably from malolactic fermentation. Give it until the middle of 1994 and partner it with grilled chicken wings.

STYLE dry
QUALITY 🍷🍷🍷½
VALUE ★★★+
GRAPES chardonnay
REGION Canterbury
CELLAR 1-3
PRICE $16-18

St Jerome Chardonnay

Owner/winemaker Davorin Ozich is having fun producing huge, inky reds and idiosyncratic whites at his old-established West Auckland winery. This chardonnay typifies his style.

CURRENT RELEASE 1991 I get a hint of honey on the nose, along with the more usual grapefruit characters. On the palate it is grainy, spicy and mouth-filling. Good wine for a seafood-topped pizza.

STYLE dry
QUALITY 🍷🍷🍷🍷
VALUE ★★★
GRAPES chardonnay
REGION Hawke's Bay
CELLAR 🍾 3
PRICE $24-26

Alan Scott Chardonnay

For many years Alan Scott was a Marlborough-based viticulturalist for Corbans, so he knows the area well. His wines are new on the market, but already they have found a keen following.

CURRENT RELEASE 1992 Chardonnay's classic citric characters are quite subtle on the nose, but come into play once you get the wine into your mouth. It's not as big as the '91 version, but is soft, clean and agreeable.

STYLE dry
QUALITY ▼▼▼▼
VALUE ★★★
GRAPES chardonnay
REGION Marlborough
CELLAR ▌ 2
PRICE $19-21

Seibel Reserve Chardonnay

This used to be the only barrel-fermented chardonnay in the country that sold for under $15. The price has now risen slightly, but it's still possible to buy it for $15 at the winery.

CURRENT RELEASE 1990 The nose is delightfully toasty and the flavours on the palate are soft and approachable. This is quite a rich wine, with the usual citric tones staying away until the finish.

STYLE dry
QUALITY ▼▼▼▼
VALUE ★★★★+
GRAPES chardonnay
REGION Hawke's Bay
CELLAR ▬ 1-3
PRICE $15-19

Seifried Estate Chardonnay

There used to be a lot of vintage variation in Hermann Seifried's chardonnays, but he and former winemaker Saralinda MacMillan really got things sorted out for the last couple of vintages.

CURRENT RELEASE 1992 The nose is great — all mealy and toasty, just the way I like it. The wine is quite big but very frisky in the mouth, and it boasts a pleasantly spicy finish.

STYLE dry
QUALITY ▼▼▼▼▼
VALUE ★★★★★
GRAPES chardonnay
REGION Nelson
CELLAR ▬ 2-4
PRICE $15-17

Selaks Founder's Selection Matador Vineyard Marlborough Chardonnay

A slightly new name for the wine known until the 1990 vintage as Marino Selak Founder's Selection Chardonnay. Some of that model can still be found on the shelves, alongside this newer version.

CURRENT RELEASE 1991 This is a *big* wine, with sweet loam and apricots vying for attention with chardonnay's more usual lemon/lime aromas. The wine starts sweet in the mouth, and fills out admirably before finishing with a touch of oaky spice. Enjoy it with veal — the genuine white variety, if you can find it — in a light creamy sauce.

STYLE dry
QUALITY ♛♛♛♛
VALUE ★★★+
GRAPES chardonnay
REGION Marlborough
CELLAR ▬ 2-4
PRICE $22-25

Selaks Marlborough Chardonnay

Both the 1991 and 1992 versions of this wine can be found on retail shelves. The 1991 is probably tasting better because of its extra bottle age, but this vintage is no slouch.

CURRENT RELEASE 1992 The bouquet smells of figs, which is fine by me because they're my favourite fruit. There's some nice spice on the palate and a crisp, clean finish.

STYLE dry
QUALITY ♛♛♛♛
VALUE ★★★+
GRAPES chardonnay
REGION Marlborough
CELLAR ▮ 2
PRICE $15-18

Shingle Peak Chardonnay

One of a range of attractively packaged and well-priced Marlborough wines produced by Auckland-based Matua Valley.

CURRENT RELEASE 1992 The nose is nicely mealy, and I pick up grapefruit and apricots in there as well. In the mouth it's creamy and moderately rich, and has a lingering finish. A good match for seafood-topped pasta.

STYLE dry
QUALITY ♛♛♛♛
VALUE ★★★★
GRAPES chardonnay
REGION Marlborough
CELLAR ▮ 2
PRICE $16-18

Stonecroft Hawke's Bay Chardonnay

Alan Limmer's vineyard is situated on stonier soil than most in the area, giving his wines a hot-climate intensity as a result of the sun's reflective rays.

CURRENT RELEASE 1991 I get figs on the nose of this attractive wine, followed by hints of vanilla from its sojourn in French oak barrels. In the mouth the richness of ripe fruit is balanced by crisp acids, and there is an impressively big, long-lasting finish.

STYLE dry
QUALITY �♟♟♟
VALUE ★★★
GRAPES chardonnay
REGION Hawke's Bay
CELLAR ■■■- 2-3
PRICE $18-22

Stoneleigh Marlborough Chardonnay

Marlborough sauvignon blanc has made such a name for itself overseas that many punters must presume it's a one-grape province. This widely exported Corbans-made chardonnay is helping to keep things in perspective.

Previous outstanding vintages: '89

CURRENT RELEASE 1991 The nose is reminiscent of lemon zest in this fruit-led wine. On the palate the same citric characters keep things refreshing and give it a zingy finish.

STYLE dry
QUALITY ♟♟♟♟
VALUE ★★★
GRAPES chardonnay
REGION Marlborough
CELLAR ▌ 2
PRICE $17-19

Te Kairanga Chardonnay

The biggest winery in the officially designated central Martinborough area, Te Kairanga began slowly but should be worth watching in the future.

CURRENT RELEASE 1992 There's a hint of the sort of mealiness I like on the nose, and on the palate this wine really goes for it. It's big, chunky and moreish, but lacks finesse on the finish.

STYLE dry
QUALITY ♟♟♟♟
VALUE ★★★
GRAPES chardonnay
REGION Martinborough
CELLAR ▌ 3
PRICE $25-28

Te Kairanga Reserve Chardonnay

Te Kairanga has the distinction of having a winery building partly built by social activist and Invercargill mayor Tim Shadbolt. Winemaker Chris Buring uses only his very best fruit for this wine.

CURRENT RELEASE 1991 The nose carries a hint of mealiness from its barrel-fermentation, and some of the same character is carried though onto the palate. The wine is big, complex and appealing, but lacks elegance right at the end. Good with barbecued pork spareribs.

STYLE dry
QUALITY ♛♛♛♛
VALUE ★★★
GRAPES chardonnay
REGION Martinborough
CELLAR ▬ 2-4
PRICE $22-26

Te Mata Elston Chardonnay

The Te Mata name is most often associated with the near-legendary red wine Coleraine, named after John and Wendy Buck's Ian Athfield-designed home, but this chardonnay has also had considerable praise heaped upon it.

Previous outstanding vintages: '87, '89

CURRENT RELEASE 1992 Balance is what this splendidly made wine is all about. Immaculately clean fruit gives it a richly citric tang, and there is evidence of intelligent oak treatment — but nothing dominates. Enjoy it with Nelson Bay oysters or a butter-roasted chicken.

STYLE dry
QUALITY ♛♛♛♛♛
VALUE ★★★
GRAPES chardonnay
REGION Hawke's Bay
CELLAR ▬ 2-5
PRICE $24-28

Totara Chardonnay

The Chan family's vineyard at Thames, on the Coromandel Peninsula, has been little heard of in recent years, but this and the Reserve-labelled chardonnay that follows give notice that Totara is worth watching again.

CURRENT RELEASE 1991 The nose is so reminiscent of coconut that it's like sniffing a Pina Colada. There's a bit of the same sensation on the palate, but it is backed up by more traditional citric tastes. Try it alongside a poached chicken breast topped with a mustard cream sauce.

STYLE dry
QUALITY ♛♛♛♛
VALUE ★★★+
GRAPES chardonnay
REGION Hawke's Bay
CELLAR ▮ 2
PRICE $16-18

Totara Chardonnay Reserve

Made from the best Hawke's Bay fruit the winery can get, this wine is a cut above the 'standard' version reviewed earlier. This vintage was awarded the trophy for top chardonnay at last year's Air New Zealand National Wine Awards.

CURRENT RELEASE 1990 There's a touch of that coconut character in this version as well, but it's overridden by the vanilla flavours of oak and the richness of ripe grapes. The wine is faintly viscous and has a long finish.

STYLE dry
QUALITY ♟♟♟♟
VALUE ★★★
GRAPES chardonnay
REGION Hawke's Bay
CELLAR ▮ 2
PRICE $30-33

Vavasour Chardonnay

The Vavasour winery in the Awatere Valley, Marlborough, has got one of the best vineyard/winery teams in the country in viticulturalist Richard Bowling and winemaker Glenn Thomas. This bottle arrived with 'only just bottled!' scrawled all over it, but I didn't need to make allowances — it's great.

Previous outstanding vintages: '89, '91

CURRENT RELEASE 1992 The peach, spice and melon-skin aromas on the bouquet are beautifully balanced, and there are equally good things happening on the palate. The wine is full-flavoured but smooth, and has a long finish. Try it with a rabbit pie.

STYLE dry
QUALITY ♟♟♟♟♟
VALUE ★★★
GRAPES chardonnay
REGION Marlborough
CELLAR ▬ 2-4
PRICE $24-26

Vidal Private Bin Hawke's Bay Chardonnay

Vidal, part of the Villa Maria group, achieved considerable medal success under previous winemaker Kate Marris. Her replacement, Elise Montgomery, seems to be continuing the tradition.

CURRENT RELEASE 1992 Mealy, peachy characters on the nose and a spicy, melon-like palate make an attractive package of this mid-range wine. Enjoy it with pan-fried snapper and almonds.

STYLE dry
QUALITY ♟♟♟
VALUE ★★★+
GRAPES chardonnay
REGION Hawke's Bay
CELLAR ▮ 2
PRICE $12-15

Vidal Reserve Hawke's Bay Chardonnay

The Vidal winery shares with Villa Maria a reputation for top chardonnay and cabernet sauvignon, and uses all Hawke's Bay fruit. This latest Reserve chardonnay scored a silver medal at the 1992 Air New Zealand National Wine Awards.

Previous outstanding vintages: '86, '89

CURRENT RELEASE 1991 The wood is subdued in the bouquet, overridden at this stage by clean, citric fruit characters. The taste is all about ripe, rich fruit, and there is an appealingly spicy finish.

STYLE dry
QUALITY ▼▼▼▼▼
VALUE ★★★★
GRAPES chardonnay
REGION Hawke's Bay
CELLAR ▇▬ 2-3
PRICE $20-25

Villa Maria Cellar Selection Chardonnay

One of three mid-priced wines (the others are a sauvignon blanc and a cabernet/merlot) that have done well for the Villa team since their release in the middle of 1992.

CURRENT RELEASE 1991 Nice wine! The nose has light toast backing up the citrics, and there are some delightfully fruity tones on the palate. It managed only a bronze medal at the Air New Zealand Wine Awards, but I rate it higher than that.

STYLE dry
QUALITY ▼▼▼▼
VALUE ★★★+
GRAPES chardonnay
REGION Marlborough
CELLAR ▌ 3
PRICE $16-18

Villa Maria Private Bin Chardonnay (Gisborne Region)

A steady seller for the company, and invariably top value. In good years it has more than an echo of the much-praised Reserve series' style.

CURRENT RELEASE 1992 Apricots and lemons provide an attractive welcome on the nose. The palate is pleasantly spicy and peachy, but the wine finishes a bit short. Enjoy it with a chicken salad.

STYLE dry
QUALITY ▼▼▼▼
VALUE ★★★
GRAPES chardonnay
REGION Gisborne
CELLAR ▌ 2
PRICE $11-14

Villa Maria Reserve Chardonnay Barrique-Fermented (Gisborne Region)

A regular medal winner for the company, going back to the mid-'80s, and a deserved winner of a gold at the 1992 Air New Zealand Wine Awards. The origin of the grapes varies from vintage to vintage. This year they are all from Gisborne.

CURRENT RELEASE 1991 Pears and nectarines form a nice part of the bouquet in this gold medal-winning wine. In the mouth it is rich, spicy, beautifully rounded and complete. Enjoy it with fresh oysters.

STYLE dry
QUALITY ♟♟♟♟♟
VALUE ★★★
GRAPES chardonnay
REGION Gisborne
CELLAR ■■- 2-4
PRICE $23-27

Villa Maria Reserve Chardonnay Ihumatao

Ihumatao is a few kilometres down the road from the Villa Maria winery in Mangere, adjacent to Auckland International Airport. This wine scored gold at the 1992 Liquorland Royal Easter Wine Awards.

CURRENT RELEASE 1991 There's plenty of timber on the nose but oodles of sweet, ripe fruit to keep it company. The wine fills the mouth with citric and fig sensations, and it has a long, lingering finish.

STYLE dry
QUALITY ♟♟♟♟♟
VALUE ★★★★
GRAPES chardonnay
REGION Auckland
CELLAR ■■- 2-3
PRICE $23-28

Villa Maria Reserve Chardonnay Marlborough Region

This is the Villa's first Marlborough chardonnay, and it looks set to follow on the heels of its Hawke's Bay and Auckland cousins with medal success.

CURRENT RELEASE 1991 The keynote is stylish elegance — the citrus characters of chardonnay are there on the nose, but they are so beautifully integrated with sweet oak aromas that they are quite hard to pick out. On the palate limes, ripe grapefruit and mealy tastes all vie for attention and form a most harmonious finish.

STYLE dry
QUALITY ♟♟♟♟♟
VALUE ★★★
GRAPES chardonnay
REGION Marlborough
CELLAR ■■- 2-4
PRICE $21-24

Voss Estate Chardonnay

Gary Voss entered just two wines in last year's Air New Zealand Wine Awards — this chardonnay and a merlot — and came away with two silver medals for his trouble. Not bad!

CURRENT RELEASE 1992 The nose is perfumed but clean, and offers a nice touch of spice. The wine starts sweet in the mouth and is nicely mealy from its barrel fermentation. Partner it with casseroled chicken thighs and drumsticks.

STYLE dry
QUALITY ▼▼▼▼▼
VALUE ★★★
GRAPES chardonnay
REGION Martinborough
CELLAR ▬ 2-3
PRICE $19-23

Wairau River Chardonnay

The Wairau River winery makes only two wines, a sauvignon blanc and this chardonnay. Both are exported extensively — in fact, more is sold overseas than in this country.

CURRENT RELEASE 1992 There's a nice touch of spice in with the mealy characters on the bouquet, and something of the same flavour on the palate. The wine is soft, quite smooth and boasts a clean, medium-acid finish. Enjoy it with pan-fried hapuka steaks.

STYLE dry
QUALITY ▼▼▼▼
VALUE ★★★
GRAPES chardonnay
REGION Marlborough
CELLAR ▬ 1-3
PRICE $22-26

Whitecliff Chardonnay

Whitecliff is a mid-range label for Sacred Hill, of Hawke's Bay. The wines stand out on the shelf because they are packaged in frosted bottles.

CURRENT RELEASE 1992 There are some citric characters in the bouquet, but they're pretty shy about coming forward. In the mouth the wine is grainy, spicy and pleasant. Try with smoked beef on lettuce leaves.

STYLE dry
QUALITY ▼▼▼▼
VALUE ★★★
GRAPES chardonnay
REGION Hawke's Bay
CELLAR ▮ 2
PRICE $17-19

Chenin Blanc and Chenin Blanc/Chardonnay Blends

Chenin blanc is a high-acid grape, which makes its wines ungenerous and austere when they are young but gives them the ability to age with grace and poise. Not widely grown in New Zealand, chenin is nevertheless responsible for a handful of very good wines and, often anonymously, a number of crisp-finishing, undemanding quaffers. It combines well with less-than-perfect chardonnay and is often used for low-priced wines one step up from plain 'dry white' status.

Akarangi Hawke's Bay Chenin Blanc

The Akarangi tasting room is in an old church in Havelock North. It's difficult to find, but well worth a visit. Phone the owner, Morton Osborne, and ask for directions.

CURRENT RELEASE 1992 The nose is perfumed but earthy — a combination I found rather appealing. In the mouth it starts sweet, rounds out in the middle and finishes with an appley zing. Good wine for a salad of outdoor tomatoes drizzled with extra-virgin olive oil.

STYLE dry
QUALITY ▼▼▼▼
VALUE ★★★★
GRAPES chenin blanc
REGION Hawke's Bay
CELLAR ▮ 3-5
PRICE $10-13

Collards Chenin Blanc Dry

The Collard family has done better than any other New Zealand winery with chenin blanc, winning regular medals and other awards both here and overseas.

CURRENT RELEASE 1992 This spicy, rich, ripe wine is about as far removed from the average chenin as you can get. It fills the mouth and lingers for a long time after it has been swallowed. Enjoy it with Chinese stir-fried pork.

STYLE dry
QUALITY ▼▼▼▼▼
VALUE ★★★★+
GRAPES chenin blanc
REGION Te Kauwhata and Hawke's Bay
CELLAR ▭- 3-5
PRICE $11-16

Corbans White Label Hawke's Bay Chenin Blanc

The chenin blanc wines of Vouvray, in France's Loire Valley, age gracefully for a decade or more. This Corbans example is a fraction of the price of a good Vouvray, but the company believes it has at least some of the same ageing ability.

CURRENT RELEASE 1992 With a nose like melon skins and a crisp, clean, just off-dry taste, this well-made wine is enjoyable drinking now and should age well for three or four years — and just might last a lot longer. The good thing is that it's cheap enough for you to put some away for curiosity.

STYLE off-dry
QUALITY ▼▼▼▽
VALUE ★★★★
GRAPES chenin blanc
REGION Hawke's Bay
CELLAR ▬ 2-7
PRICE $6-9

Esk Valley Private Bin Chenin Blanc (Wood-Aged)

Spending a bit of time in oak barrels helps chenin's acids blend back into the overall flavour. Esk Valley winemaker, Grant Edmonds, has done well with the style.

CURRENT RELEASE 1991 There are floral spices on the nose, along with a touch of tangelo. The wine is quite big and rich in the mouth, with plenty of the variety's trademark crisp acids, but it finishes a bit short.

STYLE dry
QUALITY ▼▼▼
VALUE ★★★+
GRAPES chenin blanc
REGION Hawke's Bay
CELLAR ▬ 1-2
PRICE $10-12

Esk Valley Reserve Chenin Blanc

Villa Maria, of which Esk Valley is a part, makes Reserve wines only when they can get exceptionally good examples of a particular grape variety. That gives an indication of how seriously Grant Edmonds takes chenin blanc.

CURRENT RELEASE 1991 A faintly medicinal nose gives notice that this wine is different from the norm. It is quite firm in the mouth and doesn't give a lot away. The finish is slightly bitter but not unpleasant. Leave it for a couple of years and partner it with rabbit, pan-fried with olives.

STYLE dry
QUALITY ▼▼▼▽
VALUE ★★★
GRAPES chenin blanc
REGION Hawke's Bay
CELLAR ▬ 2-4
PRICE $16-19

Lincoln Chenin Blanc

Lincoln's Nick Chan is one of a handful of winemakers in New Zealand to bother barrel-fermenting chenin blanc, and he has had some quite good results.

CURRENT RELEASE 1992 Things are mainly citric on the nose, but there's a dash of oak character in there as well from the wine's sojourn in used French and new American barrels. On the palate it starts sweet, rounds out in the middle but ends up quite austere on the finish. Partner it with a toasted mozzarella cheese sandwich.

STYLE dry

QUALITY ▼▼▼▼

VALUE ★★★

GRAPES chenin blanc

REGION Waikato

CELLAR ▦— 2-3

PRICE $13-15

Matawhero Chenin/Chardonnay

Most blends of these two varieties are sold young, but Matawhero's Denis Irwin believes in holding them back to get a bit of bottle age.

CURRENT RELEASE 1989 There's some nice spice on the nose and clean, fresh tastes on the palate. Nice wine for Chinese-style chicken cooked with a load of ginger and garlic.

STYLE dry

QUALITY ▼▼▼▼

VALUE ★★★+

GRAPES
chardonnay 70%,
chenin blanc 30%

REGION Gisborne

CELLAR ▯ 2

PRICE $16-19

Millton Gisborne Chenin Blanc

James Millton takes chenin blanc more seriously than most winemakers, but he says it is not a grape for viticulturalists who control the vineyard from their tractor seat. Its habit of ripening unevenly means you've got to get in amongst the bunches to sort things out. His dedication shows.

CURRENT RELEASE 1991 Spice, flowers and melon characters form an attractive trio on the nose, while the tastes are round, spicy and mouth-filling. The wine is drinking well now but needs time to be at its best. Give it until at least the end of 1994 and partner it with a chicken and tomato salad dressed with home-made mayonnaise.

STYLE dry

QUALITY ▼▼▼▼

VALUE ★★★

GRAPES chenin blanc

REGION Gisborne

CELLAR ▦— 1-5

PRICE $19-23

St Aubyns Chenin Blanc/Chardonnay

Mostly chenin but with enough chardonnay to give it a bit of extra depth, this wine is popular and well priced. The two varieties add up to more than the sum of their parts.
CURRENT RELEASE 1992 The bouquet is distinctly limey, and that citric crispness carries through onto the palate. The wine seems sweet in the middle but finishes dry. Enjoy it with snacks like gherkins and biersticks.

STYLE dry

QUALITY ♟♟♟

VALUE ★★★+

GRAPES
chenin blanc 85%, chardonnay 15%

REGION Hawke's Bay

CELLAR ▊ 2

PRICE $7-10

Seibel Chenin Blanc Hawke's Bay Barrel-Fermented Classic Dry

Norbert Seibel says he makes this chenin for the confirmed chardonnay drinker. He certainly gives it the full treatment; this model has had a partial malolactic fermentation and spent fifteen months in oak barrels.
CURRENT RELEASE 1990 The delightfully toasty, mealy nose reminded me of cornflakes, and I was equally pleased with the taste. The wine is well rounded, spicy and warm, and would be a fine companion to a plate of Bluff oysters — which means you'll have to put it away for a season.

STYLE dry

QUALITY ♟♟♟♟

VALUE ★★★★

GRAPES chenin blanc

REGION Hawke's Bay

CELLAR ▊ 3

PRICE $12-14

Totara Chenin Blanc

After a time in the wilderness, it is good to see this long-established winery getting back into the quality-wine market.
CURRENT RELEASE 1990 This wine is so perfumed it smells like aftershave, but things come more into perspective on the palate. There's a bit of Granny Smith character in there, particularly on the finish, but overall the fruit is quite nicely rounded. Try it with crumbed squid rings.

STYLE dry

QUALITY ♟♟♟♟

VALUE ★★★★+

GRAPES chenin blanc 90%, sauvignon blanc 10%

REGION Hawke's Bay

CELLAR ▊ 2

PRICE $8-10

West Brook Hawke's Bay Chenin Blanc

This West Auckland company, once known as Panorama Vineyards, is producing a sound range of well-priced wines.

CURRENT RELEASE 1991 The nose is appley and the taste clean and crisp, with nice zingy acids to balance the touch of sweetness left in by winemaker Anthony Ivicevich. Try it with roast pork and apple sauce.

STYLE off-dry

QUALITY ♟♟♟

VALUE ★★★★

GRAPES chenin blanc

REGION Hawke's Bay

CELLAR ▬▬ 2-4

PRICE $7-9

Yelas Estate Selection (Pleasant Valley) Chenin/Chardonnay

This Henderson vineyard was established in 1895, but until recently it has been known mostly for sherry and port. Under the direction of Stephan Yelas, however, a selection of table wines is being produced and some medal success has been achieved.

CURRENT RELEASE 1990 The nose is floral, and there's something of the same sensation on the palate. The wine is appealing, but the finish drops off a bit suddenly.

STYLE dry

QUALITY ♟♟♟

VALUE ★★★

GRAPES
chenin blanc 55%,
chardonnay 45%

REGION Hawke's Bay

CELLAR ▮ 2-3

PRICE $10-12

Gewürztraminer

This is the most distinctive grape variety of them all, making wines that are strongly aromatic, spicy and floral. Gewürztraminer is a 'wow!' wine, but it is so definite that after a glass or two most winelovers call out for something a little less exuberant. It is difficult to place with food, but I have had reasonable success pairing it with lightish curries and chilli-spiced Thai dishes.

Black Ridge Gewürztraminer

First vintage for this Central Otago winery was 1988. Since then the wines — and the winemaker — have had a constant shake-up from earthworks for the nearby Clyde Dam.

CURRENT RELEASE 1992 Things are quite subdued on the nose, but there's plenty of lively spice on the palate. The wine is an approachable middleweight and finishes crisply, but with a quick belt of bitterness right at the end.

STYLE dry

QUALITY ▼▼▼▼

VALUE ★★+

GRAPES gewürztraminer

REGION Central Otago

CELLAR ▬ 2-4

PRICE $16-22

Brookfields Gewürztraminer

Winemaker and owner Peter Robertson is more famous for his rich, flavoursome red wines than his whites, but gewürztraminer is a steady seller with locals visiting his attractively landscaped Hawke's Bay vineyard.

CURRENT RELEASE 1992 The bouquet has only gentle spice, and the taste seems a little flat at first, but then things get going and round out for a reasonably crisp finish. Sip it with nuts and dried fruit.

STYLE dry

QUALITY ▼▼▼

VALUE ★★★

GRAPES gewürztraminer

REGION Hawke's Bay

CELLAR ▮ 2

PRICE $12-18

Coopers Creek Gewürztraminer

Owners Andrew and Cyndy Hendry and winemaker Kim Crawford have had moderate medal success with gewürztraminer over the years. This model won them a silver at the 1992 Air New Zealand Wine Awards.
CURRENT RELEASE 1990 Kim says the bouquet is like rose petals, and that sums it up very neatly. It smells sweet but is in fact quite dry on the palate and full of crisp, clean but properly spicy fruit. Try it with a classy ham sandwich.

STYLE off-dry
QUALITY ▼▼▼▼
VALUE ★★★+
GRAPES gewürztraminer
REGION Gisborne
CELLAR 2
PRICE $14-17

Crab Farm Gewürztraminer Dry

One of two versions of the style. The other (see *Overflow*) has a bit of residual sugar, while this model is almost bone dry.
CURRENT RELEASE 1992 The nose isn't at all typical — I found it quite toasty. Things are more conventional in the mouth, with plenty of spice and a long finish. If you've got a BYO Malaysian restaurant anywhere near you, try it with Nasi Lemak.

STYLE dry
QUALITY ▼▼▼▼
VALUE ★★★
GRAPES gewürztraminer
REGION Hawke's Bay
CELLAR 2
PRICE $14-18

Cross Roads Gewürztraminer

This new Hawke's Bay winery made an immediate impact at the 1991 Air New Zealand Wine Awards by taking one silver and four bronze medals from five wines entered. I reckon the dry riesling is the pick of their range, but the gewürztraminer is no slouch.
CURRENT RELEASE 1991 Strong ginger characters dominate the bouquet of this stylish gewürz. In the mouth it is fresh and spicy, and boasts a delightfully clean finish with no trace of bitterness. The debut 1990 version was good wine. This is better.

STYLE dry
QUALITY ▼▼▼▼
VALUE ★★★★
GRAPES gewürztraminer
REGION Hawke's Bay
CELLAR 2
PRICE $11-15

Dry River Gewürztraminer (Dry River Estate)

Dry River's Neil McCallum has made something of a crusade of producing top-class gewürztraminer. He loves the variety's outspokenness, and believes that if winemakers aren't prepared to spend time on it, they should pull the vines out.

Previous outstanding vintages: '91

CURRENT RELEASE 1992 The bouquet is rich, spicy and delicious, but it's also beautifully focused. In the mouth the wine is complete and elegant, and deserves to be enjoyed alongside a roast of pork, served with roasted potatoes, buttered baby beans and kumara, tossed in butter and chopped ginger to bring out that character in the wine.

STYLE dry
QUALITY ♟♟♟♟♟
VALUE ★★★
GRAPES gewürztraminer
REGION Martinborough
CELLAR ▣– 2-5
PRICE $21-24

Dry River Gewürztraminer 'Lawson's' Marlborough

This is Neil's 'other' gewürz, made from grapes grown on the far side of Cook Strait. It is an interesting exercise to try the two together.

CURRENT RELEASE 1992 Ginger and lychees are much in evidence on the nose, along with an elegant touch of spice. The taste starts with a dash of honey and moves through gewürz's range of spices before bunching for a clean, faintly sweet finish. Enjoy it with dried pears.

STYLE off-dry
QUALITY ♟♟♟♟♟
VALUE ★★★
GRAPES gewürztraminer
REGION Marlborough
CELLAR ▣– 2-5
PRICE $21-25

Forest Flower Collection Gewürztraminer

From one of several low-to-medium-priced Villa Maria collections. Part of the proceeds from each sale go towards saving native trees, so you can do your bit for the ecology movement while you're enjoying the wine.

CURRENT RELEASE 1991 The appropriate floral, spicy keynotes are in the bouquet, but they're quite subdued on the palate. A lighter style that is probably enjoyed, well chilled, on its own.

STYLE medium
QUALITY ♟♟♟♟
VALUE ★★★+
GRAPES gewürztraminer
REGION Gisborne
CELLAR ▌1
PRICE $9-11

Giesen Marlborough Old Renwick Road Gewürztraminer

Made in Canterbury from Marlborough fruit, this wine is less intense than many of the genre and is therefore easier to place with food.
CURRENT RELEASE 1991 Gewürzrtraminer grapes are a faintly bronze-pink colour, and there is an echo of the same tint in this wine. The bouquet is classic gewürz, with lychees, cinnamon and honey-glazed pineapple all very much in evidence. The taste doesn't quite deliver what the nose promises — the same flavours are there, but they're too subdued.

STYLE dry
QUALITY ▼▼▼▼
VALUE ★★★+
GRAPES gewürztraminer
REGION Marlborough
CELLAR ▬ 1-2
PRICE $11-13

Grove Mill Gewürztraminer

Grove Mill winemaker David Pearce makes quite a fuss of his gewürztraminer, fermenting it in barrels and leaving it in contact with the yeast cells. It seems to be a lot of trouble to go to for a variety that isn't a big seller in New Zealand, but it certainly adds interest to the wine.
CURRENT RELEASE 1991 That distinctive gewürz spiciness is joined by a dash of fresh-bread aromas in this idiosyncratic wine. The taste is fresh and spicy and not at all over the top — always a danger with this exuberant variety — and the finish is clean and slightly sweet.

STYLE off-dry
QUALITY ▼▼▼▼
VALUE ★★★
GRAPES gewürztraminer
REGION Marlborough
CELLAR ▮ 2
PRICE $16-18

Lawson's Dry Hills Gewürztraminer

Dr Neil McCallum, from Dry River Wines in Martinborough, used fruit from this vineyard for one of his two 1992 gewürztraminers. When Neil joined Dry Hills' Ross and Barbara Lawson in a Wine Options team, they called themselves 'The Dry Horrors'.
CURRENT RELEASE 1992 The nose is earthy, but it also contains a healthy dose of gewürz's spicy attributes. Interestingly, the taste features a bit of the sort of graininess found in Dry River examples. Nice wine, and a good companion to a Cajun-spiced chicken breast.

STYLE dry
QUALITY ▼▼▼▼
VALUE ★★★
GRAPES gewürztraminer
REGION Marlborough
CELLAR ▮ 3
PRICE $15-18

Lintz Estate Spicy Traminer

This new winery in Martinborough is the only one in the country to part-translate the name of the grape variety — gewürz means spicy in German.

CURRENT RELEASE 1992 The spice on the nose is broad and backed by some toasty characters. The palate is rich and mouth-filling, and there is a nice, grainy finish. It should go well with a lamb curry.

STYLE off-dry

QUALITY ▼▼▼▼

VALUE ★★+

GRAPES gewürztraminer

REGION Marlborough

CELLAR █ 2

PRICE $19-22

Martinborough Vineyards Gewürztraminer

The Martinborough area — and this vineyard in particular — has made a name for itself with pinot noir, but other varieties also grow well in the valley. Gewürztraminer is one of them.

CURRENT RELEASE 1992 Winemaker Larry McKenna reckons this is the best gewürz he's ever made. It's certainly impressive. The characteristic spicy flavours are there, but unusually for the variety, the wine has a lot of elegance. Partner it with roast pork.

STYLE dry

QUALITY ▼▼▼▼▼

VALUE ★★★

GRAPES gewürztraminer

REGION Martinborough

CELLAR █ 3

PRICE $15-17

Matawhero Gewürztraminer

Matawhero owner Denis Irwin is a larger-than-life character who has adopted some of the organic grape-growing principles of his near-neighbours the Milltons. A decade ago his gewürztraminers were considered the best in the country, but consistency has been a problem with recent vintages.

CURRENT RELEASE 1990 The nose is gorgeously rich and chock-full of cinnamon, cloves and ginger. In the mouth the wine is drier than this opulent introduction suggests. It is rounded to the point of being soft and has a slightly bitter finish. This is an idiosyncratic wine you will either love or hate.

STYLE dry

QUALITY ▼▼▼

VALUE ★★★

GRAPES gewürztraminer

REGION Gisborne

CELLAR █ 1

PRICE $15-18

Matua Valley Gewürztraminer

The Spence brothers were among the first to grow gewürztraminer, and over the years their efforts with the grape have won them a stack of medals.
CURRENT RELEASE 1991 Crystallised ginger is the overriding aroma on the nose of this charming wine, followed by hints of spice and pineapple. The taste is strongly varietal but not over the top, thanks to a good dose of crisp acid, and the finish is clean and sweet. Match it with a lightish chicken curry.

STYLE off-dry
QUALITY ♥♥♥♥♥
VALUE ★★★★★
GRAPES gewürztraminer
REGION Hawke's Bay
CELLAR ▮ 2
PRICE $10-13

Merlen Gewürztraminer

Merlen's ebullient owner/winemaker, Almuth Lorenz, has done well with gewürz, winning quite a few awards in the last few years. The judges at last year's Air New Zealand Wine Awards, however, decided this model didn't rate highly enough.
CURRENT RELEASE 1992 There's some nice cinnamon-like spice on the nose, and the taste is quite broad and pleasantly frisky, with an interestingly grainy finish. Try it with smoked fish in a herb-laced sauce.

STYLE dry
QUALITY ♥♥♥
VALUE ★★★
GRAPES gewürztraminer
REGION Marlborough
CELLAR ▮ 3
PRICE $15-17

Mills Reef Traminer/Riesling

I wasn't that rapt in the straight Mills Reef gewürz I reviewed for last year's *Penguin Guide*, so from my point of view adding riesling was a great idea!
CURRENT RELEASE 1991 Riesling's floral character wins out on the nose, with gewürz's celebrated spiciness bringing up the rear. The wine starts sweet and stays ripe and clean right to the end. Nice with a spicy Thai chicken salad.

STYLE medium
QUALITY ♥♥♥♥
VALUE ★★★
GRAPES gewürztraminer 50%, riesling 50%
REGION Hawke's Bay
CELLAR ▮ 2
PRICE $12-14

Mission Gewürztraminer

Manager Warwick Orchiston and winemaker Paul Mooney produce a large number of well-priced wines. The gewürz is one of the least expensive on the market. CURRENT RELEASE 1992 Last year's model had a subdued bouquet, but this wine is so strongly perfumed it reminds me of aftershave. The tastes are clean but not as clearly defined as I would like.

STYLE off-dry

QUALITY ▼▼▼

VALUE ★★★+

GRAPES gewürztraminer

REGION Hawke's Bay

CELLAR 🍾 2

PRICE $9-11

Nobilo Gewürztraminer

The company that pioneered müller-thurgau in New Zealand has also done a nice line in gewürztraminer over the years. The Nobilo style is drier than many, and therefore goes well with food. CURRENT RELEASE 1990 There's a swag of ginger on the nose that carries through onto the palate. This is stylish wine, nicely rounded but with enough acid zing to ensure a refreshing finish. Partner it with roast pork, and put something spicy in the gravy.

STYLE medium

QUALITY ▼▼▼▼

VALUE ★★★+

GRAPES gewürztraminer

REGION Gisborne

CELLAR 🍾 3

PRICE $13-15

Penfolds Clive River Traminer/Riesling

This wine is the pick of the inexpensive Penfolds Clive River range, offering a nice bit of gewürztraminer spice to complement the floral riesling grape — and it's often on special at around $5. CURRENT RELEASE 1991 The nose is fruity and floral with a gentle bit of gewürz spice right at the back. On the palate the wine is medium-sweet and satisfyingly mouth-filling.

STYLE medium

QUALITY ▼▼▼

VALUE ★★★★

GRAPES gewürztraminer, riesling

REGION Gisborne

CELLAR 🍾

PRICE $6-8

Phoenix Gewürztraminer

An earlier version of this wine took a gold medal and the trophy for top gewürz at the Air New Zealand Wine Awards.
CURRENT RELEASE 1991 This is very clean, stylish wine. The palate is quite big, with all of gewürztraminer's considerable attributes in perfect balance. Enjoy it on its own.

STYLE off-dry

QUALITY ☘☘☘☘☘

VALUE ★★★

GRAPES gewürztraminer

REGION Gisborne

CELLAR ▮ 2

PRICE $12-14

Rippon Vineyard Gewürztraminer

The Rippon vineyard, on the shores of Lake Wanaka, has been called the most picturesque site in New Zealand. This wine was made by Rudi Bauer, who has since left Rippon and moved to the Giesen winery in Canterbury.
CURRENT RELEASE 1992 There's steely spice on the nose, which I rather like. The taste is rich and honeyed, with traces of lychee and cloves coming through, and the finish is clean and memorable. Share it, on its own, with good friends.

STYLE off-dry

QUALITY ☘☘☘☘

VALUE ★★★+

GRAPES gewürztraminer

REGION Central Otago

CELLAR ▮ 3

PRICE $16-18

Robard & Butler Gewürztraminer

A couple of vintages ago, this wine was made from Gisborne grapes. In 1990 the blend was part Gisborne, part Marlborough, and now it is all from Marlborough.
CURRENT RELEASE 1991 The nose is all about lychees and crystallised ginger — classic gewürz characteristics. The same flavours are in evidence on the palate, but the overall impression is of balance, and that's quite a trick with so assertive a variety. Enjoy it with Thai chicken curry.

STYLE dry

QUALITY ☘☘☘☘

VALUE ★★★★★

GRAPES gewürztraminer

REGION Marlborough

CELLAR ▮ 3

PRICE $11-13

St George Estate Gewürztraminer

This small winery in Havelock North boasts one of the most pleasant vineyard restaurants in the country, and sells many of its wines there.

CURRENT RELEASE 1990 The gewürztraminer spice is there on the bouquet, but it's a bit flat. On the palate the wine is quite dry and finishes cleanly, but with a jarring dose of bitterness.

STYLE dry
QUALITY ♈♈
VALUE ★★½
GRAPES gewürztraminer
REGION Hawke's Bay
CELLAR ▮
PRICE $11-13

St Jerome Gewürztraminer (Medium)

St Jerome is the patron saint of the Ozich family, owners and winemakers at the winery that bears his name. I doubt that he ever tasted gewürztraminer, but you never know.

CURRENT RELEASE 1990 Ginger and lychees do their thing on the nose, as is only right and proper with this variety, and their luscious, spicy characters linger onto the palate. The wine starts with a real belt of flavour, dries out in the middle but stays fresh and clean right to the end. Partner it with a not-too-fiery curry.

STYLE medium
QUALITY ♈♈♈♈
VALUE ★★★+
GRAPES gewürztraminer
REGION Hawke's Bay
CELLAR ▮ 2
PRICE $14-16

Seibel Hawke's Bay Gewürztraminer (Semi-Dry)

Norbert Seibel, once winemaker at Corbans, has won a number of medals over the years with a series of gewürztraminers.

CURRENT RELEASE 1990 The nose is floral rather than spicy, and suggests the wine will be sweet. In fact, it is off-dry on the palate, boasts some pleasant lychee-like flavours in the middle but suffers from a slightly bitter finish. Norbert says it is an absolute must with crayfish.

STYLE off-dry
QUALITY ♈♈♈
VALUE ★★★
GRAPES gewürztraminer
REGION Hawke's Bay
CELLAR ▮ 2
PRICE $14-17

Seifried Estate Nelson Gewürztraminer

This non-Reserve version is one of several variations on the gewürz theme from winery owner Hermann Seifried and former winemaker Saralinda Macmillan.

CURRENT RELEASE 1992 I get cracked pepper on pineapple when I sniff this charming wine, but maybe that's my odd nose, not the wine's. In the mouth it's a middleweight, with lots of spicy, frisky flavours and a clean finish.

STYLE medium
QUALITY ▼▼▼▼
VALUE ★★★+
GRAPES gewürztraminer
REGION Nelson
CELLAR ▯ 2
PRICE $11-13

Seifried Estate Nelson Gewürztraminer (Reserve Dry)

Using the name 'Reserve Dry' suggests the wine is a step up in price, but in fact its recommended retail price is the same as for the slightly sweeter version reviewed above.

CURRENT RELEASE 1991 Ginger is the most dominant aroma on the nose, and the same character helps make the flavour big and sumptuous. Dry it may be, but this is still a full-flavoured style with a crisp, clean finish.

STYLE dry
QUALITY ▼▼▼▼
VALUE ★★★★
GRAPES gewürztraminer
REGION Nelson
CELLAR ▯ 2
PRICE $11-13

Stonecroft Gewürztraminer

This is the first time Stonecroft owner-winemaker Alan Limmer has made a totally dry gewürztraminer. Previous vintages have been medium in style.

CURRENT RELEASE 1991 The change in style hasn't affected the quality. The bouquet is grainy, spicy and rich — like honey on wholemeal toast. On the palate it is broad but with good crisp acids and the finish is clean and refreshing. Enjoy it, well chilled, on its own.

STYLE dry
QUALITY ▼▼▼▼
VALUE ★★★
GRAPES gewürztraminer
REGION Hawke's Bay
CELLAR ▯ 4
PRICE $17-19

Torlesse Gewürztraminer

The winery is in Canterbury, but winemaker Kym Rayner bought Marlborough fruit to make this stylish gewürz. It paid off — the wine won a silver medal at the 1992 Air New Zealand Wine Awards.

CURRENT RELEASE 1992 The bouquet is quite understated, which makes it classier than some over-the-top versions. It is bigger on the palate than this subdued start suggests, with lychees, ginger and cloves coming into play. The end is nicely spicy and not at all bitter. Partner it with herbed lamb chops.

STYLE dry
QUALITY ▼▼▼▼
VALUE ★★★
GRAPES gewürztraminer
REGION Marlborough
CELLAR 3
PRICE $15-18

Vidal Private Bin Hawke's Bay Gewürztraminer

This mid-priced wine is consistently good value — not as rich as the big-brother Reserve version, but offering a fair belt of spicy character for your money.

CURRENT RELEASE 1992 Good, clean spice and a taste like spiced apples make this wine an attractive mouthful. Partner it with the sort of curry that has diced fruit in the sauce.

STYLE dry
QUALITY ▼▼▼▼
VALUE ★★★+
GRAPES gewürztraminer
REGION Hawke's Bay
CELLAR 2
PRICE $10-12

Vidal Reserve Gewürztraminer

Top-of-the-line wine from a company that has been winning medals for gewürztraminer for a decade or more.

Previous outstanding vintages: '88

CURRENT RELEASE 1991 Ginger, pineapple and lychees are all there in the bouquet of this richly scented wine. The taste is rich and full and the finish lingering and pleasant.

STYLE dry
QUALITY ▼▼▼▼
VALUE ★★★
GRAPES gewürztraminer
REGION Hawke's Bay
CELLAR 4
PRICE $16-19

Villa Maria Private Bin Gewürztraminer (Gisborne Region)

Villa's mid-range Private Bin wines are often good value and don't always deserve to be regarded as poor relations of the Reserve series.

CURRENT RELEASE 1992 The nose is a little shy, but there are some nice grainy qualities on the palate, along with the usual floral spiciness. Good with Chinese sweet-and-sour pork.

STYLE off-dry

QUALITY ▼▼▼

VALUE ★★★+

GRAPES gewürztraminer

REGION Gisborne

CELLAR ▮ 3

PRICE $10-13

Villa Maria Reserve Gewürztraminer (Ihumatao)

A regular medal-winner for the company, and a wine with an enthusiastic following.

Previous outstanding vintages: '85, '86

CURRENT RELEASE 1991 A gingery bouquet is a Villa trademark, and this wine has heaps of it. The taste is quite dry, and a good acid balance gives it a pleasant crispness. Enjoy it with pineapple-glazed ham steaks.

STYLE dry

QUALITY ▼▼▼▼▼

VALUE ★★★★

GRAPES gewürztraminer

REGION South Auckland

CELLAR ▮ 4

PRICE $16-19

West Brook Gewürztraminer

West Brook's Tony Ivecivich cellars his gewürztraminer for a couple of years before releasing it. It obviously pays — he won a silver medal with this model at the 1992 Air New Zealand Wine Awards.

CURRENT RELEASE 1990 The bouquet is quite chunky, with spiced peaches, cinnamon and cloves all doing a bit of attention-seeking. The wine starts sweet but dries out towards the end. It would be a good partner for Indonesian Nasi Goreng.

STYLE medium

QUALITY ▼▼▼▼

VALUE ★★★

GRAPES gewürztraminer

REGION West Auckland

CELLAR ▮ 3

PRICE $13-15

Müller-Thurgau

Müller-thurgau, occasionally called riesling-sylvaner, is New Zealand's most widely planted variety. Müller is to the wine scene what the song 'Ten Guitars' is to parties. It will never make a *great* wine, but it is happily able to produce large numbers of pleasant, fresh and instantly appealing beverage styles that are perfect for the hot summer months. There are few food recommendations in this section — müller-thurgau is best on its own or with simple nibbles.

Babich Dry Riesling-Sylvaner

There used to be an unwritten rule that dry müller-thurgau would be labelled riesling-sylvaner. Babich is one of the few wineries to continue the tradition.

CURRENT RELEASE 1992 There are some nice lemony/floral hints on the nose that remind me more of riesling than müller. The taste is spicy and quite full. Enjoy it with a whole pan-fried flounder.

STYLE off-dry

QUALITY ▼▼▼▼

VALUE ★★★+

GRAPES müller-thurgau

REGION Gisborne

CELLAR ▮ 2

PRICE $7-9

Babich Müller-Thurgau

Same grape, different name. Babich wines are always clean, impeccably made and good value. Müller-thurgau has been a steady seller for the company over the years, and today the fruit is better than ever. The 1990 vintage picked up the trophy for best müller-thurgau at the 1992 Air New Zealand Wine Awards.

CURRENT RELEASE 1992 There are flowers and a touch of honey on the nose, and some sweet, nectar-like flavours on the palate. Crisp acids stop things getting too cloying. Best on its own.

STYLE medium

QUALITY ▼▼▼

VALUE ★★★

GRAPES müller-thurgau

REGION Gisborne

CELLAR ▮

PRICE $7-10

Brookvale Müller-Thurgau

Often the first wine released each year, Brookvale, from the Villa Maria stable, is consistently fresh, clean and fruity, medium-sweet and instantly appealing on a hot day.

CURRENT RELEASE 1992 What fun! This wine smells like flowers and honey, and tastes a bit like peaches, and on a hot summer's day that's not all bad. Partner it with — what else — a chilled peach.

STYLE medium
QUALITY ▼▼▼
VALUE ★★★+
GRAPES müller-thurgau
REGION Gisborne
CELLAR ▐
PRICE $5-8

Forest Flower Müller-Thurgau

Another Villa Maria series, this one wearing various native flowers on the labels. American tourists have been heard to wonder aloud whether the wine was made from native flowers!

CURRENT RELEASE 1992 There's a hint of ginger mixed in with the usual aromas of honey and flowers, and some nectar-like fruit on the palate. This model seems fuller-flavoured than last year's and boasts a rich but clean finish.

STYLE medium
QUALITY ▼▼▼
VALUE ★★★+
GRAPES müller-thurgau
REGION Gisborne
CELLAR ▐
PRICE $5-7

Martinborough Müller-Thurgau

Fans of this beautifully made müller had better be in quick — this is the last of the line. Winemaker Larry McKenna has pulled out the vines to make way for new plantings of pinot gris, which he believes suits the area better.

CURRENT RELEASE 1992 What a shame this is the last one — it's a beaut. It's got all the usual honey and floral characters, but there's some lovely spice in there as well, and firm, crisp acids to hold everything together. Enjoy it in the garden with summer nibbles.

STYLE off-dry
QUALITY ▼▼▼▼
VALUE ★★★★
GRAPES müller-thurgau
REGION Martinborough
CELLAR ▐ 2
PRICE $9-11

Mission St Mary Riesling-Sylvaner

Only a handful of wineries still use the alternative name for müller-thurgau. Mission calls this off-dry wine riesling-sylvaner to distinguish it from the slightly sweeter müller-thurgau (see *Overflow*).

CURRENT RELEASE 1992 Honey and clove-like aromas make for an interesting introduction. The taste is sweetish, clean and pleasant. Best on its own.

STYLE medium

QUALITY ▼▼▼▼

VALUE ★★★

GRAPES müller-thurgau

REGION Hawke's Bay

CELLAR ▮ 1

PRICE $7-9

Montana Wohnsiedler Müller-Thurgau

Dismissed by most serious wine drinkers as a bit of harmless frippery, Wohnsiedler suddenly demanded to be taken a little more seriously when, in 1984 colours (it used to be vintaged), it took a gold medal at the National Wine Awards a couple of years ago.

CURRENT RELEASE (non-vintage) Wohnsiedler varies little from year to year, and true to form the current model is fresh, delightfully fruity and on the sweet side of medium. Take a bottle on your next picnic.

STYLE medium

QUALITY ▼▼▼▼

VALUE ★★★½

GRAPES müller-thurgau

REGION Gisborne and Marlborough

CELLAR ▮ 2

PRICE $6-7

Morton Estate Müller-Thurgau (White Label)

Few people realise Morton Estate makes a müller, but this simply structured wine is a winner with the locals.
CURRENT RELEASE 1991 The nose is lightly honeyed and impeccably clean, and on the palate the acids are just crisp enough to keep the variety's natural fruitiness in check. Nice wine for summer.

STYLE medium

QUALITY ▼▼▼

VALUE ★★★

GRAPES müller-thurgau

REGION Gisborne

CELLAR ▮

PRICE $8-10

Nobilo Müller-Thurgau

Nobilo was the first company to introduce the slightly sweet style of müller-thurgau to New Zealanders back in the mid-'70s.

CURRENT RELEASE 1992 The nose is properly floral and honeyed and the taste is nicely balanced between sugar and acid. Good with a roast-pork sandwich.

STYLE medium

QUALITY ▼▼▼

VALUE ★★★

GRAPES müller-thurgau

REGION Gisborne

CELLAR 🍾

PRICE $8-10

Okahu Estate Müller-Thurgau

This pleasant müller is made under contract by Nick Chan, of Lincoln Vineyards. The winery is in the Far North, but the fruit comes from Gisborne.

CURRENT RELEASE 1992 The nose has a steely edge that makes this müller different from most. The taste is more typical, with plenty of floral notes and some nice crisp acids on the finish.

STYLE off-dry

QUALITY ▼▼▼▼

VALUE ★★★

GRAPES müller-thurgau

REGION Gisborne

CELLAR 🍾 2

PRICE $8-10

Riverpoint Riesling-Sylvaner

A new label for Matawhero of Gisborne, and a wine with promise which took a bronze medal at the 1992 Liquorland Royal Easter Wine Awards.

CURRENT RELEASE 1991 On the nose this wine is so richly honeyed that it is easy to take for a dessert style. The taste echoes the sensation of honey, but the wine is medium in sweetness, pleasantly smooth and very approachable.

STYLE medium

QUALITY ▼▼▼▼

VALUE ★★★

GRAPES müller-thurgau

REGION Gisborne

CELLAR 🍾

PRICE $15–17

St Aubyns Müller-Thurgau

St Aubyns is yet another Villa Maria series, this one near the bottom of the price heap. The company must have access to an awful lot of müller-thurgau grapes to produce so many variations on the theme.

CURRENT RELEASE 1992 There's a field of flowers in the bouquet and a reasonable amount of depth on the palate. The wine is on the sweeter side of medium but finishes with at least a touch of crispness.

STYLE medium
QUALITY ▼▼▼
VALUE ★★★
GRAPES müller-thurgau
REGION Gisborne
CELLAR 🍾
PRICE $5-8

Seifried Estate Müller-Thurgau

Müller-thurgau is the most widely planted variety in New Zealand and also in Germany, where Austrian-born Hermann Seifried did some of his training, so he has an affinity with the grape.

CURRENT RELEASE 1992 The usual floral/honey notes are in good form on the nose. The wine tastes so sweet it borders on lusciousness, but it finishes clean and crisp.

STYLE medium
QUALITY ▼▼▼▼
VALUE ★★★+
GRAPES müller-thurgau
REGION Nelson
CELLAR 🍾 2
PRICE $8-10

Villa Maria Private Bin Müller-Thurgau

Designed to be a cut above Villa's Brookvale, St Aubyns and Forest Flower müllers, this Private Bin bottling has won a few minor medals over the years.

CURRENT RELEASE 1992 There's a hint of steel in with the flowers, which I don't mind at all. The wine is on the sweet side of medium but is nice and crisp on the finish.

STYLE medium
QUALITY ▼▼▼
VALUE ★★★
GRAPES müller-thurgau
REGION Gisborne
CELLAR 🍾 1
PRICE $6-8

Pinot Gris

In last year's *Penguin Guide* we listed pinot gris in with 'Unusual Whites'. It's still unusual, but we decided to give it its own section for 1993, albeit a small one. It deserves it. At its best, pinot gris has a delightfully grainy character, along with an appealing touch of spice, and it has the advantage of producing relatively full-bodied wines in regions where lighter styles are the norm.

Brookfields Pinot Gris

The Brookfields tasting room is one of the most pleasant spots in the Bay, and this pinot gris is a popular choice for people bringing their own picnic lunch with them. CURRENT RELEASE 1992 That classic graininess is much in evidence on the nose of this charming wine, and the taste is smooth and mouth-filling with a spicy finish. Partner it with a ham salad spiked with grainy mustard, or even a ham and mustard sandwich.

STYLE dry
QUALITY 🍷🍷🍷🍷
VALUE ★★★
GRAPES pinot gris
REGION Hawke's Bay
CELLAR 🍷 3
PRICE $16-18

Dry River Pinot Gris

Dry River's Neil and Dawn McCallum have become the gurus for pinot gris in New Zealand. Neil has a great love for the styles of Alsace, and models this wine after them. The vintage was an awkward one in Martinborough, so this latest model doesn't quite reach the splendid heights of previous versions — but it's still nice drinking.
CURRENT RELEASE 1992 The nose is so citric the wine could be taken for chardonnay, but a touch of graininess gives the game away. In the mouth it starts sweet but settles down to display rich, satisfying flavours that finish firmly.

STYLE dry
QUALITY 🍷🍷🍷🍷
VALUE ★★+
GRAPES pinot gris
REGION Martinborough
CELLAR ▬ 2-3
PRICE $23-26

Gibbston Valley Estate Reserve Pinot Gris

The grapes for this wine were from some of the first vines planted by Alan Brady when he established the vineyard in 1982. It won a silver medal at last year's Air New Zealand Wine Awards.

CURRENT RELEASE 1992 The bouquet is grainy and mealy in the classic pinot gris style, and that's followed by some delightfully frisky notes on the palate. Enjoy it with a ham steak and garlic potatoes.

STYLE dry
QUALITY ᵂᵂᵂᵂᵂ
VALUE ★★★+
GRAPES pinot gris
REGION Central Otago
CELLAR 4
PRICE $17-21

Mission Pinot Gris

Mission Vineyards have a number of unusual varieties scattered around Hawke's Bay. This pinot gris used to be labelled under one of its alternative names, tokay d'Alsace.

CURRENT RELEASE 1992 The bouquet is like toasted nuts and the taste is nicely spicy and grainy, making this wine a fine companion for chicken satay.

STYLE dry
QUALITY ᵂᵂᵂᵂ
VALUE ★★★★+
GRAPES pinot gris
REGION Hawke's Bay
CELLAR 3
PRICE $9-11

St Helena Pinot Gris

Pinot gris not only grows well in France's Alsace region, but it seems suited to the colder parts of New Zealand. St Helena has been producing one for several years.

CURRENT RELEASE 1991 The colour is faintly pink and the bouquet like unfermented grape juice, and there's a bit of that same character on the palate. The wine is soft and pleasant, but doesn't have the exciting graininess I associate with the variety.

STYLE dry
QUALITY ᵂᵂᵂ
VALUE ★★★
GRAPES pinot gris
REGION Canterbury
CELLAR 2
PRICE $12-14

Riesling

Riesling, often labelled Rhine riesling, is a Cinderella variety in New Zealand, and that's a shame. Our cool ripening climate suits it well, and our best producers are able to create delightfully floral, gently flavoursome wines that are perfect for summer when they're young but cellar well for three or four years. In fact, a good four-year-old riesling is one of the world's great vinous taste experiences.

Babich Rhine Riesling

The Babich name is better known for other varieties, but over the years winemaker Joe Babich has produced a series of crisp, clean rieslings that are always excellent value. Recent versions have been made from fruit grown in the highly rated Gimblett Road area in Hawke's Bay.

CURRENT RELEASE 1992 This charming wine starts steely yet fruity — like sniffing a honeydew melon. It tastes clean and is quite well rounded, but good crisp acids make sure things stay refreshing. Enjoy it on its own — or with a honeydew melon.

STYLE off-dry
QUALITY ♥♥♥♥
VALUE ★★★★★
GRAPES riesling
REGION Hawke's Bay
CELLAR ▌ 4
PRICE $8-10

Black Ridge Riesling

This Central Otago winery is appropriately named. It is surrounded by ridges of black rock that give it the appearance of a moonscape.

CURRENT RELEASE 1992 The nose is strongly lemony, and the taste starts sweet but evens out with good crisp acids. Partner it with a fish salad.

STYLE dry
QUALITY ♥♥♥
VALUE ★★
GRAPES riesling
REGION Central Otago
CELLAR ▌ 5
PRICE $17-23

Collards Marlborough Rhine Riesling

Collards was the first winery to score gold with riesling, back in 1978. This model only managed a bronze medal at the '92 Air New Zealand Wine Awards, but a few weeks later was given a gold in Canberra. I've got to say I'm with the Aussies.

Previous outstanding vintages: '86, '87, '89

CURRENT RELEASE 1992 There's a deliciously floral nose and lots of spicy fruit, but the thing that makes this wine a standout for me is its depth of flavour. Enjoy it with melon and prosciutto ham.

STYLE dry
QUALITY ♥♥♥♥♥
VALUE ★★★★★
GRAPES riesling
REGION Marlborough
CELLAR ▌4
PRICE $11-13

Collards Rhine Riesling

This blend from three areas did better with the local judges, scoring a silver medal at the Air New Zealand awards.

CURRENT RELEASE 1991 There's plenty of honeysuckle on the nose, along with the beginnings of Aussie-style kerosene. That probably sounds pretty weird, but it works. The wine tastes honeyed but fresh, and has a luscious finish. Best on its own.

STYLE medium
QUALITY ♥♥♥♥♥
VALUE ★★★★★
GRAPES riesling
REGION Hawke's Bay, Marlborough, Henderson
CELLAR ▌4
PRICE $11-13

Conders Bend Riesling

Winemaker and owner Craig Gass says he moved to Marlborough from Nelson (where he ran Korepo Wines, now called Ruby Bay) specifically to make white wines. This riesling is a good example of his skills.

CURRENT RELEASE 1991 The nose is strongly floral with a hint of honey and oranges. On the palate it has a touch of spice, boasts zingy acids and finishes cleanly. Partner it with a nut-stuffed chicken breast.

STYLE off-dry
QUALITY ♥♥♥♥♥
VALUE ★★★+
GRAPES riesling
REGION Marlborough
CELLAR ▌5
PRICE $13-15

Coopers Creek Riesling (Hawke's Bay)

Marlborough was once regarded as a home away from home for the riesling grape, but Kim Crawford at Coopers Creek is one of several winemakers to defy the pundits by producing a series of medal-winning examples from Hawke's Bay vineyards. Kim's success is well deserved — his rieslings are fresh, floral and instantly appealing.

Previous outstanding vintages: '87, '91

CURRENT RELEASE 1992 The nose is so citric it reminds me of lemon cordial. The wine starts sweet in the mouth, but evens out in the middle palate. It's still rich, but it has enough clean, crisp acids to carry the day. Best on its own.

STYLE off-dry
QUALITY �♜♛
VALUE ★★★+
GRAPES riesling
REGION Hawke's Bay
CELLAR ▐ 2
PRICE $14-16

Corbans White Label Marlborough Johannisberg Riesling

Named for the US market, where Johannisberg is the common prefix for the grape, this wine is consistently one of the great bargains of the wine world. It's gone up a couple of dollars this year, but it's still excellent buying.

CURRENT RELEASE 1992 The nose is clean and floral, and the taste is crisp, faintly spicy and just plain enjoyable. Partner it with scallops in a creamy sauce.

STYLE off-dry
QUALITY ♛♛♛♜
VALUE ★★★★★
GRAPES riesling
REGION Marlborough
CELLAR ▭▬ 3-4
PRICE $7-9

Cross Roads Riesling (Dry)

Massey University lecturer and wine writer Malcolm Reeves and his partner Lester O'Brien have established a solid reputation for quality since they launched their Hawke's Bay winery just three vintages ago. This dry riesling is one of two they make.

CURRENT RELEASE 1992 The wine has a sort of musk perfume nose and is round and spicy on the palate. It is quite a rich style, despite its dryness, and would go well alongside a piece of pan-fried gurnard topped with a light cream sauce.

STYLE dry
QUALITY ♛♛♛♛
VALUE ★★★
GRAPES riesling
REGION Hawke's Bay
CELLAR ▐ 3
PRICE $12-16

Cross Roads Riesling (Medium)

The medium version has had a longer time in contact with the skins, which gives it a bit of extra complexity, and is a weightier wine.

CURRENT RELEASE 1992 Despite the extra sweetness, I find this wine lean on the nose and very citric. Things change after that, however. The taste is quite honeyed and rich, and there is an enjoyably fresh finish.

STYLE medium
QUALITY ♛♛♛♛
VALUE ★★★
GRAPES riesling
REGION Hawke's Bay
CELLAR ▮ 4
PRICE $10-14

deRedcliffe Marlborough Rhine Riesling

A new wine for this company, which boasts the only winery in New Zealand attached to a major hotel, in the form of the plush, Japanese-owned Hotel du Vin. Since the change of ownership, winemaker Mark Compton has been able to buy pretty well every bit of equipment he's ever wanted, and it is beginning to show in his wine.

CURRENT RELEASE 1991 Hints of green in the colour suggest youth, and a bouquet reminiscent of citrus flowers continues the impression. On the palate the wine seems quite sweet at first, but a good dose of acid straightens things out, and it finishes clean, crisp and dry. Enjoy it with poached Golden Bay scallops.

STYLE off-dry
QUALITY ♛♛♛♛
VALUE ★★★★
GRAPES riesling
REGION Marlborough
CELLAR ▮ 2
PRICE $11-16

Dry River Riesling (Craighall Estate)

Dry River owner/winemaker Neil McCallum makes two rieslings, this one from Martinborough, and another using Marlborough fruit. Like all his wines, this model needs time.

CURRENT RELEASE 1992 Dry River wines all seem to be beautifully controlled, and this riesling is no exception. On the nose it is firm and together, while on the palate it is rich and smooth. The only drawback to my taste is a slightly cloying finish.

STYLE off-dry
QUALITY ♛♛♛♛
VALUE ★★+
GRAPES riesling
REGION Martinborough
CELLAR ▬▬ 2-5
PRICE $21-24

Dry River Riesling Rocenvin Estate

Neil McCallum has been criticised for buying out-of-area grapes, but when you have people constantly wanting to buy your product and the home vineyard supply is exhausted, what else are you to do?

CURRENT RELEASE 1992 The bouquet is grainy and rich, and the taste is honeyed and sweeter than the Martinborough version, with the result that that cloying finish is exacerbated.

STYLE medium
QUALITY ♥♥♥
VALUE ★★
GRAPES riesling
REGION Marlborough
CELLAR ▮ 2
PRICE $21-24

Duke of Marlborough Riesling

Allen and Joyce Hogan's wines are usually available only by mail order, but they're well worth searching out. Check the address list at the back of the book. Riesling is one of their favourite grapes.

CURRENT RELEASE 1992 This is quite a luscious wine, with honey and dried fruit characters on the nose and sweet, rich tastes on the palate. The acids are there to keep things reasonably crisp, but the overall impression is of mouth-filling roundness. Try it with pork fillet in a fruit-based sauce.

STYLE medium
QUALITY ♥♥♥♥
VALUE ★★★★
GRAPES riesling
REGION Marlborough
CELLAR ▮ 4
PRICE $12-14

French Farm Riesling

The winery is in Akaroa, on Banks Peninsula, but the grapes for this shy but pleasant riesling come from Marlborough.

CURRENT RELEASE 1992 The nose is steely, with riesling's floral characters just discernible at the back. The wine is nicely balanced on the palate with good, crisp acids and a clean, fresh finish.

STYLE dry
QUALITY ♥♥♥
VALUE ★★★+
GRAPES riesling
REGION Marlborough
CELLAR ▮ 3
PRICE $13-16

Gibbston Valley Riesling (Southern Selection)

The words Southern Selection mean the grapes come from Marlborough, not the home vineyard at Queenstown.

CURRENT RELEASE 1992 The nose is faintly steely, but there's a good dose of riesling's more usual lemon characters in there as well. The wine is quite light in style, which makes it a good choice for lunch, and finishes cleanly.

STYLE dry
QUALITY ▼▼▼▼
VALUE ★★★
GRAPES riesling
REGION Marlborough
CELLAR █ 5
PRICE $14-18

Giesen Riesling Dry

Predictably, this family of German winemakers does well with riesling, the great grape of their homeland. Previous outstanding vintages: '87

CURRENT RELEASE 1992 There's some appealing muscat-like spice in the bouquet that carries through onto the palate to add a touch of friskiness to the wine's well-rounded flavours. Good with pan-fried pork chops.

STYLE dry
QUALITY ▼▼▼▼
VALUE ★★★+
GRAPES riesling
REGION Canterbury
CELLAR █ 4
PRICE $14-16

Gladstone Riesling

Gladstone's Dennis Roberts abandoned a professional career to establish this Wairarapa winery a few years ago. First vintage was 1991, and the three wines produced that year were pretty impressive, particularly the riesling. (If you can find any, it's still drinking splendidly.)

CURRENT RELEASE 1992 The nose is perfumed and carries hints of melon skin. The wine starts sweet in the mouth and has a bit of frisky spiciness in the middle. It's good wine, but to my mind not quite up to the superb standard of the 1991. Partner it with pan-fried scallops.

STYLE off-dry
QUALITY ▼▼▼▼
VALUE ★★★
GRAPES riesling
REGION Wairarapa
CELLAR █ 3
PRICE $18-22

Grape Republic Waterfall Bay Rhine Riesling (Dry)

Tricky stuff here. There are two Grape Republic rieslings, this dry version and the medium model reviewed below, but the only way to tell them apart is from a slight change to the text on the back label.

CURRENT RELEASE 1992 The bouquet is gently honeyed and the taste round, stylish and pleasant. Not your run-of-the-mill riesling, but none the worse for that.

STYLE dry
QUALITY ♥♥♥♥
VALUE ★★★+
GRAPES riesling
REGION Hawke's Bay and Horowhenua
CELLAR ▮ 4
PRICE $14-18

Grape Republic Waterfall Bay Rhine Riesling (Medium)

The colourful Grape Republic labels are designed by Richard Johansen, creative director for Kelly Gee FCB Advertising in Brisbane.

CURRENT RELEASE 1992 The nose is shier than the off-dry version's, which is surprising, but on the palate things start with a good belt of floral richness, although they quieten down again on the finish. Best on its own.

STYLE medium
QUALITY ♥♥♥
VALUE ★★★
GRAPES riesling
REGION Hawke's Bay and Horowhenua
CELLAR ▮ 3
PRICE $12-16

Grove Mill Riesling

Enjoying a dish of Marlborough seafood accompanied by a glass of this stylish riesling at the pleasant Grove Mill winery/restaurant in Blenheim is one of life's great summer pleasures.

CURRENT RELEASE 1992 Honeysuckle and limes are both discernible in the bouquet of this beautifully made wine. The taste is sweet and luscious at first, but then the zingy acids cut in and emphasise the clean fruit.

STYLE medium
QUALITY ♥♥♥♥♥
VALUE ★★★+
GRAPES riesling
REGION Marlborough
CELLAR ▮ 5
PRICE $16-19

Highfield Estate Marlborough Riesling

Highfield has Japanese and British owners, but wine-maker Tony Hooper was trained at Roseworthy Agricultural College in South Australia.
CURRENT RELEASE 1992 The nose is citric and steely, while in the mouth the wine is fresh but a little austere on the finish.

STYLE dry
QUALITY ▼▼▼
VALUE ★★★
GRAPES riesling
REGION Marlborough
CELLAR 🍾 3
PRICE $11-13

Hunter's Riesling

The Hunter's name is strongly associated with world-beating sauvignon blanc, but other varieties are treated equally well by the company. This riesling deserves to be better known.
CURRENT RELEASE 1992 What a charmer! The nose is lemony with a dash of the florals lurking at the back, and the taste is clean, well rounded but still delightfully crisp. Take it on a picnic and cool it in a stream, then enjoy it with the chicken salad.

STYLE off-dry
QUALITY ▼▼▼▼
VALUE ★★★+
GRAPES riesling
REGION Marlborough
CELLAR 🍾 5
PRICE $14-18

Lincoln Rhine Riesling

Made from grapes grown at the interestingly named Gunn vineyard in Hawke's Bay, this is a popular lunch-time wine at Lincoln's de Vines restaurant in Lincoln Road, Henderson.
CURRENT RELEASE 1992 A perfumed, musky nose is followed by a load of fresh lime characters on the palate. The wine offers a reasonable amount of depth for your dollar and goes nicely with Paul Hogan-style barbecued prawns.

STYLE medium
QUALITY ▼▼▼▼
VALUE ★★★+
GRAPES riesling
REGION Hawke's Bay
CELLAR 🍾 4
PRICE $10-14

Martinborough Vineyards Riesling

This company has done so well with pinot noir that winemaker Larry McKenna's skills with other grapes tend to be forgotten. They shouldn't be; Martinborough rieslings are consistently flavoursome and attractive.
CURRENT RELEASE 1992 This full-bodied style has enough acid to ensure it will last five years or more. Right now it is quite fresh, but it will round out and become rich and luscious.

STYLE medium
QUALITY ▼▼▼▼▼
VALUE ★★★+
GRAPES riesling
REGION Martinborough
CELLAR 🍾 5
PRICE $14-17

Merlen Rhine Riesling

Owner/winemaker Almuth Lorenz has had moderate medal success with her riesling wines, and they sell well through the company's mail-order Cellar Club.
CURRENT RELEASE 1992 The nose reminds me of rock melons, but the taste is more typical and richly mouth-filling. Enjoy it with a chicken salad dressed with home-made mayonnaise.

STYLE medium
QUALITY ▼▼▼▼
VALUE ★★★★
GRAPES riesling
REGION Marlborough
CELLAR 🍾 4
PRICE $13-15

Mills Reef Dry Riesling

Last year I didn't rate this wine as highly as the 1990 vintage, but it has improved markedly in the bottle over the last twelve months. Now, I love it!
CURRENT RELEASE 1991 The nose is like spicy oranges, and things are gloriously rich and full in the mouth, but with enough acids to keep that lively crispness right to the end. Enjoy it with stir-fried vegetables and savoury rice.

STYLE off-dry
QUALITY ▼▼▼▼▼
VALUE ★★★★+
GRAPES riesling
REGION Hawke's Bay
CELLAR 🍾 5
PRICE $13-15

Mills Reef Medium Riesling

The Preston family, which owns and operates Mills Reef, also runs a successful kiwifruit wine business, but the two operations are kept totally separate.

CURRENT RELEASE 1992 There's a nice touch of spiced honey on the nose and some rich characters on the palate, but the wine isn't as zingy as its older stablemate. Best on its own.

STYLE medium
QUALITY 🍷🍷🍷
VALUE ★★★
GRAPES riesling
REGION Hawke's Bay
CELLAR 2
PRICE $13-15

Millton Gisborne Riesling (Opou Vineyard)

The Opou vineyard is in the area where Poverty Bay's first vines were planted in 1890. This riesling is grown according to the Milltons' organic principles, with pests kept at bay by companion plantings of hyssop and other herbs. Previous outstanding vintages: '87

CURRENT RELEASE 1992 Flowers, honey, lemons and limes — all the classic riesling characteristics are there in the bouquet of this nicely made wine. Once you get it in your mouth, it is soft, spicy and quite rich, but boasts a crisp, fresh finish. James and Annie Millton suggest partnering it with fresh Gisborne crayfish. I won't argue — particularly if they shout.

STYLE medium
QUALITY 🍷🍷🍷🍷½
VALUE ★★★
GRAPES riesling
REGION Gisborne
CELLAR 5
PRICE $16-18

Mission Rhine Riesling

The deep-terracotta-coloured label is different from most of the Mission range, and carries the words 'satin sweetness' under the grape variety. Very poetic.

CURRENT RELEASE 1992 The bouquet is honeyed and lightly spicy, and the palate is sweet and rich, but with enough acid to keep everything clean and respectable. Best, well chilled, on its own.

STYLE medium
QUALITY 🍷🍷🍷
VALUE ★★★★
GRAPES riesling
REGION Hawke's Bay
CELLAR 2
PRICE $9-12

Montana Marlborough Rhine Riesling

Riesling from Montana's Brancott Estate Vineyard has done well — the 1990 version picked up a silver at the 1992 Air New Zealand Wine Awards, as did the 1991 vintage at the '92 Liquorland Royal Easter Wine Awards. Previous outstanding vintages: '86, '89

CURRENT RELEASE 1992 The nose is floral and steely with a bit of honey lurking at the back. In the mouth it is a middleweight, boasts plenty of clean fruit and has a touch of richness on the finish.

STYLE dry
QUALITY ▼▼▼�؟
VALUE ★★★+
GRAPES riesling
REGION Marlborough
CELLAR ▮ 3
PRICE $10-13

Morton Estate Marlborough Riesling (White Label)

Morton's John Hancock has in the past sourced his riesling grapes from Hawke's Bay, but this year he found some Marlborough fruit that took his fancy.

CURRENT RELEASE 1992 The classic riesling flower tints on the nose also display a bit of spice, which is nice. The wine starts sweet but rounds out in the middle palate and boasts well-integrated acids. Good with steamed flounder.

STYLE off-dry
QUALITY ▼▼▼؟
VALUE ★★★+
GRAPES riesling
REGION Marlborough
CELLAR ▮ 3
PRICE $9-11

Neudorf Moutere Riesling

Tim and Judy Finn's Neudorf Vineyard is tiny, but its reputation has spread far beyond the Nelson boundaries and even as far as Australia. Riesling suits the area well.
CURRENT RELEASE 1992 I like this wine! The nose is delicately scented and the taste is fresh, crisp, and beautifully clean. Enjoy it on its own in the company of good friends.

STYLE dry
QUALITY ▼▼▼▼▼
VALUE ★★★+
GRAPES riesling
REGION Nelson
CELLAR ▮ 4
PRICE $14-17

Ohinemuri Estate Riesling

Another Hawke's Bay wine from Horst and Wendy
Hillerich's just-completed winery in the picturesque
Karangahake Gorge, near Paeroa.

CURRENT RELEASE 1992 The wine has been made in a
medium style, yet the bouquet is quite sharp-edged. On
the palate it tastes citric and frisky. Try it with grilled
chicken wings.

STYLE medium
QUALITY ♟♟♟
VALUE ★★★
GRAPES riesling
REGION Hawke's Bay
CELLAR ▮ 3
PRICE $14-16

Okahu Estate Rhine Riesling

The winery is in the Far North, the grapes came from
Hawke's Bay and the wine was bottled at Lincoln
Vineyards in Henderson. It seems like a lot of trouble,
but the result is a pretty smart wine.

CURRENT RELEASE 1992 There are some limey and faintly
musky sensations happening in the bouquet, along with
enough fresh, crisp acids to make this wine a pleasant
drop from sip to swallow. Enjoy it with stir-fried pork
and vegetables.

STYLE dry
QUALITY ♟♟♟♟
VALUE ★★★+
GRAPES riesling
REGION Hawke's Bay
CELLAR ▮ 4
PRICE $13-16

Palliser Estate Marlborough Rhine Riesling

This nicely crafted wine isn't the biggest seller for
Palliser, but it has a keen following with the many
Wellingtonians who make weekend treks across the
hills to buy it by the case load.

CURRENT RELEASE 1992 The citric bouquet is reminiscent of chardonnay, except that it is backed up by spice
and flowers. The taste is rich, mouth-filling and wonderfully clean. Best on its own.

STYLE off-dry
QUALITY ♟♟♟♟♟
VALUE ★★★
GRAPES riesling
REGION Marlborough
(88%) and
Martinborough
CELLAR ▮ 5
PRICE $19-22

Penfolds Lightfoot Hill Rhine Riesling

Riesling grows well in Marlborough, where this unassuming example comes from, and the Montana group, of which Penfolds is a part, has more of it planted than anyone else.

CURRENT RELEASE 1991 There's a honeyed, floral and spicy bouquet, just as there should be, and some nice ripe fruit on the palate. The wine is crisp, undemanding but pleasant, with a crisp acid ending.

STYLE off-dry
QUALITY ▼▼▼
VALUE ★★★+
GRAPES riesling
REGION Marlborough
CELLAR ▮ 1-2
PRICE $9-11

Rippon Riesling

Like many Central Otago wines, this riesling comes in an unusual tall bottle with a lip at the top. It stands out, but retailers find it difficult to store.

CURRENT RELEASE 1992 The bouquet has something of the granite character I fancy I can detect in many Central Otago wines, along with a hint of riesling's pretty floral bouquet at the back. On the palate it starts quite sweet and develops into a mouth-filling style before finishing with a nice touch of crispness. Enjoy it alongside steamed prawns.

STYLE off-dry
QUALITY ▼▼▼
VALUE ★★+
GRAPES riesling
REGION Central Otago
CELLAR ▮ 3
PRICE $20-25

Robard & Butler Amberley Rhine Riesling

This Canterbury wine has done extraordinarily well for the Corbans-owned Robard & Butler label since its first vintage in 1986.

Previous outstanding vintages: '86, '89

CURRENT RELEASE 1990 The bouquet is honeyed and rich with an appealing touch of spice, and the palate doesn't disappoint. The wine is drier than the bouquet suggests, but it is still mouth-fillingly smooth and has a long, citric finish.

STYLE dry
QUALITY ▼▼▼▼
VALUE ★★★+
GRAPES riesling
REGION Amberley/ Waipara, Canterbury
CELLAR ▮ 3-4
PRICE $16-18

Rongopai Te Kauwhata Riesling

The Rongopai winery shop at Te Kauwhata sells not only wine but also beautifully hand-crafted kauri furniture. Winemaker Tom van Dam says this wine made itself; he believes it is the best one yet to wear the company label.

CURRENT RELEASE 1991 There are plenty of flowers and a touch of honey on the nose, just to make sure you know this is riesling. The wine starts with more honey characters in the mouth, then rounds out for an acceptable but slightly disjointed finish.

STYLE dry
QUALITY ▼▼▼
VALUE ★★★
GRAPES riesling
REGION Te Kauwhata
CELLAR ▮ 3
PRICE $13-15

St George Estate Rhine Riesling

St George's Mike Bennett used to make wine for Te Mata Estate, just down the road. Nowadays he and his wife, Jill, are kept busy running their pleasant winery restaurant, where this riesling is a popular lunchtime choice.

CURRENT RELEASE 1991 The nose has a touch of mustiness, but once you get past that there are some refreshingly crisp, limey characters on the nose and the palate. The wine is bone dry, so goes well with raw oysters.

STYLE dry
QUALITY ▼▼▼▼
VALUE ★★★
GRAPES riesling
REGION Hawke's Bay
CELLAR ▭ 3-5
PRICE $12-14

St Jerome Rhine Riesling (Dry)

St Jerome is a relatively new name for an old-established West Auckland winery — it used to be called Nova Wines, then Ozich Wines. Winemaker Davorin Ozich has made a name for himself with huge, inky cabernet/merlot blends, but he also handles delicate whites pretty well.

CURRENT RELEASE 1990 There's a touch of Aussie-style kerosene on the nose of this full-flavoured riesling. That's not a character everyone likes, but I have no objection to it. In the mouth the wine is full-flavoured, floral and spicy, finishing with a nice dash of crispness.

STYLE dry
QUALITY ▼▼▼▼
VALUE ★★★+
GRAPES riesling
REGION West Auckland
CELLAR ▮ 3
PRICE $11–16

St Jerome Rhine Riesling (Medium)

Many winemakers opt to leave just a little bit of sugar in their riesling wines in the belief that a touch of sweetness suits the variety. At St Jerome they hedge their bets by marketing two versions.

CURRENT RELEASE 1989 Like its stablemate, the wine has a lovely, floral, dry honey nose with a whiff of kerosene character. On the palate it's slightly sweet without being cloying, and boasts a reasonably long finish.

STYLE medium
QUALITY ▼▼▼
VALUE ★★★
GRAPES riesling
REGION West Auckland
CELLAR ▮ 2
PRICE $11–16

Alan Scott Marlborough Rhine Riesling

The Alan Scott winery in Blenheim boasts a very pleasant vineyard restaurant made from compressed earth, a popular building material in the area.

CURRENT RELEASE 1992 The usual floral bouquet is joined by a touch of spice in this nicely crafted riesling. The wine tastes round and clean in the mouth, and has some moreishly zingy acids. Try it with Chinese stir-fried roast pork and vegetables.

STYLE dry
QUALITY ▼▼▼▼
VALUE ★★★★
GRAPES riesling
REGION Marlborough
CELLAR ▮ 4
PRICE $12-15

Seibel Hawke's Bay White Riesling (Medium-Dry)

Norbert Seibel and his wife, Silvia, have recently been joined in the business by their daughter, Elke, who handles marketing for the company.

CURRENT RELEASE 1991 The bouquet is floral and lightly honeyed, and the taste soft but pleasant. A German food writer who tried the wine recommended it for rabbit in phyllo pastry, lamb's liver on Savoy cabbage, or venison with mushrooms.

STYLE medium-dry
QUALITY ▼▼▼▼
VALUE ★★★+
GRAPES riesling
REGION Hawke's Bay
CELLAR ▮ 1
PRICE $12-15

Seibel White Riesling (Barrel-Fermented)

In last year's *Penguin Guide*, I said labelling wines white riesling hardly seemed necessary, as there was no red riesling. I got a response from Norbert Seibel, who politely (and correctly) pointed out that white riesling is the official name for the variety in Germany, and that there *is* a red riesling, usually known as black riesling. My apologies, Norbert!

CURRENT RELEASE 1990 Apricots, flowers and vanilla share honours on the nose of this unusual wine. The taste is spicy and clean, and quite different from any other riesling on the market. Norbert suggests pairing it with a herb-laced soup, scallops or a trout fillet.

STYLE dry
QUALITY ♆♆♆♆
VALUE ★★★+
GRAPES riesling
REGION Hawke's Bay
CELLAR ▐ 3
PRICE $12-14

Seifried Estate Nelson Riesling

Hermann Seifried has an affinity with the riesling grape, and he uses it to produce everything from an inexpensive carbonated sparkling wine to a series of super-sweet dessert styles.

CURRENT RELEASE 1992 Spice, honey and wild flowers form an attractive trio on the nose. The wine is citric enough to be reminiscent of orange juice, but it has good acids to keep it crisp. Best on its own.

STYLE off-dry
QUALITY ♆♆♆♆
VALUE ★★★★★
GRAPES riesling
REGION Nelson
CELLAR ▐ 2
PRICE $9-11

Seifried Estate Nelson Riesling (Reserve Dry)

Hermann sure has fun with this grape! This is a drier version of the 'standard' riesling, but without the oak treatment given to the 'oak-aged' model.

CURRENT RELEASE 1991 The nose is more like grapefruit than lemon, and the taste is rich, quite soft but with enough acids to carry things off. Enjoy it with barbecued prawns.

STYLE dry
QUALITY ♆♆♆♆
VALUE ★★★★+
GRAPES riesling
REGION Nelson
CELLAR ▐ 1
PRICE $9-11

Seifried Estate Rhine Riesling (Oak-Aged)

Seifried is one of the few producers in the country to make an oak-aged riesling. The result isn't to everyone's taste, but it makes an interesting talking point at the dinner table.

CURRENT RELEASE 1991 The acids have softened a little since I reviewed this wine for last year's guide, but there are enough left to ensure the wine will be good drinking for another year or so. The nose is spicy and boasts a hint of vanilla, but it is now quite soft on the palate. Next time you are about to open a chardonnay for a dinner party, try this instead.

STYLE dry
QUALITY 🍷🍷🍷
VALUE ★★★+
GRAPES riesling
REGION Nelson
CELLAR 1
PRICE $11-13

Selaks Marlborough Rhine Riesling

This is only the second riesling out of the Matador vineyard, which the Selak family owns in partnership with Nobilo wines. The wine is made at Vintech, a free-lance winery in Blenheim.

CURRENT RELEASE 1992 There's a touch of the sort of herbaceousness you find in Marlborough sauvignon on the nose, but the taste is all riesling. The wine is nicely rounded and full of floral notes, and the finish is crisp and long. Michael Selak tells me it goes magnificently with crayfish.

STYLE dry
QUALITY 🍷🍷🍷½
VALUE ★★★+
GRAPES riesling
REGION Marlborough
CELLAR 4
PRICE $13-15

Shingle Peak Rhine Riesling

One of a new range of stylishly packaged Marlborough wines from the entrepreneurial Brothers Spence of Matua Valley fame. The whites are all good, but the riesling offers the best value.

CURRENT RELEASE 1992 Honey and limes combine well in the bouquet. The wine is soft on the palate but has enough acid to keep things under control. Try it alongside a chicken salad dressed with home-made mayonnaise.

STYLE dry
QUALITY 🍷🍷🍷½
VALUE ★★★+
GRAPES riesling
REGION Marlborough
CELLAR 2
PRICE $11-14

Stoneleigh Marlborough Rhine Riesling

In my book, riesling ties most years with sauvignon blanc for top honours in Corbans' Stoneleigh collection. It used to be the slowest seller in the range, but nowadays, it is right up there with the others.

Previous outstanding vintages: '85, '86

CURRENT RELEASE 1992 Corbans' Stoneleigh vineyard in Marlborough is covered in river pebbles, and I fancy I could smell them on the nose of this gently floral wine. In the mouth it starts sweet but finishes dry, which is great, but it doesn't have the fruit intensity of previous vintages.

STYLE off-dry
QUALITY ▼▼▼
VALUE ★★★
GRAPES riesling
REGION Marlborough
CELLAR ▌ 2-3
PRICE $13-15

Villa Maria Rhine Riesling

Villa produced their first riesling for several years in 1991. It was much praised and sold well, and this latest model should be equally successful.

CURRENT RELEASE 1992 The nose is floral and quite soft, but good acids give a nice lift to the palate. The wine starts sweet, then finishes refreshingly dry and citric. Partner it with poached flounder in a light creamy sauce.

STYLE medium
QUALITY ▼▼▼▼
VALUE ★★★+
GRAPES riesling
REGION Marlborough
CELLAR ▌ 5
PRICE $12-14

West Brook Hawke's Bay Riesling

Riesling is fresh and fruity when it's young, but develops great character after three or four years in a quiet spot. This West Brook example is nice now but will be well worth putting away for a while.

CURRENT RELEASE 1991 There are some nice dry-honey characters on the nose, along with a hint of dried apricots. The taste is fresh and fruity but so obvious it's in danger of being clumsy. Try it with scallops in a sauce containing just a dash of Pernod.

STYLE off-dry
QUALITY ▼▼▼▼
VALUE ★★★★
GRAPES riesling
REGION Hawke's Bay
CELLAR ▌ 4
PRICE $10–12

West Brook Marlborough Rhine Riesling

A new label for this West Auckland-based winery. In the past, riesling grapes were sourced exclusively in Hawke's Bay.

CURRENT RELEASE 1992 The nose is properly honeyed and floral, and the tastes are fresh, clean and most appealing. Given that 1992 wasn't a very good year in Marlborough, this is an impressive debut.

STYLE medium
QUALITY 🍷🍷🍷🍷
VALUE ★★★+
GRAPES riesling
REGION Marlborough
CELLAR 🍷 4
PRICE $12-15

Yelas Estate Riesling (Pleasant Valley)

One of the few Henderson rieslings on the market. The climate isn't ideally suited to the variety — it prefers less humidity — but Pleasant Valley's Stephan Yelas has made a pretty good job of putting this one together.

CURRENT RELEASE 1992 The wine is floral and slightly honeyed on the nose and quite rich in the mouth, if a little reedy right at the end. It would go well with lightly spiced Chinese food.

STYLE off-dry
QUALITY 🍷🍷🍷
VALUE ★★★★
GRAPES riesling
REGION West Auckland
CELLAR 🍷 3
PRICE $9-12

Sauvignon Blanc and Semillon

Sauvignon blanc, sometimes bottled as fumé blanc, is the variety that has put New Zealand on the world wine map. We have a cool climate by viticultural standards, so the grapes have plenty of time to hang around on the vine and concentrate their flavour. When it comes to sauvignon blanc, that means the finished wine fairly screams of varietal character.

At first, Marlborough seemed to be the spiritual home of this distinctive grape variety, and certainly it is the Marlborough styles that have made it big overseas. Lately, however, Hawke's Bay has been making a determined bid for top sauvignon blanc honours. As consumers, we can sit back and enjoy the fight. Both areas make good wines, but they are distinctly different. Marlborough sauvignons are grassy, herbaceous and highly aromatic. Hawke's Bay versions are softer, rounder and often have tropical fruit characters. Take your pick.

On its own, semillon makes wine that shares many of sauvignon blanc's characteristics, but when the two are blended together the wine often takes on a new life that is greater than the sum of its parts.

Babich Hawke's Bay Sauvignon Blanc

This Henderson winery produces two sauvignons – one from Hawke's Bay, one from Marlborough. Both have achieved medal success.

Previous outstanding vintages: '89

CURRENT RELEASE 1992 The nose is more perfumed than grassy at first, and boasts a pleasant amount of tropical fruit character. In the mouth it is sweet, clean and refreshing, and finishes with a spicy twist. It's good with pan-fried fillets of sole.

STYLE dry

QUALITY ▼▼▼▼

VALUE ★★★★

GRAPES sauvignon blanc

REGION Hawke's Bay

CELLAR ▋ 1

PRICE $9-11

Babich Marlborough Sauvignon Blanc

The 1991 version of this wine was the first the company had made from Marlborough fruit, and it took a gold medal at that year's Air New Zealand Wine Awards. This vintage managed only a silver at last year's awards, but won gold and the A&G Trophy for 'Best White Table Wine' at the ACI Australian Wine Show.
CURRENT RELEASE 1992 There are some classic Marlborough scents on the nose — capsicums, cut grass and all that — but also the sort of passionfruit characters more often found in Hawke's Bay. In the mouth it is rich and so smooth it seems almost unctuous, with a medium-length finish. Try it with smoked salmon and strips of roasted capsicum on rye toast.

STYLE dry
QUALITY ▼▼▼▼▼
VALUE ★★★★+
GRAPES sauvignon blanc
REGION Marlborough
CELLAR ▮ 1
PRICE $10-14

Brookfields Sauvignon Blanc

Owner/winemaker Peter Robertson has won a lot of well-deserved kudos for his big, flavoursome reds, but watch out for his whites — they're getting better every year.
CURRENT RELEASE 1992 The wine is warm and spicy on the nose, thanks to its sojourn in oak barrels. It is not a super-crisp style, rather it tastes rich and smooth and boasts a lingering finish. Partner it with smoked snapper roe on toast.

STYLE dry
QUALITY ▼▼▼▼
VALUE ★★★
GRAPES sauvignon blanc
REGION Hawke's Bay
CELLAR ▮ 2
PRICE $14-17

Chard Farm Barrique-Ferment Sauvignon Blanc

In last year's guide, I expressed doubt as to whether sauvignon blanc suited this vineyard, but after tasting this latest model I'm changing my mind.
CURRENT RELEASE 1992 The nose is all cut grass and gooseberries in the approved sauvignon fashion, but the usual Central Otago high acids have been tempered by the barrel fermentation. The wine is crisp, clean and lively, and has a touch of mealy spice on the finish. Enjoy it with Chinese stir-fried chicken and vegetables.

STYLE dry
QUALITY ▼▼▼▼
VALUE ★★★+
GRAPES sauvignon blanc
REGION Central Otago
CELLAR ▮ 1
PRICE $16-19

Clearview Sauvignon Blanc

Clearview partners Tim Turvey and Helma Van den Burg offer Mediterranean lunches at their seaside winery during the summer months.
CURRENT RELEASE 1992 The nose has more depth than many of the genre. In the mouth it starts sweet but then dries out for a nice, clean finish. An uncomplicated wine that cries out for a seafood salad.

STYLE dry
QUALITY 🍷🍷🍷
VALUE ★★+
GRAPES sauvignon blanc
REGION Hawke's Bay
CELLAR 🍷 1
PRICE $18-20

Cloudy Bay Sauvignon Blanc

This wine has done an enormous amount to put New Zealand on the world wine map. The easy-to-remember name and simple label have caught the public imagination in Australia, Europe, the US and the Far East, with the result that there's not a lot left for us.
Previous outstanding vintages: '88, '89, '91
CURRENT RELEASE 1992 Spicy cloves, freshly cut capsicums and flowers are the attractive flavour components in the bouquet of this beautifully made wine. The taste is rich and mouth-filling, but with nicely integrated acids keeping everything in balance. Partner it with a whole baked Marlborough salmon stuffed with herbed mushrooms.

STYLE dry
QUALITY 🍷🍷🍷🍷🍷
VALUE ★★★
GRAPES sauvignon blanc 95%, semillon 5%
REGION Marlborough
CELLAR 🍷 3
PRICE $20-26

Collards Barrique-Fermented Semillon

The team at Collards uses a mixture of two types of French oak to ferment and age their Henderson-grown semillon juice.
CURRENT RELEASE 1992 There's some nice spice on the nose and a clean, frisky, faintly limey character on the palate. It should be good with Cajun-spiced chicken.

STYLE dry
QUALITY 🍷🍷🍷
VALUE ★★★+
GRAPES semillon
REGION West Auckland
CELLAR 🍷 3
PRICE $14-18

Collards Marlborough Sauvignon Blanc

Impeccable cleanliness is a hallmark of wines from this respected West Auckland producer, and that quality is epitomised by this refreshing sauvignon.

CURRENT RELEASE 1992 Capsicum characters mark this wine as a classic Marlborough style, but the lads have managed to get a bit more fruit depth than many of their competitors in this difficult vintage. It's rich, satisfying and boasts a medium-long finish. Try it with a ham sandwich.

STYLE dry

QUALITY ▼▼▼▼▼

VALUE ★★★★

GRAPES sauvignon blanc

REGION Marlborough

CELLAR ▯ 2

PRICE $13-17

Collards Rothesay Vineyard Sauvignon Blanc

The Rothesay vineyard is at Waimauku, a few kilometres away from the Henderson winery. It has spawned some highly successful wines, including this regular medal-winner.

Previous outstanding vintages: '89, '90

CURRENT RELEASE 1992 Hay, honeysuckle and asparagus — they're all there in the bouquet. The wine is soft and quite mouth-filling, and would be a good partner for a chicken salad with home-made mayonnaise.

STYLE dry

QUALITY ▼▼▼▼▼

VALUE ★★★★

GRAPES sauvignon blanc

REGION West Auckland

CELLAR ▯ 3

PRICE $14-18

Conders Bend Sauvignon Blanc

Winemaker Craig Gass aimed for a riper style than most of the genre for this vintage, and he succeeded.

CURRENT RELEASE 1992 The bouquet starts with a touch of passionfruit, but that is overtaken pretty smartly by some gently grassy characters. On the palate the wine is softly herbaceous. Lovely wine for a Mediterranean salad topped with baked capsicums.

STYLE dry

QUALITY ▼▼▼▼

VALUE ★★★

GRAPES sauvignon blanc

REGION Marlborough

CELLAR ▯ 2

PRICE $16-18

Cooks Winemaker's Reserve Sauvignon Blanc

Cooks was one of the first New Zealand labels to appear in any quantity in the UK. Nowadays, the company is part of the Corbans fold.

Previous outstanding vintages: '89

CURRENT RELEASE 1991 The nose is a little shy, but if you sniff deeply enough there is evidence of very ripe fruit. There's nothing shy, however, about the taste; honeysuckle and gooseberry flavours occupy every corner of your mouth and linger long after the wine has been swallowed. Great with a whole baked salmon or trout.

STYLE dry
QUALITY ♥♥♥♥
VALUE ★★★+
GRAPES sauvignon blanc
REGION Marlborough
CELLAR 🍾 3
PRICE $19-22

Coopers Creek Fumé Blanc

This barrel-fermented and oak-aged Gisborne sauvignon has done well for Coopers Creek, picking up a few medals and proving popular with the punters.

Previous outstanding vintages: '89

CURRENT RELEASE 1992 Capsicum and toast share the honours on the nose. The taste is soft, well rounded and spicy, and the finish crisply citric. Partner it with an aubergine and capsicum casserole.

STYLE dry
QUALITY ♥♥♥♥
VALUE ★★★+
GRAPES sauvignon blanc
REGION Gisborne
CELLAR 🍾 2
PRICE $14-17

Coopers Creek Marlborough Sauvignon Blanc

Delightfully fresh, crisp acids are a hallmark of Coopers Creek whites; the Marlborough sauvignon is no exception.

CURRENT RELEASE 1992 Passionfruit on the nose is more common in Hawke's Bay sauvignons, but it is a strong influence on this Marlborough version. The taste is clean, fresh and invigorating, thanks largely to a delightfully zingy finish. Best on its own.

STYLE dry
QUALITY ♥♥♥♥
VALUE ★★★★
GRAPES sauvignon blanc
REGION Marlborough
CELLAR 🍾 2
PRICE $14-16

Corbans Private Bin Fumé Blanc

Private Bin fumés have been pretty successful for Corbans — they've been winning medals since the mid-1970s. The latest model continued the tradition with a gold at the 1992 Air New Zealand Wine Awards.

Previous outstanding vintages: '85, '88

CURRENT RELEASE 1990 Hay and freshly baked bread both waft out of the glass, while on the palate a most attractive mealiness takes over. The flavours are mature and well rounded, and the finish is impressively long.

STYLE dry

QUALITY ♟♟♟♟♟

VALUE ★★★

GRAPES sauvignon blanc

REGION Marlborough

CELLAR ▌2

PRICE $23-25

Crab Farm Sauvignon Blanc Barrel-Fermented

Winemaker Hamish Jardine ferments this wine in French barrels and leaves it there for seven months, stirring it from time to time to get the flavour of the yeast through it. The result is certainly more interesting than the non-wooded version (see *Overflow*).

CURRENT RELEASE 1992 There are plenty of dry oak characters on the nose, with bread smells from the yeast lurking at the back. The wine starts sweet in the mouth and stays fruity in the middle palate, but has a slightly bitter finish.

STYLE dry

QUALITY ♟♟♟

VALUE ★★★

GRAPES sauvignon blanc

REGION Hawke's Bay

CELLAR ▌2

PRICE $15-17

Cross Roads Sauvignon Blanc

This is only the third vintage for this newish Hawke's Bay winery. The name will be one to watch — already, owners Malcolm Reeves and Lester O'Brien have had considerable medal success.

CURRENT RELEASE 1992 The lads produce two sauvignons — this is the unwooded model. On the nose it smells of passionfruit and figs, and in the mouth it starts sweet, develops quite a lot of roundness in the middle palate then finishes with a respectable amount of length. Enjoy it with asparagus quiche.

STYLE dry

QUALITY ♟♟♟♟

VALUE ★★★★

GRAPES sauvignon blanc

REGION Hawke's Bay

CELLAR ▌2

PRICE $13-15

Cross Roads Sauvignon Blanc (Barrel-Fermented)

The grapes for this wine came from two Hawke's Bay vineyards. The resultant juice was then fermented in French oak barrels and put through a malolactic fermentation.

CURRENT RELEASE 1992 The wine was very new when I tried it, and was dominated by the taste of the oak barrels in which it had been fermented and aged. In the mouth, however, it displayed some nice, sweet fruit and ended with a good dash of style.

STYLE dry

QUALITY ♛♛♛♛

VALUE ★★★+

GRAPES sauvignon blanc

REGION Hawke's Bay

CELLAR ▬ 1-3

PRICE $15-17

Dashwood Sauvignon Blanc

Winemaker Glenn Thomas was able to use all his own fruit for the 1991 vintage of this label, but in 1992 he had to blend it with grapes brought in from the nearby Wairau Valley.

CURRENT RELEASE 1992 The nose is classic Marlborough — all grassy and smelling of capsicums. The wine is quite simple, but crisp and clean enough to go well with steamed mussels.

STYLE dry

QUALITY ♛♛♛

VALUE ★★+

GRAPES sauvignon blanc 90%, semillon 10%

REGION Marlborough

CELLAR ▮ 1

PRICE $17-19

Delegat's Hawke's Bay Sauvignon Blanc

The Delegat winery is in Henderson, but the company's grapes are drawn from Hawke's Bay and Marlborough. Previous outstanding vintages: '86, '89

CURRENT RELEASE 1992 There's a nice touch of pineapple on the nose, leading into a clean, refreshing mouthful of wine. It's not a 'biggie', but it's no less enjoyable for that.

STYLE dry

QUALITY ♛♛♛

VALUE ★★★

GRAPES sauvignon blanc

REGION Hawke's Bay

CELLAR ▮ 2

PRICE $13-15

Delegat's Proprietor's Reserve Hawke's Bay Fumé Blanc

The Proprietor's Reserve wines are top of the heap for this company, and winemaker Brent Marris lavishes all sorts of loving care and attention on them.
Previous outstanding vintages: '86, '89
CURRENT RELEASE 1991 Passionfruit and honeysuckle get together for a pleasant introduction to this generously flavoured wine. The taste is spicy, mealy and rich. Enjoy it with Mexican nachos.

STYLE dry
QUALITY ▼▼▼▼
VALUE ★★★+
GRAPES sauvignon blanc
REGION Hawke's Bay
CELLAR ▬ 1-3
PRICE $16-21

deRedcliffe Fumé-style Semillon/Sauvignon Blanc

The grapes for this European-style wine came from vineyards in Mangatawhiri, Mangere and Hawke's Bay. They were blended and finished at the deRedcliffe winery, which is part of the Hotel du Vin complex.
CURRENT RELEASE 1991 This wine is grainier and earthier on the nose than a straight sauvignon, which is no bad thing. It tastes clean and frisky at both ends but is quite round in the middle. Partner it with a cheese-topped veal schnitzel.

STYLE dry
QUALITY ▼▼▼▼
VALUE ★★★+
GRAPES semillon 65%, sauvignon blanc 35%
REGION Mangatawhiri, Mangere and Hawke's Bay
CELLAR ▬ 1-3
PRICE $14-16

deRedcliffe Marlborough Sauvignon Blanc

Winemaker Mark Compton bought his first Marlborough sauvignon grapes for the 1991 vintage and was immediately rewarded with a gold medal at the Air New Zealand Wine Awards. This version took a silver medal at last year's awards.
CURRENT RELEASE 1992 The nose is classic Marlborough, with capsicum and gooseberry notes fighting for attention. It is equally charming on the palate, giving evidence of ripe fruit treated well. Partner it with a breast of turkey.

STYLE dry
QUALITY ▼▼▼
VALUE ★★★+
GRAPES sauvignon blanc
REGION Marlborough
CELLAR ▮ 2
PRICE $12-14

deRedcliffe Semillon/Chardonnay

Blends of semillon and chardonnay are common in Australia but not often seen here, except for wines produced exclusively for mail-order sale to New Zealand Wine Society members. We should have more of them, because the two varieties work well together. CURRENT RELEASE 1991 Semillon's herbaceousness starts the ball rolling in the bouquet, with a touch of the chardonnay citrics not far behind. On the palate the wine is spicy and more mouth-filling than would be expected from either variety on its own. Enjoy it with a salad based on raw mushrooms and smoked chicken.

STYLE dry

QUALITY �

VALUE ★★★+

GRAPES semillon 55%, chardonnay 45%

REGION Mangatawhiri and Hawke's Bay

CELLAR ▋ 2

PRICE $13-15

Discovery Sauvignon Blanc

The inexpensive Discovery range is made by Cooks, part of the Corbans group. In the past, the company has used Hawke's Bay fruit, but Corbans' Marlborough winemaker Allan McCorkindale had so much fruit for the 1992 vintage that this wine was also sourced there. CURRENT RELEASE 1992 The nose is all cut grass and capsicums in the classic Marlborough style. The taste is equally attention-grabbing, and there are some nice crisp acids on the finish. It's a bit too obvious to place with food, so enjoy it, well chilled, on its own.

STYLE dry

QUALITY ♥♥♥♥

VALUE ★★★+

GRAPES sauvignon blanc

REGION Marlborough

CELLAR ▋

PRICE $10-12

Dry River Sauvignon Blanc

Most sauvignon blanc is at its best when it is young and fresh, but Dry River's Neil McCallum makes all his wines to cellar. His sauvignons are good young, but inevitably better after a year or so.
Previous outstanding vintages: '88, '89
CURRENT RELEASE 1992 The bouquet is not unlike the Marlborough benchmark, but this wine has an added undertone of earthiness. The taste, however, is all about clean, lean fruit, and the finish is like biting into a chilled Gala apple. Give it at least a year in a quiet place, then partner it with sushi.

STYLE dry

QUALITY ♥♥♥♥

VALUE ★★★

GRAPES sauvignon blanc

REGION Martinborough

CELLAR ➡ 1-3

PRICE $17-19

Esk Valley Private Bin Sauvignon Blanc

The Esk Valley winery, on the coast road leading to Napier, is being turned into a showcase by its owners, the Villa Maria group. The Private Bin sauvignon is consistently good and has picked up a few medals.

CURRENT RELEASE 1992 The wine is faintly grassy and boasts a touch of the Hawke's Bay tropicals on the nose, then follows this with some sweet, ripe fruit tastes and a clean, soft, but reasonably crisp finish.

STYLE dry

QUALITY ♟♟♟♟

VALUE ★★★

GRAPES sauvignon blanc

REGION Hawke's Bay

CELLAR ▌ 1

PRICE $11-13

Forrest Estate Barrel-Fermented Semillon

John Forrest, one of the new players on the Marlborough winemaking scene, matures his semillon for five months in a mixture of French and American oak, and he reckons the 1991 model should be cellared for three years, 'if,' he adds, 'you've got the patience'.

CURRENT RELEASE 1991 This wine has developed a smokey character on the nose since I tasted it for last year's guide. The palate has broadened out, but the crisp acids are still very much in evidence and help give the wine a refreshing limey finish. It's great with a chunky pork paté.

STYLE dry

QUALITY ♟♟♟♟

VALUE ★★★

GRAPES semillon

REGION Marlborough

CELLAR ■■► 3-4

PRICE $17-21

Forrest Estate Sauvignon Blanc

Locals refer to the ever-growing stone wall taking shape outside the nicely laid-out Forrest winery as 'the great wall of Renwick'. It does bear some resemblance to its namesake, but John assures us it won't be as long.

CURRENT RELEASE 1992 Capsicums are obvious on the nose in the approved Marlborough fashion, but I fancy I could detect a (pleasant!) touch of garlic as well. The taste is round, quite soft and very drinkable. Partner it with a pan-fried salmon steak.

STYLE dry

QUALITY ♟♟♟♟

VALUE ★★★

GRAPES sauvignon blanc

REGION Marlborough

CELLAR ▌ 2

PRICE $16-19

French Farm Oaked Sauvignon

When the French first settled at Akaroa, on Banks Peninsula, they planted vines with the intention of making wine. Little came of the enterprise, but now Tony Bish has established a vineyard and restaurant in the area.This sauvignon blanc is made from Marlborough fruit.
CURRENT RELEASE 1992 Grassy Marlborough grapes and the French oak barrels in which part of the wine was fermented have given it a bouquet reminiscent of fresh hay. In the mouth it is spicy, well rounded and clean, with a crisp acid finish. Partner it with steamed asparagus topped with butter and fresh parsley.

STYLE dry
QUALITY ♟♟♟♟
VALUE ★★★
GRAPES sauvignon blanc
REGION Marlborough
CELLAR ▮ 3
PRICE $17-20

Gibbston Valley Sauvignon Blanc

One of two sauvignons produced by this Queenstown winery. This one is made from owner Alan Brady's own grapes, the other uses grapes from Marlborough.
CURRENT RELEASE 1992 The bouquet is grassy and capsicummy in the approved South Island fashion, while on the palate the wine is crisp and clean with a lot of acid zing. Partner it with snacks like gherkins and olives.

STYLE dry
QUALITY ♟♟♟♟
VALUE ★★★
GRAPES sauvignon blanc
REGION Central Otago
CELLAR ▮ 2
PRICE $16-18

Gibbston Valley Sauvignon Blanc Southern Selection

This wine caused a fair bit of controversy when it picked up one of only two gold medals awarded to 1992 sauvignons at the Air New Zealand Wine Awards. Most people thought it was made from Central Otago fruit; only the fine print on the back label identifies it as from Marlborough, and winemakers from there cried 'foul'.
CURRENT VINTAGE 1992 Controversy aside, this is splendid wine. On the nose it is floral, spicy and more reminiscent of hay than the usual fresh grass. The tastes are ripe and rich in the middle but fresh and zingy on the finish. Partner it with warm hot-smoked salmon.

STYLE dry
QUALITY ♟♟♟♟♟
VALUE ★★★+
GRAPES sauvignon blanc
REGION Marlborough
CELLAR ▮ 3
PRICE $17-22

Giesen Marlborough Rapaura Road Sauvignon Blanc

The Giesens are certainly not chauvinistic about their home territory of Canterbury; several of their wines are made from out-of-area fruit.

CURRENT RELEASE 1992 Last year it was all capsicums, but this year I pick up spicy asparagus on the nose. The taste is frisky in front but rounds out more in the middle than the '91 version. Good wine for steamed asparagus with Hollandaise sauce.

STYLE dry

QUALITY ▼▼▼▼

VALUE ★★★+

GRAPES sauvignon blanc

REGION Marlborough

CELLAR █ 1

PRICE $17-19

Gladstone Sauvignon Blanc

I couldn't get a handle on the 1991 version of this wine, but either my tastes or the wine have changed for the 1992 vintage – I like it a lot, and that's despite 1992 being a lousy year in Martinborough.

CURRENT RELEASE 1992 The bouquet has a touch of parmesan about it, which is something I've never struck in a sauvignon before — or in any other wine for that matter. The taste is different from the norm as well — a bit earthy but with plenty of sauvignon's hay-like characters also in residence, and the finish is crisp and faintly spicy. Try it with seafood lasagne.

STYLE dry

QUALITY ▼▼▼▼

VALUE ★★★

GRAPES sauvignon blanc

REGION Wairarapa

CELLAR █ 2

PRICE $18-22

Grape Republic Waterfall Bay Sauvignon Blanc

Waterfall Bay is a picturesque spot on Kapiti Island, which is clearly visible from this Horowhenua winery.

CURRENT RELEASE 1991 Putting the wine through a partial malolactic fermentation and ageing it in oak has diffused the varietal character in the bouquet, but there's obviously some good fruit in there. Things are more typical of sauvignon on the palate, and there are some good acids. Altogether, it's a refreshing mouthful.

STYLE dry

QUALITY ▼▼▼▼

VALUE ★★★

GRAPES sauvignon blanc

REGION Horowhenua

CELLAR █ 2

PRICE $14-18

Grape Republic Waterfall Bay Semillon

Winemaker and partner Alastair Pain says he has had very favourable comments on this wine from people visiting the winery.

CURRENT RELEASE 1992 There's a nice bit of spice on the nose, which blends well with semillon's natural herbaceousness. On the palate the wine is frisky, mealy and quite mouth-filling. It goes well with veal schnitzel topped with grilled cheese.

STYLE dry
QUALITY 🍷🍷🍷🍷🍷
VALUE ★★★★
GRAPES semillon 92%, sauvignon blanc 8%
REGION Hawke's Bay
CELLAR 🍾 4
PRICE $14-18

Grove Mill Sauvignon Blanc

Grove Mill is the only winery right in the township of Blenheim, and shares its premises with a very good restaurant. The 1991 version of this wine scored a silver medal at that year's Air New Zealand Wine Awards, and this vintage repeated the trick at the 1992 Awards.

CURRENT RELEASE 1992 There are some nice tropical fruit and gooseberry tones on the nose, and they are followed on the palate by evidence of rich, ripe grapes. Partner this mouth-filling wine with a plate of Marlborough Sounds mussels.

STYLE dry
QUALITY 🍷🍷🍷🍷🍷
VALUE ★★★+
GRAPES sauvignon blanc
REGION Marlborough
CELLAR 🍾 3
PRICE $16-18

Highfield Estate Sauvignon Blanc

Founded by Marlborough grape grower Bill Walsh, Highfield is now owned by Wellington businessman Neil Buchanan in partnership with UK-based Tom Tenurewa and Japan-based Shin Yokoi, both of whom have connections with the French Champagne house of Drappier.

CURRENT RELEASE 1992 The touch of the tropicals on the nose of this pleasant sauvignon give it more of a Hawke's Bay feel than most Marlborough models. On the palate it is clean and quite multi-faceted, thanks partly to winemaker Tony Hooper's habit of sourcing grapes from more than one vineyard. Try it with a salad of outdoor tomatoes dressed with good olive oil.

STYLE dry
QUALITY 🍷🍷🍷🍷
VALUE ★★★
GRAPES sauvignon blanc
REGION Marlborough
CELLAR 🍾 2
PRICE $15-18

Highfield Estate Sauvignon Blanc (Oak-Aged)

You have to look closely to distinguish this wine from the unwooded version reviewed earlier. The words 'oak aged' are printed in gold across the label illustration, and are quite hard to pick up.

CURRENT RELEASE 1992 The bouquet is classic Marlborough cut grass and gooseberries, backed up by the vanilla characters of French oak barrels. On the palate the wine starts sweet before settling down to show off clean, fresh, crisp characters that make it a natural match for raw oysters.

STYLE dry
QUALITY ▼▼▼▼▼
VALUE ★★★+
GRAPES sauvignon blanc
REGION Marlborough
CELLAR ▮ 4
PRICE $18-22

Hunter's Sauvignon Blanc

Hunter's, along with Cloudy Bay, has done wonders for the name of New Zealand wine in the tough UK export market. This is the unwooded version of the company's big-selling sauvignon.

Previous outstanding vintages: '89

CURRENT RELEASE 1992 The nose is great — it's warm and inviting, with a hay-like character rather than the aggressive grassiness of some of its competitors. Balance is the key word on the palate. The acids give it a lot of zing, but they are so well integrated that the overall impression is quite round. Impressive wine that deserves to accompany a whole baked Marlborough salmon.

STYLE dry
QUALITY ▼▼▼▼▼
VALUE ★★★★
GRAPES sauvignon blanc
REGION Marlborough
CELLAR ▮ 2
PRICE $17-19

Hunter's Sauvignon Blanc (Oak-Aged)

This is the wine which, in 1985 colours, was voted top wine of the show for an unprecedented three days in succession at a major London exhibition. In those days it was labelled Fumé Blanc, but that name has been outlawed in Europe under EC regulations.

Previous outstanding vintages: '87, '88

CURRENT RELEASE 1991 Marlborough sauvignon blanc doesn't come any better than this splendid example. The bouquet is full of the same capsicum characters as the unwooded version, but they are joined by a hint of lime and vanilla. Share it with your best friend.

STYLE dry
QUALITY ▼▼▼▼▼
VALUE ★★★
GRAPES sauvignon blanc
REGION Marlborough
CELLAR ▮ 2
PRICE $19-24

Jackson Estate Sauvignon Blanc

The 1991 first release of this Marlborough sauvignon created quite a stir by top-scoring in a *Cuisine* magazine sauvignon tasting conducted by three Masters of Wine, Bob Campbell, Kym Milne and Michael Brajkovich. Previous outstanding vintages: '91

CURRENT RELEASE 1992 The current wine doesn't quite measure up to the splendid standards of the 1991, but it is still crisp, clean, stylish and frighteningly drinkable. Share it with good friends and a plate of hot-smoked Marlborough salmon with buttered toast triangles.

STYLE dry
QUALITY ♟♟♟♟
VALUE ★★★
GRAPES sauvignon blanc
REGION Marlborough
CELLAR 🍾 2
PRICE $19-21

Kumeu River Sauvignon

Michael Brajkovich makes the most unusual sauvignon blanc in the country, sometimes using great doses of botrytised fruit and nearly always putting the wine through a full malolactic fermentation.
Previous outstanding vintages: '86, '89

CURRENT RELEASE 1991 I get toast and a wee hint of chocolate on the nose, which makes things different for a start. The wine is muted, smooth and quite rich, and would be a fine companion to a piece of smoked kahawai (optimistically called sea trout in some quarters).

STYLE dry
QUALITY ♟♟♟♟
VALUE ★★+
GRAPES sauvignon blanc
REGION West Auckland
CELLAR 🍾 2
PRICE $20-25

Limeburners Bay Sauvignon Blanc

The Limeburners Bay vineyard is off the 'standard' West Auckland wine trail, but the company has a loyal following of fans who regularly make the trek out to Hobsonville.

CURRENT RELEASE 1991 The nose is a sort of combination of Marlborough herbaceousness and Hawke's Bay hay. On the palate it starts with a belt of sweet, ripe fruit before softening out somewhat, but it has good enough acid to keep things in perspective.

STYLE dry
QUALITY ♟♟♟♟
VALUE ★★★★
GRAPES sauvignon blanc 92%, semillon 8%
REGION West Auckland
CELLAR 🍾 1
PRICE $11-13

Limeburners Bay Semillon/Chardonnay

Semillon and chardonnay combine well together, and Alan and Jetta Laurenson of Limeburners Bay have made a nice job of this one.
CURRENT RELEASE 1991 Semillon's herbaceous character shoves chardonnay out of the way in the bouquet, but things are rather quieter on the palate. The wine is well rounded and pleasant, and would go well with smoked kahawai in a creamy sauce.

STYLE dry
QUALITY ♟♟♟
VALUE ★★★+
GRAPES semillon 60%, chardonnay 40%
REGION West Auckland
CELLAR ▊ 2
PRICE $10-12

Lincoln Sauvignon Blanc (Hawke's Bay)

Winemaker Nick Chan fermented a third of this wine in new French barrels to soften the variety's exuberance and emphasise the ripe fruit characters.
CURRENT RELEASE 1992 There's a whiff of perfumed lollies on the nose along with pleasant floral characters. On the palate it reeks of ripe fruit, a feature that gives it the sort of roundness Nick was presumably aiming for, but it still has plenty of zing. It works well with a piece of tarakihi topped with brown butter and parsley.

STYLE dry
QUALITY ♟♟♟♟
VALUE ★★★★
GRAPES sauvignon blanc
REGION Hawke's Bay
CELLAR ▊ 3
PRICE $10-13

Lintz Estate Sauvignon Blanc

Owner and winemaker Chris Lintz likes to give sauvignon blanc quite a lot of wood treatment. This version has been fermented and aged in oak barrels.
CURRENT RELEASE 1992 The bouquet seems chewy — if that's not a contradiction in terms — and quite earthy. In the mouth the wine is soft, perhaps too much so at first, but the acids cut in to give it a reasonably crisp finish. Good with cheese-topped pasta.

STYLE dry
QUALITY ♟♟♟
VALUE ★★★
GRAPES sauvignon blanc
REGION Martinborough
CELLAR ▊ 2
PRICE $16-18

Martinborough Vineyards Sauvignon Blanc

Sauvignon blanc wines from Martinborough manage to combine something of the herbaceousness of their Marlborough counterparts with the tropical fruit characters associated with Hawke's Bay versions.

CURRENT RELEASE 1992 There's some great fruit in this pungent little number. Cut grass, capsicums, gooseberries — they're all in there somewhere. Despite this upfront introduction, however, the wine is quite full and round once you get it swirling around your tonsils. Best as an aperitif.

STYLE dry
QUALITY 🍷🍷🍷
VALUE ★★+
GRAPES sauvignon blanc
REGION Martinborough
CELLAR 1
PRICE $17-19

Matua Fumé Blanc

There's no official ruling on this, but most New Zealand winemakers label their sauvignon as fumé blanc when it's spent time in wood. Matua reverses this system and labels the unwooded sauvignon as fumé, claiming it tastes smokier than the wooded version (fumé means smoky in French).

CURRENT RELEASE 1992 I can't pick up any smokiness on the nose, but there are some fresh, steely characters in there. The wine is quite fruity but very clean and refreshing. Enjoy it with something using braised leeks.

STYLE dry
QUALITY 🍷🍷🍷🍷
VALUE ★★★+
GRAPES sauvignon blanc
REGION Hawke's Bay
CELLAR 2
PRICE $9-13

Matua Sauvignon Blanc Reserve

This is the top sauvignon for the Matua team, although lately the less-expensive Shingle Peak version has been equalling it in the medal stakes.

Previous outstanding vintages: '86, '89

CURRENT RELEASE 1992 Grass and a bit of vanilla start things off with a flourish. It's not an aggressive sort of sauvignon, but offers nicely rounded, stylish flavours that would suit a smoked salmon salad.

STYLE dry
QUALITY 🍷🍷🍷🍷½
VALUE ★★★+
GRAPES sauvignon blanc
REGION West Auckland
CELLAR 3
PRICE $15-19

Merlen Sauvignon Blanc

Winemaker Almuth Lorenz is better known for her chardonnay and riesling, but this sauvignon is also a good seller for her.

CURRENT RELEASE 1992 Cut capsicums are evident on the nose, as is only right and proper for a Marlborough sauvignon. On the palate the wine is rounder than the bouquet suggests, and it finishes quite smoothly.

STYLE dry

QUALITY ▼▼▼▼

VALUE ★★★

GRAPES sauvignon blanc

REGION Marlborough

CELLAR ▌ 2

PRICE $15-17

Mills Reef Clifton Road Sauvignon Blanc

Winemaker Paddy Preston now makes two styles of sauvignon blanc — this tank-fermented version, and the barrel-fermented model reviewed below.

CURRENT RELEASE 1992 Honeysuckle and pineapple characters join forces on the nose and take your taste buds through to a fresh, fruity and clean wine with instant appeal. Match it with barbecued vegetables, particularly eggplant.

STYLE dry

QUALITY ▼▼▼▼

VALUE ★★★+

GRAPES sauvignon blanc

REGION Hawke's Bay

CELLAR ▌ 2

PRICE $13-16

Mills Reef Sauvignon Blanc Barrel-Fermented

Last year the barrel fermentation wasn't mentioned on the label, but this year it has been added to differentiate this wine from the tank-fermented model above.

CURRENT RELEASE 1992 The nose has the same honeysuckle character, but this time it is joined by passionfruit aromas and a nice bit of mealiness. In the mouth it is smooth and well rounded, and boasts a lingering finish. Good with braised chicken legs.

STYLE dry

QUALITY ▼▼▼▼

VALUE ★★★

GRAPES sauvignon blanc

REGION Hawke's Bay

CELLAR ▌ 2

PRICE $15-17

Millton Te Arai River Sauvignon Blanc

Millton wines proudly wear the Bio-Gro symbol on their labels, certifying that the grapes are grown without the use of artificial pesticides, fertilisers or herbicides. This pleasant wine is a blend of sauvignon blanc and semillon.

CURRENT RELEASE 1992 The semillon has added a touch of honeysuckle to sauvignon's tropical fruit characters. On the palate it is fresh, appley but with some depth, and boasts a clean, crisp finish. James and Annie Millton suggest it is best as an aperitif. I agree.

STYLE dry
QUALITY ♟♟♟♟
VALUE ★★★+
GRAPES sauvignon blanc 85%, semillon 15%
REGION Gisborne
CELLAR 2
PRICE $17-20

Mission Fumé Blanc

Mission are to be commended for putting the words 'smoky sauvignon' under the main title on the label; few people realise sauvignon and fumé are two names for the same grape.

CURRENT RELEASE 1992 The nose is closer to a Marlborough model than that of most Hawke's Bay sauvignons, but that distinctive grassiness is tempered by a dash of sweet oak. On the palate it is quite frisky and clean, with a touch of spice from being aged in small barrels. It would be good with a piece of smoked blue cod.

STYLE dry
QUALITY ♟♟♟
VALUE ★★★+
GRAPES sauvignon blanc
REGION Hawke's Bay
CELLAR 2
PRICE $12-14

Mission Sauvignon Blanc

Someone enjoys dreaming up romantic subtitles for some of the Mission wines. This one carries the words 'whisper of medium sweetness'. Isn't that nice?

CURRENT RELEASE 1992 The bouquet is grassy with a touch of honey, while on the palate the wine is fresh, a little apple-like but with some depth. The finish is clean and refreshing. Enjoy it with poached or pan-fried scallops.

STYLE off-dry
QUALITY ♟♟♟
VALUE ★★★+
GRAPES sauvignon blanc
REGION Hawke's Bay
CELLAR 1
PRICE $8-11

Mission Sugar Loaf Semillon (Nevers Oak Reserve)

The great oak-aged semillons of Australia's Hunter Valley often live for a decade or more. This Mission example is unlikely to have that sort of longevity, but it would be worth taking a gamble on four or five years' cellaring.

CURRENT RELEASE 1989 Gentle spice and subtle oak characters on the nose form an inviting start to this nicely structured wine. On the palate there are refreshingly crisp acids and a good dose of well-rounded flavours. The finish is quite fruity and lasts well.

STYLE dry
QUALITY ♥♥♥♥
VALUE ★★★★
GRAPES semillon
REGION Hawke's Bay
CELLAR 🍷 5
PRICE $14-16

Montana Estates Brancott Estate Sauvignon Blanc

The four Montana Estates wines (two chardonnays and a cabernet, plus this sauvignon) are seen more often on restaurant lists than on retail shelves.

CURRENT RELEASE 1991 This superb wine shows just what a great vintage 1991 was for Marlborough. Sure, it's got Marlborough grassiness in the bouquet, but it's so well balanced with spicy oak that it seems elegant. In the mouth it is so soft it leans towards richness, and it boasts a silky-smooth finish. Enjoy it on its own or with a Niçoise salad.

STYLE dry
QUALITY ♥♥♥♥♥
VALUE ★★+
GRAPES sauvignon blanc
REGION Marlborough
CELLAR 🍷 3
PRICE $27-31

Montana Marlborough Sauvignon Blanc

One of the best-known New Zealand wines in the UK, probably only second in public awareness to the near-legendary Cloudy Bay, and the recipient of heaps of praise from that part of the world.

Previous outstanding vintages: '86, '89

CURRENT RELEASE 1992 This is a much quieter wine than the bombastic 1991 version. The nose is grassy, but not aggressively so, and the tastes are relatively rounded. Sip it on its own on a hot summer's evening.

STYLE dry
QUALITY ♥♥♥
VALUE ★★★+
GRAPES sauvignon blanc
REGION Marlborough
CELLAR 🍷
PRICE $10-13

Morton Estate Hawke's Bay Fumé Blanc (Black Label)

This top-of-the-range wine from Australian-owned Morton Estate unaccountably missed out on a medal at the 1991 Air New Zealand Wine Awards, but the balance was redressed last year when it picked up a well-deserved silver.

CURRENT RELEASE 1991 Lovely, sweet oak stands out on the nose, along with toasty, mealy and dried-fruit characters. The taste is equally rich and mouth-fillingly delicious. Enjoy it with a plate of vegetables such as capsicums, tomatoes, courgettes and eggplant, all barbecued or grilled and served at room temperature dressed with Balsamic vinegar and extra-virgin olive oil.

STYLE dry
QUALITY ♟♟♟♟♟
VALUE ★★★
GRAPES sauvignon blanc
REGION Hawke's Bay
CELLAR ▮ 4
PRICE $20-24

Morton Estate Hawke's Bay Fumé Blanc (White Label)

The Morton Estate winery at Katikati, near Tauranga, has only a small vineyard of its own, but manager John Hancock and winemaker Steve Bird have great confidence in Hawke's Bay grapes.

CURRENT RELEASE 1992 The bouquet is spicy, only slightly grassy and has taken on the aroma of dried figs during its sojourn in oak barrels — no bad thing. The same spicy/grassy double act does its thing on the palate and helps give the wine a crisp, clean finish. Partner it with smoked mullet.

STYLE dry
QUALITY ♟♟♟♟
VALUE ★★★+
GRAPES sauvignon blanc
REGION Hawke's Bay
CELLAR ▮ 2
PRICE $12-14

Morton Estate Hawke's Bay Sauvignon Blanc (White Label)

The Morton Estate team picks the grapes for this wine over a four-week period, to obtain various degrees of ripeness. This vintage has had a little bit of residual sugar left in to lift the fruit character.

CURRENT RELEASE 1992 The nose is steely rather than grassy. That characteristic waits until you get the wine into your mouth. The taste is crisp, flinty and refreshing, and the finish is light but clean.

STYLE off-dry
QUALITY ♟♟♟
VALUE ★★★
GRAPES sauvignon blanc
REGION Hawke's Bay
CELLAR ▮ 1
PRICE $12-14

Nautilus Marlborough Sauvignon Blanc

Last year the grapes came from Hawke's Bay; this year Marlborough was the source and another label, Twin Islands, has been launched by the wine's distributors, Negociants, to showcase the Hawke's Bay product.
CURRENT RELEASE 1992 The bouquet is clean, with both cut-grass and gooseberry characters vying for attention. The wine tastes fresh and stimulating, and would be good with snapper or cod in a creamy sauce.

STYLE dry
QUALITY ♟♟♟♟
VALUE ★★★
GRAPES sauvignon blanc
REGION Marlborough
CELLAR ▮ 1
PRICE $18-21

Neudorf Moutere Semillon

This semillon from one of the country's most picturesque vineyards demonstrates that the variety has adapted well to the sunny hillsides of Nelson.
CURRENT RELEASE 1991 The bouquet is herbaceous, but it's not all upfront — there's a bit of depth behind it. There is plenty of ripe fruit on the palate and good acids to add a bit of friskiness. A good match for Chinese stir-fried pork and asparagus.

STYLE dry
QUALITY ♟♟♟♟
VALUE ★★★
GRAPES semillon
REGION Nelson
CELLAR ▮ 2
PRICE $13-16

Neudorf Nelson Sauvignon Blanc

Last year's equivalent of this wine was made from both Nelson and Marlborough grapes, but this year Tim and Judy Finn grew enough of their own.
CURRENT RELEASE 1992 The wine has a classic South Island bouquet — all grassy and pungent. The taste is only slightly less exuberant, and keeps things clean and fresh until the wine is swallowed. Partner it with a crab salad (using real crab meat, not surimi).

STYLE dry
QUALITY ♟♟♟♟
VALUE ★★★+
GRAPES sauvignon blanc
REGION Nelson
CELLAR ▮ 2
PRICE $16-19

Nobilo Marlborough Sauvignon Blanc

The Nobilos get the fruit for this wine from their Matador vineyard, which they own fifty-fifty with Selaks.

CURRENT RELEASE 1992 The bouquet is grassy, but not aggressively so. The wine is rounder in the mouth than last year's model, though there's still an ample amount of clean, frisky fruit in there.

STYLE dry

QUALITY ♟♟♟♟

VALUE ★★★★+

GRAPES sauvignon blanc

REGION Marlborough

CELLAR ▊ 1

PRICE $10-12

Ohinemuri Estate Hawke's Bay Sauvignon Blanc

This winery near Waihi draws grapes from several parts of the North Island. It is a popular spot for tourists passing through the picturesque gorge where it is situated.

CURRENT RELEASE 1992 The grassy tones on the nose lean more to the hay end of the spectrum, and they are accompanied by a touch of tropical fruit in classic Hawke's Bay style. The wine tastes herbaceous and offers a pleasantly spicy finish.

STYLE dry

QUALITY ♟♟♟

VALUE ★★★

GRAPES sauvignon blanc

REGION Hawke's Bay

CELLAR ▊ 2

PRICE $14-16

Oyster Bay Sauvignon Blanc

Oyster Bay is a label used by Delegat's for Marlborough-sourced wines. The first release (1990) of this wine was awarded the trophy for top sauvignon blanc at a major international competition in London.

CURRENT RELEASE 1992 Grass and capsicums are both on the bouquet in the approved Marlborough fashion, but the taste is rounder than many of the genre can boast. The wine is nicely proportioned and would do justice to a whole baked snapper.

STYLE dry

QUALITY ♟♟♟♟♟

VALUE ★★★

GRAPES sauvignon blanc

REGION Marlborough

CELLAR ▊ 2

PRICE $18-21

Palliser Estate Martinborough Sauvignon Blanc

Palliser was established a couple of years after the five original Martinborough vineyards had made an impressive name for themselves in competition, but the newcomer was quick to catch up.

Previous outstanding vintages: '91

CURRENT RELEASE 1992 All the classic sauvignon calling cards are there in the pungent, herbaceous bouquet. The taste is quite rich but with plenty of acid zing, and the finish long and satisfying.

STYLE dry
QUALITY 🍷🍷🍷🍷🍷
VALUE ★★+
GRAPES sauvignon blanc
REGION Martinborough
CELLAR 🍷 2
PRICE $28-32

C. J. Pask Sauvignon Blanc

Chris Pask's winemaker, Kate Bradburnd, won a stack of awards for her previous employer, Vidal Wines. Kate believes in letting sauvignon fruit do the talking, rather than masking its appealingly fresh flavours with wood and other distractions.

CURRENT RELEASE 1992 Passionfruit and nectarines are the characters I find on the nose. On the palate it is fruity and quite rich, making it an easy-to-drink style that is good on its own or alongside a chicken sandwich with home-made mayonnaise.

STYLE dry
QUALITY 🍷🍷🍷🍷
VALUE ★★★
GRAPES sauvignon blanc
REGION Hawke's Bay
CELLAR 🍷 2
PRICE $14-16

Penfolds Cottle Bush Sauvignon Blanc

This wine is part of an everyday range for Penfolds, yet this first vintage equalled the more expensive Winemakers Reserve model with a silver medal at last year's Air New Zealand Wine Competition.

CURRENT RELEASE 1991 The clean, grassy nose is classic Marlborough. On the palate it is frisky at first, rounder in the middle but boasts a nice, spicy finish. It's good with a Mediterranean salad featuring capsicums and eggplant.

STYLE dry
QUALITY 🍷🍷🍷🍷
VALUE ★★★★
GRAPES sauvignon blanc
REGION Marlborough
CELLAR 🍷
PRICE $9-11

Penfolds Sauvignon Blanc Winemakers Reserve

The top-of-the-line sauvignon for Penfolds, and one of four wines in this series.

CURRENT RELEASE 1991 The aromas of fresh hay are evident on the nose, the result of the barrel fermentation the wine was put through. The wine is soft and round in the mouth and has a medium-length finish. Partner it with crumbed pork schnitzels and buttered new potatoes.

STYLE dry

QUALITY ♟♟♟♟

VALUE ★★★

GRAPES sauvignon blanc

REGION Marlborough

CELLAR ▮ 2-3

PRICE $15-17

Rippon Vineyards Sauvignon Blanc

I wasn't overly impressed with the 1991 version of this wine, but either my palate or the wine has taken a quantum leap for 1992 — this one's great!

CURRENT RELEASE 1992 There's a touch of ice and granite about the nose of this stylish sauvignon, which is appropriate to the landscape it comes from. On the palate it starts sweet, rounds off into a crisp middle and finishes with a limey farewell. It's impressive wine that needs a salad based around baked and skinned capsicums to set it off.

STYLE dry

QUALITY ♟♟♟♟♟

VALUE ★★★+

GRAPES sauvignon blanc

REGION Central Otago

CELLAR ▮ 3

PRICE $16-18

Robard & Butler Marlborough Fumé Blanc

Robard & Butler has established a solid reputation with wood-aged sauvignons, several of which have won medals. Winemaker Allan McCorkindale picked up a silver medal for this wine at the 1992 Air New Zealand Wine Awards.

CURRENT RELEASE 1991 Vanilla and melons stand out on the nose, along with a touch of sauvignon's more common grassy characters. The wine is well rounded on the palate and has a frisky finish. Enjoy it with wiener schnitzel.

STYLE dry

QUALITY ♟♟♟♟

VALUE ★★★★

GRAPES sauvignon blanc

REGION Marlborough

CELLAR ▮ 1-2

PRICE $13-15

Robard & Butler Marlborough Sauvignon Blanc

The unwooded version of the fumé blanc reviewed earlier and, in this case, the lesser wine. That was partly because 1991 was a much better vintage than 1992 — in years to come the two wines may well swap places on the quality scale.

CURRENT RELEASE 1992 There are some classy cut-grass aromas on the nose, but although the taste is frisky, it is also a bit thin. Partner it with snacks like gherkins and olives.

STYLE dry

QUALITY ♥♥♥

VALUE ★★★

GRAPES sauvignon blanc

REGION Marlborough

CELLAR ▮

PRICE $13-15

St George Estate Fumé Blanc

The French oak-fermented version of the 'plain' sauvignon (see *Overflow*), more complex and probably worth short-term cellaring.

CURRENT RELEASE 1992 The bouquet is lean but clean, with a touch of spice from the wine's barrel fermentation. In the mouth it is soft and easy to drink, but it finishes a bit flat.

STYLE dry

QUALITY ♥♥♥

VALUE ★★★

GRAPES sauvignon blanc

REGION Hawke's Bay

CELLAR ▮ 1

PRICE $12-14

St Jerome Sauvignon Blanc Hawke's Bay

Owner/winemaker Davorin Ozich has made a name for himself with a couple of blockbuster reds, but this nicely flavoured sauvignon shows he can handle white grapes as well.

CURRENT RELEASE 1992 I get passionfruit and pineapples on the nose of this pleasant sauvignon. This is Davorin Ozich's best yet. The wine is clean, nicely rounded without being flabby, and has a nice, zingy acid finish. Partner it with pan-fried squid.

STYLE dry

QUALITY ♥♥♥♥

VALUE ★★★+

GRAPES sauvignon blanc

REGION Hawke's Bay

CELLAR ▮ 2

PRICE $18-21

Sacred Hill Fumé Blanc

Winery owners Dave and Mark Mason make sauvignon blanc like nobody else in New Zealand. Not everybody likes it — notably competition judges — but it has a large following.

CURRENT RELEASE 1991 The nose has hints of apples along with a good measure of toasty graininess from the wine's barrel fermentation. The taste is muted, pleasant enough, but marred by a faint bitterness.

STYLE dry

QUALITY ▼▼▼

VALUE ★★+

GRAPES sauvignon blanc

REGION Hawke's Bay

CELLAR 🍾 2

PRICE $17-19

Alan Scott Marlborough Sauvignon Blanc

The label is relatively new, but winemaker Alan Scott has been on the Marlborough wine scene for close to a decade and had a lot to do with Corbans Stoneleigh Sauvignon Blanc.

CURRENT RELEASE 1992 The usual cut grass and capsicum are all there on the nose, and the taste is clean, fresh and pleasant. Not a glass-leaper, but nice enough for casual summer sipping.

STYLE dry

QUALITY ▼▼▼

VALUE ★★+

GRAPES sauvignon blanc

REGION Marlborough

CELLAR 🍾 1

PRICE $16-18

Seibel Hawke's Bay Mere Road Sauvignon Blanc Reserve

Norbert Seibel has been 'borrowing' wineries to make his wine for the last few vintages. Now he has bought his own premises in West Auckland, so things should get a bit easier for him.

CURRENT RELEASE 1992 There are plenty of sauvignon's crisp, grassy notes on the nose, but the wine is soft and well rounded on the palate. Partner it with an avocado-stuffed chicken breast.

STYLE dry

QUALITY ▼▼▼▼

VALUE ★★★+

GRAPES sauvignon blanc

REGION Hawke's Bay

CELLAR 🍾 3

PRICE $13-15

Seibel Sauvignon Blanc Fumé

Norbert Seibel is probably best known for his riesling and gewürztraminer, but he particularly enjoys working with sauvignon blanc. He promotes this full-flavoured example of his skills as a good food wine.

CURRENT RELEASE 1989 This wine has softened out since I reviewed it for last year's *Penguin Guide*. It still boasts spicy vanilla characters on the nose, but the taste is less assertive than it was a year ago. Enjoy it with smoked chicken and mayonnaise.

STYLE dry

QUALITY ▼▼▼▼

VALUE ★★★+

GRAPES sauvignon blanc

REGION Hawke's Bay

CELLAR 🍾

PRICE $12-15

Seifried Estate Nelson Sauvignon Blanc

Nelsonians say their climate is quite different from Marlborough's, but when it comes to sauvignon blanc their wine styles are virtually indistinguishable.

CURRENT RELEASE 1992 Cut-grass characters in the bouquet and a clean, crisp taste make this wine a good choice for the summer season. The finish has medium length, and the overall impression is of freshness. Partner it with raw marinated scallops.

STYLE off-dry

QUALITY ▼▼▼▼

VALUE ★★★★

GRAPES sauvignon blanc

REGION Nelson

CELLAR 🍾 1

PRICE $13-15

Marino Selak Founder's Selection Sauvignon Blanc (Oak-Aged)

This wine won a gold medal at the 1991 Air New Zealand Wine Awards under its alternative title, Fumé Reserve.

CURRENT RELEASE 1991 Toasty oak is the first thing you notice when you stick your nose into a glass of this stylish wine, with sauvignon characters way at the back. On the palate the charmingly sweet fruit and oak characters combine to create a round, smooth wine with a lingering finish. The ultimate wine for smoked trout on triangles of buttered wholemeal toast.

STYLE dry

QUALITY ▼▼▼▼▼

VALUE ★★★+

GRAPES sauvignon blanc

REGION Marlborough

CELLAR 🍾 2

PRICE $19-21

Selaks Gisborne Fumé Blanc

Selaks have had great success with sauvignon blanc over the years, and now produce several variations on the theme. The Gisborne version is designed for early drinking.
CURRENT RELEASE 1992 Classic sauvignon cut capsicums leap out of the glass, and there are some nice, clean, crisp flavours on the palate. Not one of the biggest sauvignons around, but pleasant drinking nevertheless. Try it with any sort of smoked fish.

STYLE dry
QUALITY ▼▼▼⬤
VALUE ★★★★
GRAPES sauvignon blanc
REGION Gisborne
CELLAR ▮ 2
PRICE $8-11

Selaks Marlborough Sauvignon Blanc

Selaks sauvignons were early pioneers on the overseas market, but their reputation was gained in Australia while other companies were concentrating on the UK. Now they are well respected in both countries as well as at home.
CURRENT RELEASE 1992 Classic Marlborough cut-grass characters are much in evidence on the nose, but there's more richness on the palate than can be said for many of the genre. Partner it with a whole baked trout, if you should be so lucky.

STYLE dry
QUALITY ▼▼▼▼
VALUE ★★★+
GRAPES sauvignon blanc
REGION Marlborough
CELLAR ▮ 2
PRICE $13-15

Selaks Marlborough Sauvignon Blanc/Semillon

The Selaks were among the first winemakers to blend these two varieties together, and they have won many medals both in New Zealand and overseas for their efforts.
Previous outstanding vintages: '86
CURRENT RELEASE 1992 The herbaceousness that both varieties bring to the bouquet is nicely accented by a touch of oak spice. The taste is soft, spicy and complex. Great wine for a Thai chicken salad.

STYLE dry
QUALITY ▼▼▼▼⬤
VALUE ★★★
GRAPES sauvignon blanc 60%, semillon 40%
REGION Marlborough
CELLAR ▮ 2
PRICE $17-19

Shingle Peak Sauvignon Blanc

The holographic artwork on the label attracts attention, but the wine is good enough to have impulse buyers coming back for another bottle.
CURRENT RELEASE 1992 The grassy, squeaky-clean bouquet screams of Marlborough sauvignon, and the same classic characters are much in evidence in the mouth. Great with gravad lax (marinated salmon).

STYLE dry
QUALITY ▼▼▼▼
VALUE ★★★
GRAPES sauvignon blanc
REGION Marlborough
CELLAR ▮ 1
PRICE $13-15

Soljans Hawke's Bay Sauvignon Blanc

Tony Soljan has been in the wine industry for many years, but his wines are known mainly to regulars at his family's Henderson tasting room and barbecue area.
CURRENT RELEASE 1992 The name may soon become better known if the quality of this new label is anything to go by. The nose starts with a nice touch of citric fruit and melon skin, and the tastes are mealy, frisky and boast a good zingy finish.

STYLE dry
QUALITY ▼▼▼▼
VALUE ★★★★
GRAPES sauvignon blanc
REGION Hawke's Bay
CELLAR ▮ 2
PRICE $10-12

Stonecroft Sauvignon Blanc

Alan Limmer's Stonecroft vineyard is on much stonier soil than most of its Hawke's Bay neighbours, so the wines are different from the norm.
CURRENT RELEASE 1992 There's a rock-melon character and a hint of spice in the bouquet. In the mouth the wine starts sweet and rounds out impressively to quite a mouth-filling style, thanks partly to the 15 per cent of it that Alan ferments and ages in French oak barrels. The finish is frisky and long-lasting.

STYLE dry
QUALITY ▼▼▼▼
VALUE ★★★
GRAPES sauvignon blanc
REGION Hawke's Bay
CELLAR ▮ 3
PRICE $16-18

Stoneleigh Marlborough Sauvignon Blanc

Stoneleigh is Corbans' prestige Marlborough vineyard. River pebbles cover the ground, reflecting the sun's ripening rays back onto the grapes and keeping the soil cosy overnight — perfect conditions for sauvignon blanc. Previous outstanding vintages: '86, '89, '91

CURRENT RELEASE 1992 The nose is pungent and grassy in the classic Marlborough style, and the palate is crisp, quite full and nicely zingy. It's good wine, but doesn't reach the heights of the previous vintage.

STYLE dry
QUALITY ▼▼▼▼
VALUE ★★★+
GRAPES sauvignon blanc
REGION Marlborough
CELLAR ▮
PRICE $13-15

Te Kairanga Sauvignon Blanc

The Te Kairanga vineyard was planted in the early 1970s by controversial publisher Alistair Taylor. Under the management of Tom and Robyn Draper it has become a popular tourist spot, and the wines are getting better each year.

CURRENT RELEASE 1992 The wine is as grassy on the nose as any Marlborough model, although it comes from the other side of the Strait. It offers plenty of clean, frisky character and a nice touch of spice at the end. Try it with crumbed chicken breasts.

STYLE dry
QUALITY ▼▼▼▼
VALUE ★★★
GRAPES sauvignon blanc
REGION Martinborough
CELLAR ▮ 1
PRICE $17-21

Te Mata Cape Crest Sauvignon Blanc

The Te Mata name is synonymous with red wine, thanks to their near-legendary Coleraine cabernet blend, but this and its sister sauvignon are good sellers for the company.

CURRENT RELEASE 1992 The nose is smoky and almost peaty — it fleetingly reminded me of whisky. In the mouth, however, it's all grape. This is clean, fresh wine with good acids and a medium-long finish. It's great with a plate of Hawke's Bay asparagus.

STYLE dry
QUALITY ▼▼▼▼
VALUE ★★★
GRAPES sauvignon blanc
REGION Hawke's Bay
CELLAR ▮ 1
PRICE $16-18

Te Mata Castle Hill Sauvignon Blanc

Cape Crest is in pretty short supply, but there's enough of the faintly fruitier Castle Hill to make it a big success in the UK.

CURRENT RELEASE 1992 The nose is more herbaceous than last year's model, and the taste is nicely rounded with a touch of spice. I enjoy it on its own, but it would certainly not be offended by a bowl of giant Chilean olives.

STYLE dry

QUALITY ♟♟♟♟

VALUE ★★★

GRAPES sauvignon blanc

REGION Hawke's Bay

CELLAR ▮ 1

PRICE $15-17

Te Whare Ra Fumé Blanc

Allen and Joyce Hogan put a different historical photograph on the label of each new vintage of this blended wine. Te Whare Ra wines are available almost exclusively by mail order — check the list at the back of the book.

CURRENT RELEASE 1991 The bouquet is crisp and classically sauvignon, and the taste is frisky, fresh and clean. Great wine for a pile of just-opened shellfish.

STYLE dry

QUALITY ♟♟♟♟

VALUE ★★★+

GRAPES sauvignon blanc 60%, semillon 40%

REGION Marlborough

CELLAR ▮ 1–2

PRICE $18–19

Totara Winemaker's Reserve Sauvignon Blanc

It's good to see this Thames-based winery, seemingly in the wilderness for a number of years, producing a range of top-class wines.

CURRENT RELEASE 1990 On the nose this big, outspoken wine is more like a barrel-fermented chardonnay, thanks to its mealy, grainy characters. Bottle age has lost it that appealing sauvignon 'zing', but that has been replaced by round, mouth-filling flavours that make it an ideal match for roast pork.

STYLE dry

QUALITY ♟♟♟♟

VALUE ★★★+

GRAPES sauvignon blanc

REGION Hawke's Bay

CELLAR ▮ 1

PRICE $16-18

Tui Vale Sauvignon Blanc

Tui Vale makes two sauvignons, this unwooded version and the wooded model reviewed below. Unusually, this one is more expensive.
CURRENT RELEASE 1992 The welcome is all passionfruit, leading into some crisp but nicely rounded tropical fruit tastes on the palate. Good wine for a smoked-salmon salad.

STYLE dry
QUALITY ▼▼▼▼
VALUE ★★★★
GRAPES sauvignon blanc
REGION Hawke's Bay
CELLAR ▮ 2
PRICE $14-16

Tui Vale Sauvignon Blanc Oak-Aged

Winemaker Keith Crone put this fruit into French barrels to give it more complexity, but he still prefers the unoaked version. So do I.
CURRENT RELEASE 1991 I get something like spiced pineapple on the nose, which indicates the fruit was very ripe before it went into oak. In the mouth the wine is round, viscous and smooth, but finishes short. Good with summer nibbles.

STYLE dry
QUALITY ▼▼▼▼
VALUE ★★★+
GRAPES sauvignon blanc
REGION Hawke's Bay
CELLAR ▮ 2
PRICE $13-15

Twin Islands Hawke's Bay Sauvignon Blanc

This is a new label being distributed by Negociants, an Australian-owned firm of wine merchants that also markets the Nautilus range.
CURRENT RELEASE 1992 The nose is like hay and passionfruit, and the taste is soft but quite rich. An impressive debut.

STYLE dry
QUALITY ▼▼▼▼
VALUE ★★★★
GRAPES sauvignon blanc
REGION Hawke's Bay
CELLAR ▮ 2
PRICE $10-12

Vavasour Reserve Sauvignon Blanc

This wine and its less expensive stablemate, Dashwood Sauvignon Blanc, were originally conceived as little more than cash-flow fill-ins until the company's red wines came on stream, but they have both been enormously successful. Now, they're here to stay.

CURRENT RELEASE 1992 Toast, vanilla and honeysuckle form a great trio on the nose and lead into a round, smooth taste with a tempting bit of spice on the finish. Good wine for hot-smoked salmon, preferably still warm from the smoker.

STYLE dry
QUALITY ????
VALUE ★★★
GRAPES sauvignon blanc
REGION Marlborough
CELLAR 3
PRICE $24-27

Vidal Private Bin Fumé Blanc

The Private Bin description is used by Vidal, Villa Maria and Esk Valley (all part of the same group) for a series of wines a step below the much-lauded Reserve series. Sauvignons thus labelled are often very good value.

Previous outstanding vintages: '89

CURRENT RELEASE 1992 There's toast, vanilla and hay on the nose, and lots of sweet fruit character on the palate. It all adds up to a pleasant wine that would go well with smoked trout, if you should be so lucky.

STYLE dry
QUALITY ????
VALUE ★★★★
GRAPES sauvignon blanc
REGION Hawke's Bay
CELLAR 2
PRICE $10-12

Vidal Reserve Fumé Blanc

The top-of-the-line sauvignon for this Hawke's Bay company has earned a reputation for elegance rather than knock-'em-dead power.

Previous outstanding vintages: '89

CURRENT RELEASE 1991 When I tasted this vintage for last year's guide, it had just been bottled and the oak was still dominant. It is still much in evidence, but it is in much better balance with the ripe fruit characters that show through on the palate. The wine is well rounded, delicately spicy and has beautifully integrated acids. Enjoy it with a smoked-eel salad.

STYLE dry
QUALITY ????
VALUE ★★★+
GRAPES sauvignon blanc
REGION Hawke's Bay
CELLAR 3
PRICE $17-20

Villa Maria Cellar Selection Sauvignon Blanc

The Cellar Selection wines are designed to sit in the middle of the market for quality and price, but this sauvignon took a silver medal at the 1992 Air New Zealand Wine Awards.

CURRENT RELEASE 1992 The grassy sauvignon nose is subdued, and the same rounded characters are evident on the palate. Good acids ensure things are kept in kilter, and give the wine a crisp finish. Great with a smoked mullet sandwich.

STYLE dry

QUALITY 🍷🍷🍷🍷

VALUE ★★★+

GRAPES sauvignon blanc

REGION Marlborough

CELLAR 🍾 2

PRICE $15-17

Villa Maria Private Bin Marlborough Sauvignon Blanc

The Villa takes its Marlborough grapes from a vineyard with a variety of soil types within its boundaries. Viticulturalist Steve Smith believes this adds complexity to the wine.

CURRENT RELEASE 1992 The bouquet is more reminiscent of Hawke's Bay than Marlborough, with tropical fruit and hay-like characters making their presence felt. The taste is crisp and clean, quite light but with good acids and a finish like a chilled Splendour apple.

STYLE dry

QUALITY 🍷🍷🍷🍷

VALUE ★★★★

GRAPES sauvignon blanc

REGION Marlborough

CELLAR 🍾 2

PRICE $11-14

Villa Maria Reserve Sauvignon Blanc

The Reserve designation marks this as the most serious sauvignon in the Villa's extensive collection. This version picked up a silver medal at the 1991 Air New Zealand Wine Awards and was rewarded for persistence with a gold at last year's awards.

Previous outstanding vintages: '86, '90

CURRENT RELEASE 1991 Spicy hay, if there is such a thing, on the nose makes for a nice introduction to this elegant wine. The palate is mouth-filling, quite rich and round, and the finish is delightfully long and lingering.

STYLE dry

QUALITY 🍷🍷🍷🍷½

VALUE ★★★+

GRAPES sauvignon blanc

REGION Marlborough

CELLAR 🍾 2

PRICE $17-20

West Brook Hawke's Bay Sauvignon Blanc

Like many Auckland wineries, West Brook brings some of its sauvignon blanc grapes in from Hawke's Bay. CURRENT RELEASE 1992 Hay and capsicums can both be found in the bouquet. Good acids give the wine a lot of zing in the mouth and ensure a clean finish.

STYLE dry

QUALITY ♥♥♥♥

VALUE ★★★★

GRAPES sauvignon blanc

REGION Hawke's Bay

CELLAR ▮ 1

PRICE $9-11

West Brook Sauvignon Blanc/Semillon

The company makes a straight semillon and a couple of variations on the straight sauvignon theme, so this blend is a logical extension.
CURRENT RELEASE 1990 The nose is surprisingly shy, given the aromatic tendencies of both varieties, and on the palate the wine starts quietly, but gathers strength for a big finish. My sample went well with a piece of smoked marlin.

STYLE dry

QUALITY ♥♥♥♥

VALUE ★★★★

GRAPES sauvignon blanc 85%, semillon 15%

REGION Hawke's Bay and West Auckland

CELLAR ▮ 2

PRICE $11-13

Whitecliff Fumé Blanc

Winery owners the Mason brothers call their Whitecliff range 'brasserie-style wines'. They are less expensive than the Dartmoor and Sacred Hill collections which sit above them.
CURRENT RELEASE 1991 The 1990 version of this wine had 20 per cent semillon blended into it, but the lads did without it for 1991. The wine has a shy nose and is austere on the palate, but may open out in a year or so. Try it with a seafood salad.

STYLE dry

QUALITY ♥♥♥

VALUE ★★+

GRAPES sauvignon blanc

REGION Hawke's Bay

CELLAR ➤ 2

PRICE $15-19

Whitecliff Sauvignon Blanc

This wine doesn't do well in competition because most judges find it has an an oxidised character. Winery owner Dave Mason says he's following French guidelines, and that's how it turns out. The bottom line is that he's selling all he can make.

CURRENT RELEASE 1991 The bouquet is certainly soft for sauvignon, with a bit of wet dog starting things off and cut-grass characters only coming in at the back. The wine has pleasant fruit flavours and good acids but seems lean. Best on its own.

STYLE dry
QUALITY ♟♟♟♟
VALUE ★★+
GRAPES sauvignon blanc
REGION Hawke's Bay
CELLAR ▯ 1
PRICE $15-19

Yelas Estate Hawke's Bay Fumé Blanc

Yelas Estate is the name used for the top wines of Pleasant Valley Vineyards, in the Auckland suburb of Henderson.

CURRENT RELEASE 1990 On the nose the wine's nine-month sojourn in French barrels has given it a vanilla/chocolate character that promises good things to come. In the mouth it starts sweet before getting back to the more familiar sauvignon grassiness. Enjoy it with smoked mussels.

STYLE dry
QUALITY ♟♟♟
VALUE ★★★
GRAPES sauvignon blanc
REGION Hawke's Bay
CELLAR ▯ 2
PRICE $11-13

Yelas Estate Hawke's Bay Late Harvest Sauvignon Blanc

The grapes for this unusual wine were picked late to optimise their sweetness. It's not a luscious dessert style, but rather a medium-sweet, hot-day quaffer.

CURRENT RELEASE 1989 The bouquet has both ginger and honey, along with a bit of sauvignon's gooseberry tones. In the mouth the wine is sweet, spicy and pleasant without being a standout. Try it alongside a chilled pear.

STYLE medium
QUALITY ♟♟♟
VALUE ★★★
GRAPES sauvignon blanc
REGION Hawke's Bay
CELLAR ▯
PRICE $12-14

Yelas Estate Oak-Matured Semillon

Semillon wines from the Hunter Valley in New South Wales age gracefully for a decade or more. This West Auckland example isn't that old yet, but it's picked up a fair bit of character in the three or so years since the grapes were picked.

CURRENT RELEASE 1989 There's quite a bit of flavour in the bouquet, with grassiness making the first impression and vanilla following on behind. The wine has a nice balance between its fruit and oak components, and it has a chunky feel to it that I find quite appealing. Try it with an asparagus and onion quiche.

STYLE dry

QUALITY ▾▾▾▾

VALUE ★★★+

GRAPES semillon

REGION West Auckland

CELLAR ▯ 2

PRICE $11-13

Yelas Estate Sauvignon Blanc

Many winemakers pick some of their sauvignon grapes early, to emphasise the variety's grassiness. Winery owner Stephan Yelas doesn't agree with that policy; he picked these grapes late enough to make sure they were fully ripe.

CURRENT RELEASE 1992 The nose is classic capsicum, but it's quite deep on the scale and almost honeyed. On the palate the wine is well rounded and easy to drink, but it lacks zing on the finish.

STYLE dry

QUALITY ▾▾▾

VALUE ★★★

GRAPES sauvignon blanc

REGION Hawke's Bay

CELLAR ▯

PRICE $10-13

Unusual and Unspecified Whites

Using the names of French regions such as Chablis and Burgundy to describe local wines is far less common in New Zealand than in Australia or California, but it still happens. The labels on these wines seldom mention the grape varieties used, and nor do wines with proprietary brands such as Blenheimer or Chablisse.

All such products are listed in this section and the similar one for red wines, and if their makers were willing to divulge the grape varieties they contain, we have listed them.

Also in this section are a number of unusual varieties, many of them made by only one or two producers.

Babich Chablis

Babich Classic Dry is a common house wine in hotel bars and restaurants around town, but for my money this similarly priced stablemate is better value.

CURRENT RELEASE 1992 There's a faint hint of spice on the nose, but mostly this wine is about simple, clean flavours. The riesling characters on the nose suggest it will be slightly sweet, but it is quite dry in the mouth. A good pre-barbecue quaffer.

STYLE off-dry

QUALITY ▼▼▼▼

VALUE ★★★★

GRAPES riesling, sylvaner, chardonnay

REGION Gisborne and Hawke's Bay

CELLAR 🍾 1

PRICE $7-9

Babich Classic Dry

This big-selling wine is one of the few bone-dry whites in its price range, making it a popular choice to partner a cheap meal.

CURRENT RELEASE 1991 There's not a lot given away in the bouquet, but things certainly smell squeaky clean. There are no dramatic fruit characters in the mouth, but the wine is crisp, refreshing and not as austere as you might expect.

STYLE dry

QUALITY ▼▼▼

VALUE ★★★★

GRAPES sylvaner, riesling, müller-thurgau

REGION Gisborne and Hawke's Bay

CELLAR 🍾 1

PRICE $7-9

Babich Fumé Vert

It sounds like a grape variety, but fumé vert means smoky green and is a proprietary name used in an attempt to describe the wine's characteristics.

CURRENT RELEASE 1992 Semillon's grassiness and sauvignon's capsicum character are easily found in the bouquet. The wine is spicy, clean and fresh on the palate but a wee bit thin on the finish. Still, it would make a fine companion to a seafood salad.

STYLE dry

QUALITY ▼▼▼▼

VALUE ★★★

GRAPES semillon 60%, sauvignon blanc 20%, chardonnay 20%

REGION Gisborne

CELLAR 🍾 1

PRICE $9-12

Collards White Burgundy

This blended white has been a top seller for the Collard family for a decade or more. The grape types vary from year to year; the aim is consistency of style.

CURRENT RELEASE 1992 Quite a steely little wine, thanks to the chenin blanc in its make-up. It is fruity, clean and refreshing but is unlikely to get you uncontrollably excited.

STYLE dry

QUALITY ▼▼▼▼

VALUE ★★★★

GRAPES chenin blanc 50%, chardonnay 50%

REGION West Auckland

CELLAR 🍾 2

PRICE $8-10

Coopers Creek Coopers Classic Dry

The same three grapes are used each year for this big-selling wine, but the percentages occasionally vary. Last year semillon seemed to dominate. This year I picked up more chenin.

CURRENT RELEASE 1992 The nose is steely and citric with just a hint of herbaceousness. The wine tastes fresh and faintly spicy and has a nice clean finish. Partner it with a bacon, lettuce and tomato sandwich.

STYLE dry

QUALITY ▼▼▼

VALUE ★★+

GRAPES semillon 40%, chenin blanc 40%, chardonnay 20%

REGION Gisborne and Hawke's Bay

CELLAR 🍾 1

Giesen Ehrenfelser

The only commercial release of wine made from this German-sourced grape, believed to be a close relation to riesling. The name comes from Ehrenfels Castle on the Rhine River at Rudesheim.

CURRENT RELEASE 1991 The nose is very floral with a hint of cloves, and the taste is soft, but with enough acid to keep it lively. Try it with a chicken breast topped by a fruity sauce.

STYLE off-dry

QUALITY ♟♟♟♟

VALUE ★★★

GRAPES ehrenfelser

REGION Canterbury

CELLAR ▯ 2

PRICE $13-15

Hunter's Breidecker

Hunter's is one of only a handful of wineries making wine from this German variety, a close relation of müller-thurgau. It is named after the viticulturalist who developed it by crossing müller-thurgau with ehren-felser.

CURRENT RELEASE 1992 The nose is floral, and I fancy I can pick up honeysuckle and pears in there somewhere. The taste is quite sweet at first, but there are enough crisp acids to keep things in proportion in the middle, although I find the finish a bit cloying.

STYLE medium

QUALITY ♟♟♟

VALUE ★★★

GRAPES breidecker

REGION Marlborough

CELLAR ▯

PRICE $10-12

Hunter's Estate Dry White

Wines called simply 'dry white' seldom have a lot to offer, but this blend offers good depth of flavour and more than a touch of class.

CURRENT RELEASE 1992 The bouquet is smoky and floral, and on the palate nicely integrated acids keep every-thing refreshing. It's a bit like biting into a chilled Gala apple. Enjoy it with barbecued squid.

STYLE dry

QUALITY ♟♟♟♟

VALUE ★★★+

GRAPES riesling 60%, chardonnay 25%, sauvignon blanc 15%

REGION Marlborough

CELLAR ▯ 2

PRICE $10-14

Jackson Estate Marlborough Dry

This wine is 100 per cent riesling, although that fact is mentioned only in the small print on the back label. Riesling isn't a big seller in New Zealand, so maybe the plan is to grab the sale before people realise what it is! CURRENT RELEASE 1992 The nose is steely at first, but there's some richness in there too. This wine is mouth-filling and faintly spicy, and would go well with pan-fried cod or snapper.

STYLE dry
QUALITY ♟♟♟♟
VALUE ★★★+
GRAPES riesling
REGION Marlborough
CELLAR ▌ 4
PRICE $15-17

Merlen Morio-Muscat

Merlen's Almuth Lorenz was about the happiest winemaker in the room at last year's Air New Zealand Wine Awards when she picked up a trophy for this unusual wine. Almuth's family grows the variety in Germany, and initially she planted a few vines 'just for fun' in Marlborough — but it seems they love the place! CURRENT RELEASE 1992 The bouquet reminds me of dried pears and honey. The wine is rich and mouth-filling, but crisp acids keep things nicely in perspective. Enjoy it on its own, or perhaps with fresh pears.

STYLE medium
QUALITY ♟♟♟♟
VALUE ★★★+
GRAPES morio-muscat
REGION Marlborough
CELLAR ▌
PRICE $13-15

Montana Blenheimer

Vying with Cooks Chasseur for the title of the biggest-selling white wine in New Zealand, Blenheimer typifies the slightly sweet müller-thurgau-based products that have introduced thousands of people to the wonders of the grape since they were first developed in the 1970s. CURRENT RELEASE (non-vintage) Plenty of floral fruit characters can be found in the bouquet, and the same sensations are carried through onto the palate. A good summer-afternoon wine.

STYLE medium
QUALITY ♟♟♟
VALUE ★★★★
GRAPES predominantly müller-thurgau
REGION Marlborough and Gisborne
CELLAR ▌
PRICE $6-8

Neudorf The Dovedale Wine

This blend of riesling and semillon — an unusual combination that would probably give the French apoplexy — took a bronze award at last year's Air New Zealand Wine Awards.

CURRENT RELEASE 1991 The herbaceousness on the nose is in the bass clef rather than the treble one populated by so many semillons, and the palate is full of sweet fruit characters that give the wine quite a mouth-filling quality. Enjoy it with a green salad topped with chunks of hot-smoked salmon.

STYLE off-dry

QUALITY ▼▼▼▼

VALUE ★★★+

GRAPES riesling 85%, semillon 15%

REGION Nelson

CELLAR 2

PRICE $13-15

Old Coach Road Classic Dry White

The wine is made by Seifried Estates, and it's named after a genuine Old Coach Road — it runs along the ridge above Nelson's Moutere Valley. The first mail deliveries were carried along this route, at first by foot, later by coach, from Nelson to Motueka.

CURRENT RELEASE (non-vintage) The wine is a blend of semillon and riesling, and it is the semillon that first grabs your attention with herbaceous aromas. Riesling comes into play on the palate, injecting some floral characters into the proceedings and adding a dry honey finish.

STYLE dry

QUALITY ▼▼▼▼

VALUE ★★★+

GRAPES riesling 60%, semillon 40%

REGION Nelson

CELLAR 1

PRICE $9-11

C. J. Pask Roy's Hill White

Roy's Hill White and Roy's Hill Red are the proprietary names for the two least expensive wines in the C. J. Pask collection.

CURRENT RELEASE 1992 The bouquet is quite big and rich, with a hint of spice at the back. In the mouth the wine is fresh and frisky with a refreshing apple-like finish. Enjoy it alongside veal bratwurst or a plate of good pork sausages.

STYLE dry

QUALITY ▼▼▼▼

VALUE ★★★

GRAPES chenin blanc

REGION Hawke's Bay

CELLAR 2

PRICE $11-13

Pleasant Valley White Burgundy

There used to be dozens of 'White Burgundies' on the New Zealand market. Nowadays, most of them come from Australia — Pleasant Valley is one of the few local producers to persist with the name.

CURRENT RELEASE (non-vintage) There is plenty of clean, lemon-like character on both the nose and palate to keep things lively. The wine starts well, turns a little mean in the middle, but finishes with a nice dose of crispness. Try it with fish fingers.

STYLE dry

QUALITY ♟♟♟

VALUE ★★★

GRAPES chenin blanc 55%, riesling 19%, chardonnay 12%, sauvignon blanc 14%

REGION Hawke's Bay

CELLAR 🍾

PRICE $7-9

Rippon Vineyard Osteiner

Try this and you can say it's the best New Zealand osteiner you've ever tasted — Otago's Rippon vineyard is the only one in the country making wine from this recently imported German variety.

CURRENT RELEASE 1992 The nose is citric and floral, like apple blossoms, and the palate is well rounded and fruity, but with enough acid crispness to keep things under control. Enjoy it on its own.

STYLE off-dry

QUALITY ♟♟♟♟

VALUE ★★★

GRAPES osteiner

REGION Central Otago

CELLAR 🍾 1

PRICE $13-15

Robard & Butler Classic Chablis

With a sugar content of just two grams per litre, this wine is one of the driest in its price bracket.

CURRENT RELEASE 1991 The nose is steely and flinty and the taste a bit apple-like, but clean and frisky enough to make it a nice summer sipper. The quality is a big step up from last year's model.

STYLE dry

QUALITY ♟♟♟♟

VALUE ★★★+

GRAPES sauvignon blanc, semillon, chardonnay

REGION East Cape

CELLAR 🍾 2

PRICE $9-11

St Jerome Chablis

Chablis or not chablis — that is the question. Well, it used to be in the days when dozens of wines on the New Zealand market were named, rather oddly, after this small region in France. Today, this example is one of only a handful to continue the practice.

CURRENT RELEASE 1992 I wasn't mad on the 1989 model I reviewed for the last *Penguin Guide*, but I like this one a lot. It's got nice steely notes on the nose and is crisp, clean and faintly spicy in the mouth. If your local delicatessen sells Greek dolmades (stuffed vine leaves), try it with them.

STYLE dry
QUALITY ▿▿▿▿
VALUE ★★★★
GRAPES breidecker 75%, riesling 25%
REGION West Auckland
CELLAR ▮ 2
PRICE $8-11

Daniel Schuster Pinot Blanc

Daniel Schuster spends a lot of time commuting between his Omihi Hills vineyard in Canterbury and various vineyards in California, for whom he acts as consultant.

CURRENT RELEASE 1992 The bouquet is so steely it's like sniffing wine in a stainless-steel tank. The taste is crisp and reminiscent of a Granny Smith apple, which means there is a good, zingy finish. Good with raw rock oysters.

STYLE dry
QUALITY ▿▿▿▿
VALUE ★★★
GRAPES pinot blanc
REGION Canterbury
CELLAR ▮ 3
PRICE $17-19

Seibel Long River Crisp Dry White

Norbert Seibel says he structures his wines to accompany food, which after all, is what it's all about — and this undemanding wine is a good example of the philosophy.

CURRENT RELEASE 1990 There are some nice toasty, spicy characters on the nose and quite a lot of richness on the palate. Semillon's apple-like herbaceousness cuts in right at the end. Enjoy it with steamed mussels.

STYLE dry
QUALITY ▿▿▿
VALUE ★★★+
GRAPES chenin blanc 50%, sauvignon blanc 25%, semillon 25%
REGION Hawke's Bay and Gisborne
CELLAR ▮
PRICE $6-9

Seibel Scheurebe

Scheurebe (pronounced shoy-ray-ba) is a German grape that makes wine with rather more character than your average müller-thurgau.

CURRENT RELEASE 1989 The nose is very Germanic — spicy, fruity and almost like a gewürztraminer. In the mouth the wine is well rounded and boasts a reasonable amount of flavour depth. Good with a ham sandwich.

STYLE dry
QUALITY 🍷🍷🍷
VALUE ★★★★
GRAPES scheurebe
REGION Gisborne
CELLAR 🍾
PRICE $8-10

Seifried Estate Chablis

Unusually for a wine designed for the 'cheap and cheerful' category, Hermann Seifried's chablis spends four months in oak barrels, albeit one-year-old ones.

CURRENT RELEASE 1991 There isn't much evidence of oak on the nose, in fact it's rather shy. The wine is crisp and dry enough to be almost austere. Partner it with bacon-topped grilled oysters.

STYLE dry
QUALITY 🍷🍷🍷
VALUE ★★★
GRAPES sylvaner, chenin blanc, chardonnay, sauvignon blanc
REGION Nelson
CELLAR 🍾 2
PRICE $8-10

Te Mata Estate Oak-Aged Dry White

This well-priced wine has more style than its name suggests, and sells like hot cakes at Te Mata's Havelock North cellar shop.

CURRENT RELEASE 1992 There's a frisky, faintly spicy nose that begs you to drink up. The taste is slightly nutty, and the finish is short but satisfying. Good with sliced tomato on crackers.

STYLE dry
QUALITY 🍷🍷🍷🍷
VALUE ★★★+
GRAPES chardonnay 55%, chenin blanc 30%, sauvignon blanc 15%
REGION Hawke's Bay
CELLAR ➡ 2
PRICE $11-13

Red Wines

Cabernet Sauvignon, Merlot, Cabernet Franc and Blends

Cabernet sauvignon, merlot and cabernet franc are the grapes from which the great reds of Bordeaux, in France, are made, and even though there is more merlot planted in the area than cabernet, it is the latter grape that is most often given the credit for their legendary quality. So how does this affect New Zealand? Fact is, many winemakers are saying we should have planted more merlot than cabernet in this country as well. On its own, cabernet sauvignon makes wines that can suffer from a 'taste hole'. They start and finish well, but go a little flat in the middle, earning them the name 'doughnut' wines. Merlot has the ability to fill in that gap and create a far more harmonious wine, and winemakers are now discovering, just as the French did many years ago, that a touch of cabernet franc helps give the wine an extra touch of class. Good wine can undoubtedly be made from cabernet sauvignon alone, but most of the recent awards have gone to those blended with merlot, and often cabernet franc as well.

Airfield Cabernet Sauvignon/Merlot

This label is seen only in years when the weather isn't so good for grapes — it's a second label used by Stephen White of Stonyridge when he considers the fruit isn't good enough to make his near-legendary Larose.
CURRENT RELEASE 1992 A second label it may be, but this wine is still big enough to impress the punters. The nose has hints of coffee and tobacco, and the taste is soft but rich and has a chocolatey finish. Enjoy it with lasagne.

STYLE dry

QUALITY ▼▼▼▼

VALUE ★★★

GRAPES cabernet sauvignon 63%, merlot 29%, cabernet franc 6%, malbec 2%

REGION Waiheke Island

CELLAR ▬▬ 2-4

PRICE $25-29

Ararimu Cabernet Sauvignon (Matua)

A new name in a stylish imported bottle for a small range of wines from Ross and Bill Spence, of Matua Valley Wines. This red took a gold medal at the 1992 Air New Zealand Wine Awards.

CURRENT RELEASE 1991 The colour is dark, and there are attractive mint/chocolate aromas on the nose, so you know you're in for something good. The taste is rich, soft and smooth, but with a powerful backbone. Great stuff! Enjoy it with a beef casserole.

STYLE dry
QUALITY ▼▼▼▼▼
VALUE ★★★
GRAPES cabernet sauvignon
REGION Hawke's Bay
CELLAR ▬▬ 2-4
PRICE $27-29

Babich Cabernet Sauvignon

This straight cabernet and its merlot-blended stablemate, both sub-labelled 'Hawke's Bay', are designed to slot in below the top-rated Babich Irongate version, but considerably above the cheap and cheerful pinotage/cabernet. Previous outstanding vintages: '85

CURRENT RELEASE 1991 The colour is good and rich, and there are some soft blackberry characters on the nose. The same soft, easy-going impression is continued in the taste. It's not a 'biggie', but it's pleasant drinking. Try it with casseroled chicken thighs.

STYLE dry
QUALITY ▼▼▼▼
VALUE ★★★★
GRAPES cabernet sauvignon
REGION Hawke's Bay
CELLAR ▌ 2
PRICE $11-13

Babich Irongate Cabernet/Merlot

This is the 'biggie' of the Babich red collection and, in various vintage colours, it has won a fistful of gold and silver medals.

Previous outstanding vintages: '87

CURRENT RELEASE 1990 The berry character of good Hawke's Bay cabernet is much in evidence in this richly flavoursome wine, along with cassis and a touch of oak spice. It is smooth, rich and frighteningly moreish. If you're feeling flush, partner it with a whole roast fillet of beef.

STYLE dry
QUALITY ▼▼▼▼▼
VALUE ★★★+
GRAPES cabernet sauvignon 78%, merlot 15%, cabernet franc 7%
REGION Hawke's Bay
CELLAR ▬▬ 2-5
PRICE $20-24

Blackbirch Cabernet Sauvignon

This is Grove Mill's top red, made from different grapes each year. Previous examples have been blends, and winemaker David Pearce reports they probably will be again in the future. The 1990 model, however, is all cabernet sauvignon.

CURRENT RELEASE 1990 Blackcurrants and cedarwood are the most upfront aromas on the bouquet, but there are all sorts of things going on in this richly coloured, chunky wine. After that big introduction, the taste is surprisingly smooth. In fact, it is the wine's velvety texture that makes it so appealing. I partnered it recently with a cheese-laden risotto, and it worked well.

STYLE dry
QUALITY ▼▼▼▼
VALUE ★★★
GRAPES cabernet sauvignon
REGION Marlborough
CELLAR ▮ 4
PRICE $23-25

Bloomfield Cabernet Sauvignon/Merlot

Winemaker David Bloomfield doesn't believe in putting too much oak flavour into his wines. This is the top-line model; the other is labelled Solway.

CURRENT RELEASE 1990 The policy of making a fruit-led wine works well. The flavours are soft and smooth enough to make this red a pleasant sipper on its own, but it is also a fine partner for a roast chicken.

STYLE dry
QUALITY ▼▼▼▼
VALUE ★★★
GRAPES cabernet sauvignon 80%, merlot 20%
REGION Wairarapa
CELLAR ▮ 2
PRICE $23-26

Blue Rock Cabernet Sauvignon

If this splendid red is any indication, this new Martinborough winery is going to be well worth watching in the future.

CURRENT RELEASE 1991 The colour is deep, the bouquet rich and berryish and the taste big and mouth-filling. This is very good wine and deserves to sit alongside a rare fillet steak topped with Béarnaise sauce.

STYLE dry
QUALITY ▼▼▼▼▼
VALUE ★★★+
GRAPES cabernet sauvignon
REGION Martinborough
CELLAR ▭- 2-5
PRICE $20-25

Brajkovich Kumeu Cabernet Franc

Michael Brajkovich is one of very few people in the country to make an unblended cabernet franc, and it's a little beauty.

CURRENT RELEASE 1992 I got a hint of spring onions on the nose, which sounds pretty weird but didn't seem to do any harm. The first impression on the palate is of ripe, sweet grapes. The wine is light, as it is designed to be, but frisky and just plain enjoyable. Michael suggests following the French example and chilling it to serve with fish. If you top the fish with a herbed tomato sauce, it should work well.

STYLE dry
QUALITY ▼▼▼▼
VALUE ★★★+
GRAPES cabernet franc
REGION West Auckland
CELLAR ▋ 1
PRICE $14-17

Brookfields Cabernet/Merlot (Gold Label)

The Gold Label is the top line for Brookfields. Down from there are the Reserve wines, then the Estate series, which owner/winemaker Peter Robertson calls his 'baby' wines. The Gold Label cabernet/merlot is consistently among the top reds in the country.

Previous outstanding vintages: '87, '89

CURRENT RELEASE 1991 Lovely Hawke's Bay berry characters on the nose and warm, rich fruit on the palate make this a very stylish wine indeed. The finish is tannic and long-lasting, indicating that cellaring for four or five years would be a good idea. After that, partner it with the best steak you can find.

STYLE dry
QUALITY ▼▼▼▼▼
VALUE ★★★
GRAPES cabernet sauvignon 75%, merlot 20%, cabernet franc 5%
REGION Hawke's Bay
CELLAR ■- 2-5
PRICE $27-32

Church Road Cabernet Sauvignon

Montana now has a connection with Cordier, French specialist red-wine makers, so we can expect big things of this label in the future.

CURRENT RELEASE 1991 The colour is inky black, and the bouquet is full of cassis and espresso characters, which all bodes well. There's plenty of ripe, sweet fruit in the mouth, balanced by some attractive oaky spice. Enjoy it with a pepperoni pizza.

STYLE dry
QUALITY ▼▼▼▼
VALUE ★★★
GRAPES cabernet sauvignon 85%, merlot 15%
REGION Hawke's Bay
CELLAR ■- 3-5
PRICE $19-23

Clearview Estate Cabernet Sauvignon

Getting a silver medal with this wine in its first showing at the 1992 Air New Zealand Wine Awards was a pretty good trick. If you call at the winery in Te Awanga, between Napier and Hastings, there might still be some left of the 1989 version, which also won a silver.

CURRENT RELEASE 1991 Cassis, coffee and liquorice share the honours on the nose, while the taste is all about oak spice and blackberries. Great wine for a Mediterranean lunch — which they just happen to specialise in at the winery.

STYLE dry

QUALITY 🍷🍷🍷🍷

VALUE ★★★+

GRAPES cabernet sauvignon 95%, merlot 5%

REGION Hawke's Bay

CELLAR 2-4

PRICE $19-24

Clearview Estate Merlot/Franc

Grapes for the cabernet sauvignon reviewed above came from three Hawke's Bay vineyards, but for this lighter model they were all from the home vineyard.

CURRENT RELEASE 1991 I get chocolate and mushrooms on the nose, which sounds odd but seems to work okay. The wine starts sweet and is quite soft in the mouth. Try it with casseroled chicken Maryland legs.

STYLE dry

QUALITY 🍷🍷🍷½

VALUE ★★★

GRAPES merlot 60%, cabernet franc 40%

REGION Hawke's Bay

CELLAR 2-4

PRICE $19-24

Cloudy Bay Cabernet/Merlot

The Cloudy Bay name is best known for whites, particularly sauvignon blanc, but this stylishly labelled red is a popular restaurant choice. Some vintages have been criticised for herbaceousness, but company founder David Hohnen says this should be accepted as a regional characteristic.

CURRENT RELEASE 1990 The bouquet suggests the wine will be lighter than previous vintages, but that's not the impression on the palate — there is a distinct feeling of big flavours that are closed in at present, but are fighting to get out. The finish is a little lean, but there are some delightfully spicy undertones.

STYLE dry

QUALITY 🍷🍷🍷½

VALUE ★★+

GRAPES cabernet sauvignon 60%, cabernet franc 30%, merlot 10%

REGION Marlborough

CELLAR 2-3

PRICE $28-32

Collards Rothesay Cabernet Sauvignon

This is the first unblended cabernet the Collards have ever made. The grapes came from their own vineyard in Waimauku, West Auckland.

CURRENT RELEASE 1990 Unblended it may be, but this is probably the best cabernet the lads have made yet. The colour is rich, the bouquet rich and minty, and the taste satisfyingly well rounded. Enjoy it with a rare roast of beef with all the extras.

STYLE dry
QUALITY ▼▼▼▼
VALUE ★★★+
GRAPES cabernet sauvignon
REGION West Auckland
CELLAR 2-5
PRICE $17-21

Cooks Winemaker's Reserve Cabernet Sauvignon

How long should red wine be left in oak barrels? It's a vexed question answered for many smaller makers by economic reality — their wines get twelve months in oak because they need the barrels for the next vintage. There are no such problems for Corbans-owned Cooks; this cabernet spent twenty months absorbing the spicy flavours of French and American oak.

Previous outstanding vintages: '86, '87

CURRENT RELEASE 1989 Berries and spicy, sweet oak form a nice introduction to this richly coloured cabernet. In the mouth the wine still tastes young; the tannins are well integrated but the fruit is a little subdued. Enjoy it with a hearty stew.

STYLE dry
QUALITY ▼▼▼▼
VALUE ★★★+
GRAPES cabernet sauvignon 85%, merlot 10%, cabernet franc 5%
REGION Hawke's Bay
CELLAR 2-5
PRICE $23-25

Coopers Creek Cabernet Franc

Another of the exceedingly rare unblended cabernet franc wines, and a pleasant, middleweight red with enough original character to make it worth seeking out as an alternative to cabernet sauvignon.

CURRENT RELEASE 1990 The wine has some Aussie-style eucalyptus characters in the bouquet and a good proportion of big, meaty flavours on the palate. The finish is a little angular, but the overall impression is warm and moreish. Good wine for a serious picnic.

STYLE dry
QUALITY ▼▼▼▼
VALUE ★★★+
GRAPES cabernet franc
REGION West Auckland
CELLAR 2
PRICE $15-18

Coopers Creek Cabernet/Merlot

Coopers Creek buys most of its grapes from contract growers around the country, but this cabernet/merlot was crafted from home vineyard grapes picked behind the winery at Huapai.

CURRENT RELEASE 1990 The nose is earthy and carries a fair bit of merlot's tobacco character. On the palate it is berryish, soft and smooth, and boasts a chocolate finish.

STYLE dry

QUALITY 🍷🍷🍷🍷

VALUE ★★★+

GRAPES cabernet sauvignon 75%, merlot 25%

REGION West Auckland

CELLAR 1-3

PRICE $16-19

Crab Farm Cabernet/Merlot

Father and son team James and Hamish Jardine love Hawke's Bay cabernet and make a handful of variations on the theme.

CURRENT RELEASE 1991 The Jardines have got a great colour into this warmly welcoming red. Sensible oak treatment has given it a nice amount of spice and enough tannin to carry it over the next four or five years. Match it with a beef or venison casserole.

STYLE dry

QUALITY 🍷🍷🍷🍷

VALUE ★★★★

GRAPES cabernet sauvignon 60%, merlot 40%

REGION Hawke's Bay

CELLAR 3-5

PRICE $16-19

Crab Farm Jardine Cabernet

This is the top Crab Farm red, named for the family and sporting a stylish grey and gold label.

CURRENT RELEASE 1991 The nose is like cassis-flavoured coffee, but the taste is all about rich, berryish Hawke's Bay cabernet. It's good wine, but I must admit I missed the merlot that gives its cheaper stablemate something extra. Nevertheless, it's good enough for a venison back steak — and put a dash in the sauce.

STYLE dry

QUALITY 🍷🍷🍷🍷

VALUE ★★★+

GRAPES cabernet sauvignon

REGION Hawke's Bay

CELLAR 3-5

PRICE $18-23

Cross Roads Cabernet/Merlot

Owners Lester O'Brien and Malcolm Reeves cut their teeth on whites for the first couple of vintages, but they're both red fans, so it was only a matter of time until they added one to their collection.
CURRENT RELEASE 1991 The mid-red colour doesn't suggest a huge wine, but there are some nice minty/chocolate characters in the bouquet. Things follow through well on the palate, with well-rounded flavours and a spicy oak finish. Enjoy it with spicy chorizo or merguez sausages.

STYLE dry
QUALITY ♥♥♥♥
VALUE ★★★
GRAPES cabernet sauvignon 75%, merlot 25%
REGION Hawke's Bay
CELLAR ▮ 3
PRICE $17-19

Dartmoor Cabernet Merlot

Winery owners David and Mark Mason are as enthusiastic about food as they are about wine, and regularly cook game for like-minded enthusiasts.
CURRENT RELEASE 1991 The nose has a bit of cassis and a lot of blueberry character. On the palate the wine is light but quite warm and rich, and has a sweetish finish. Good with venison.

STYLE dry
QUALITY ♥♥♥
VALUE ★★★
GRAPES cabernet sauvignon 80%, merlot 20%
REGION Hawke's Bay
CELLAR ▬ 2-3
PRICE $19-24

Dashwood Cabernet Sauvignon

The Vavasour winery, where this wine is made, was established with the stated aim of showing that great red wines could be made in Marlborough. This second-label red doesn't quite prove the premise, but it has much to commend it.
CURRENT RELEASE 1991 Cassis, coffee and liquorice get it together on the nose, and drift on to the palate to give the wine a soft, velvety smoothness. It's not a 'biggie', but it's thoroughly drinkable. Enjoy it with grilled liver.

STYLE dry
QUALITY ♥♥♥♥
VALUE ★★★
GRAPES cabernet sauvignon 95%, merlot 5%
REGION Marlborough
CELLAR ▮ 3
PRICE $17-19

Delegat's Hawke's Bay Cabernet/Merlot

Delegat's have won a good reputation for the quality of their reds. Both this second label and the top-rated Proprietor's Reserve get their fruit from Hawke's Bay.
Previous outstanding vintages: '86
CURRENT RELEASE 1991 You can detect lots of sweet fruit in the bouquet, with berries, cassis and oak spice all contributing to the overall effect. The wine is well rounded and has a lot of instant appeal. Partner it with a good steakburger.

STYLE dry
QUALITY ▼▼▼▼
VALUE ★★★
GRAPES cabernet sauvignon 80%, merlot 20%
REGION Hawke's Bay
CELLAR ▮ 2
PRICE $13-16

Delegat's Proprietor's Reserve Cabernet Sauvignon

A regular medal-winner, this is the top cabernet for Delegat's and, although it doesn't say so on the label, usually carries a percentage of merlot and cabernet franc.
Previous outstanding vintages: '86, '87
CURRENT RELEASE 1991 The colour is rich and the bouquet full of cabernet's trademark chocolate/berry characters. On the palate it is soft, rich and well rounded, and finishes with a nice touch of oaky spice. It works well with steak and kidney pie.

STYLE dry
QUALITY ▼▼▼▼▼
VALUE ★★★+
GRAPES cabernet sauvignon 85%, merlot 10%, cabernet franc 5%
REGION Hawke's Bay
CELLAR ▬ 2-5
PRICE $19-23

Delegat's Proprietor's Reserve Hawke's Bay Merlot

Winemaker Brent Marris has had access to so much good merlot fruit in the last couple of seasons that he has been bottling some on its own as well as blending it with the company's top cabernets.
CURRENT RELEASE 1991 There's an earthy, chunky, leathery nose on this wine that I like a lot. Must be the peasant in me. The wine fills the mouth with rich, sweet fruit that combines well with the vanilla oak characters, and the finish is long and satisfying. Enjoy it with grilled kidneys on toast.

STYLE dry
QUALITY ▼▼▼▼▼
VALUE ★★★+
GRAPES merlot
REGION Hawke's Bay
CELLAR ▬ 1-3
PRICE $17-24.

deRedcliffe Cabernet/Merlot/Franc

The deRedcliffe label has an honourable history with Bordeaux-style blends. In 1980, then-owner Chris Canning was the first winemaker in this country to blend cabernet sauvignon and merlot together.

CURRENT RELEASE 1991 The nose is a bit ungiving, but the wine starts with good, sweet fruit and ripe characters in the middle. Only the finish is a bit thin. Try it with lamb chops.

STYLE dry

QUALITY ▼▼▼▼

VALUE ★★★+

GRAPES cabernet sauvignon 45%, cabernet franc 35%, merlot 20%

REGION Hawke's Bay (98%), Mangatawhiri

CELLAR 2

PRICE $15-17

deRedcliffe Cabernet Sauvignon/Merlot

While the three-grape blend reviewed above is almost entirely made from Hawke's Bay fruit, this variation on the theme uses just over half from that region, with the rest from the home vineyard at Mangatawhiri.

CURRENT RELEASE 1990 There's a touch of herbaceousness on the nose, but the Hawke's Bay fruit largely overcomes it. The wine is pleasant enough but a little thin in the middle. One for barbecued sausages.

STYLE dry

QUALITY ▼▼▼

VALUE ★★★

GRAPES cabernet sauvignon 75%, merlot 25%

REGION Hawke's Bay (55%), Mangatawhiri

CELLAR 2

PRICE $16-19

Esk Valley Private Bin Merlot/Cabernet Sauvignon

Private Bin is the mid-range denomination for wines from the Villa Maria/Vidal/Esk Valley stable, but the Hawke's Bay reds often come close to the much-exalted Reserve series in quality.

CURRENT RELEASE 1991 This is a bigger wine than the 1990 version, with leather and cassis on the nose and rich fruit, backed by well-integrated tannins, on the palate. Good wine for a T-bone steak.

STYLE dry

QUALITY ▼▼▼▼

VALUE ★★★+

GRAPES merlot 47%, cabernet sauvignon 45%, cabernet franc 8%

REGION Hawke's Bay

CELLAR 3

PRICE $16-18

Esk Valley Reserve Merlot/Cabernet Sauvignon

Yet another variation on the Bordeaux blend theme that the Villa Maria/Vidal/Esk Valley group seems to do in such profusion.

CURRENT RELEASE 1991 The almost black colour lets you know you're in for an experience even before you stick your nose in the glass. Once you do get around to sniffing it, there are plenty of cassis and leather characters to hold your interest until you get it into your mouth. The palate is rich and smooth and the finish long and memorable. Save it for the best piece of beef you can find, but don't hurry.

STYLE dry

QUALITY ▼▼▼▼▼

VALUE ★★★

GRAPES merlot 50%, cabernet sauvignon 50%

REGION Hawke's Bay

CELLAR ▬ 3-4

PRICE $25-32

Forest Flower Collection Cabernet Sauvignon/Merlot

Another in the colourfully packaged Forest Flower series, this one wearing a pohutukawa on the label.

CURRENT RELEASE 1991 There are some nice spicy berry-ish tones and warm, ripe fruit in the bouquet and on the palate. Only the slightly green finish gives the wine's humble origins away, but it's undoubtedly good enough for party duties.

STYLE dry

QUALITY ▼▼▼

VALUE ★★★+

GRAPES cabernet sauvignon 70%, merlot 30%

REGION West Auckland

CELLAR ▐ 2

PRICE $9-11

Forrest Merlot

John and Brigid Forrest have established a pretty impressive name for their winery since they opened the doors in 1991. This merlot is John's favourite from his range.

CURRENT RELEASE 1991 Great colour and a nose like perfumed hair cream get you going. The wine tastes smooth, round and rich, and that adds up to good drinking. Partner it with something Middle Eastern, and don't spare the spice.

STYLE dry

QUALITY ▼▼▼▼▼

VALUE ★★★

GRAPES merlot 90%, cabernet sauvignon 5%, malbec 5%

REGION Marlborough

CELLAR ▬ 2-4

PRICE $25-32

French Farm Reserve Cabernet/Cabernet Franc

Plenty of winemakers are going all out to prove big reds can be made in the South Island. French Farm's Tony Bish is heading in the right direction..
CURRENT RELEASE 1991 What a colour! This inky black wine has a touch of South Island herbaceousness, but there's enough good, ripe fruit and soft oak spice to give it a lot of warmth. Enjoy it with Canterbury lamb.

STYLE dry
QUALITY ♟♟♟
VALUE ★★+
GRAPES cabernet sauvignon 85%, cabernet franc 15%
REGION Canterbury and Marlborough
CELLAR ▬- 2-4
PRICE $22-28

Giesen Mt Cass Road Cabernet Sauvignon

Many experts have said Canterbury is too cold to ripen cabernet properly, but the Giesens have done well with this label. This vintage picked up a silver medal at the 1992 Air New Zealand Wine Awards.
Previous outstanding vintages: '86
CURRENT RELEASE 1989 The colour is rich and the aromas on the nose reminiscent of spice, mint and plums. When I tasted this wine a year ago, the tannins were dominating the fruit. They're better integrated now; the wine is soft with medium weight in the mouth, but I detect a hint of leafiness on the finish.

STYLE dry
QUALITY ♟♟♟♟
VALUE ★★★
GRAPES cabernet sauvignon
REGION Burnham, Canterbury
CELLAR ▮ 1
PRICE $19-24

Gladstone Cabernet Sauvignon/Franc/Merlot

Vineyard owner Dennis Roberts retired (his word) from a professional career in Wellington with the aim of making great wine. At age fifty-one, he reckons he's got about thirty years left to prove his point.
CURRENT RELEASE 1991 The nose is earthy in the French style, and the taste is soft, velvety-smooth and rich, with a lightly spicy finish. Great wine for a Provençale-style beef and olive casserole.

STYLE dry
QUALITY ♟♟♟♟
VALUE ★★★+
GRAPES cabernet sauvignon 75%, merlot 20%, cabernet franc 5%
REGION Wairarapa
CELLAR ▬- 2-4
PRICE $23-27

Goldwater Cabernet/Merlot/Franc

Kim and Jeanette Goldwater were Waiheke Island pioneers and have turned out a series of stylish reds since they planted their first vines a decade or so ago. Previous outstanding vintages: '87, '90
CURRENT RELEASE 1991 I said it for the 1990 vintage, and I'll say it again. Wow! This richly coloured wine is full of all the cassis, cedarwood and spice characters it needs to become a classic. Power and elegance are the twin attributes for which all makers of red wine strive. This is too young yet for the elegance it will undoubtedly acquire in time, but it's got heaps of power. Put it away for four or five years and save it for a venison back steak.

STYLE dry
QUALITY 🍷🍷🍷🍷🍷
VALUE ★★★
GRAPES cabernet sauvignon 54%, merlot 35%, cabernet franc 11%
REGION Waiheke Island
CELLAR 3-6
PRICE $35-42

Grape Republic Druid Hill Cabernet Sauvignon

Partner and winemaker Alastair Pain won a silver medal with the 1990 version of this wine at the 1992 Air New Zealand Wine Awards.
CURRENT RELEASE 1991 This latest model shares something of the 1990's spicy, cassis-laden bouquet, which is no bad thing. There's a tonne of rich, sweet fruit on the palate and a fair bit of cedarwood character floating about. Not a wine for wimps!

STYLE dry
QUALITY 🍷🍷🍷🍷
VALUE ★★★+
GRAPES cabernet sauvignon
REGION Hawke's Bay
CELLAR 2-6
PRICE $16-22

Grove Mill Cabernet/Pinotage

This inky-coloured red is trying out all the medals at the Air New Zealand Wine Awards. The '89 version scored gold, the '90 managed a bronze, and this version took a silver.
CURRENT RELEASE 1991 The colour is so dark it could almost pass for a glass of that purple-black liqueur, Opal Nera. The bouquet is like sweet coffee, and the palate is full of smooth, rich berry characters. Partner it with a hearty beef casserole.

STYLE dry
QUALITY 🍷🍷🍷🍷
VALUE ★★★+
GRAPES cabernet sauvignon 50%, pinotage 50%
REGION Marlborough
CELLAR 4
PRICE $19-23

Grove Mill Cabernet Sauvignon

Winemaker David Pearce gets incredible depth of colour into all his reds. This straight cabernet follows the trend.

CURRENT RELEASE 1991 The colour is black and the bouquet like espresso coffee — all the hallmarks of a blockbuster. In fact, the flavour is surprisingly soft and round. The wine turns out to be a real smoothy, which would not frighten off a simple roast chicken.

STYLE dry
QUALITY ♥♥♥
VALUE ★★★
GRAPES cabernet sauvignon
REGION Marlborough
CELLAR ■■ 2-4
PRICE $18-23

Heron's Flight Cabernet

Another new name on the scene. The vineyard is situated at Matakana, north of Auckland, and was established in 1988 by Mary Evans and David Hoskins. This is their first wine — and it's pretty impressive.

CURRENT RELEASE 1991 The colour is inky-black and the bouquet full of chocolate and cassis. This big, tannic wine needs to sit somewhere quiet for three or four years. After that, it would make a fine companion for a sirloin steak smeared with herb butter.

STYLE dry
QUALITY ♥♥♥♥
VALUE ★★★
GRAPES cabernet sauvignon
REGION Matakana
CELLAR ■■ 3-5
PRICE $23-28

Highfield Merlot

Many people believe merlot is shaping up to be better suited to Marlborough conditions than cabernet, and this is one of the wines that has been responsible for the change of heart.

CURRENT RELEASE 1991 Leather and cassis leap out of the glass, but the wine isn't as big as this upfront introduction suggests. It is quite soft, nicely rounded and very, very drinkable. Use it to partner snacks like olives and salami.

STYLE dry
QUALITY ♥♥♥
VALUE ★★★
GRAPES merlot
REGION Marlborough
CELLAR ■■ 2-3
PRICE $20-26

Hunter's Cabernet Sauvignon

The Hunter's name is associated almost exclusively with white wines, but over the years the company has done well with a series of well-made cabernets.
CURRENT RELEASE 1991 There's a bit of a 'whole bunch' feel about the nose, as if not only the grapes had been put through the press. The wine boasts sweet fruit characters and good oaky spice but suffers from a lean finish.

STYLE dry

QUALITY ▼▼▼▼

VALUE ★★+

GRAPES cabernet sauvignon

REGION Marlborough

CELLAR ▯ 2

PRICE $18-22

Kumeu River Merlot/Cabernet

Michael Brajkovich, better known for his whites, has also produced a series of good-quality red wines, using the classic Bordeaux varieties in various combinations.
CURRENT RELEASE 1990 The nose is quite perfumed, but there are some of merlot's tobacco-like characters lurking in the background. On the palate it is soft, clean and well rounded, and finishes smoothly. Try it with an oxtail casserole.

STYLE dry

QUALITY ▼▼▼▼

VALUE ★★+

GRAPES merlot 70%, cabernet sauvignon 30%

REGION West Auckland

CELLAR ▯ 3

PRICE $23-27

Lincoln Cabernet/Merlot (The Home Vineyard)

With Hawke's Bay and Waiheke regularly taking top honours for red wines, winemakers persisting with Auckland fruit are few and far between. Lincoln's Nick Chan is one of them, and he has scored a modest pile of medals with this example of his skills.
CURRENT RELEASE 1989 When I tasted this wine (same vintage) for last year's book, I found it dominated by wood and questioned whether it would balance itself out. It hasn't yet. It has a rich colour and some soft, easygoing flavours, but that oak still calls the tune. Try it alongside a smoked-beef and mustard sandwich.

STYLE dry

QUALITY ▼▼▼▼

VALUE ★★★+

GRAPES cabernet sauvignon 66%, merlot 34%

REGION West Auckland

CELLAR ▯ 1-3

PRICE $15-17

Lincoln Merlot/Cabernet (Brighams Vineyard)

The Brighams vineyard, sometimes called Brighams Creek, is at Kumeu, about 20 minutes from the company's home base at Henderson.

CURRENT RELEASE 1991 There's a definite dungy note about the bouquet, which isn't necessarily a bad thing — many good French wines have the same character. The wine is a soft middleweight, not a palate-grabber, but will do admirably for party duties.

STYLE dry

QUALITY ▼▼▼

VALUE ★★★

GRAPES merlot 70%, cabernet sauvignon 30%

REGION West Auckland

CELLAR ▬ 2-3

PRICE $12-14

Linden Estate Merlot/Cabernet Sauvignon

This new winery in Hawke's Bay is producing a range of wines using the three classic Bordeaux varieties in various combinations.

CURRENT RELEASE 1992 The colour is light and the bouquet like spiced mushrooms. The wine tastes quite frisky and leaves an impression of sweet grapes after you swallow it. Match it with chicken satay and chilli sauce.

STYLE dry

QUALITY ▼▼▼▼

VALUE ★★★

GRAPES merlot 60%, cabernet sauvignon 40%

REGION Hawke's Bay

CELLAR ▮ 2

PRICE $13-16

Lintz Estate Cabernet/Merlot

When it comes to reds, Martinborough is best known for pinot noir, but Chris Lintz is one of a handful of makers who are keen to champion the cabernet family for the region.

CURRENT RELEASE 1991 The nose is earthy in a European style, but on the palate the cabernet franc brings soft, smooth flavours that are nicely accented by a touch of spicy oak. Good wine for a pink-roasted rack of lamb.

STYLE dry

QUALITY ▼▼▼▼

VALUE ★★★

GRAPES cabernet franc 51%, cabernet sauvignon 47%, merlot 2%

REGION Martinborough

CELLAR ▬ 2

PRICE $20-25

Lintz Estate Cabernet Sauvignon

The fine print on the label tells us this wine boasts an alcohol level of 14 per cent so don't plan on finishing a bottle before lunch!

CURRENT RELEASE 1991 The first sniff of this richly coloured wine reminded me of raspberry-flavoured coffee — well, what I imagine that would smell like. The taste is soft and easy-going but a little thin on the finish. Try it with grilled beef chipolatas.

STYLE dry

QUALITY ▼▼▼▼

VALUE ★★★

GRAPES cabernet sauvignon

REGION Martinborough

CELLAR ▭▬ 2-4

PRICE $20-25

Longridge Cabernet Sauvignon/Merlot

The first vintages of this wine were nothing to write to Mum about, but the 1989 model scored a silver medal at the 1991 Air New Zealand Wine Awards, and this version managed a bronze award at last year's contest.

CURRENT RELEASE 1991 There's a nicely balanced blend of oak dustiness and cabernet berry flavours on the nose, and they carry through onto the palate. The wine is softly tannic and quite mouth-filling and finishes with a touch of class.

STYLE dry

QUALITY ▼▼▼

VALUE ★★★

GRAPES cabernet sauvignon 80%, merlot 20%

REGION Hawke's Bay

CELLAR ▮ 3

PRICE $14-16

Matua Cabernet Sauvignon/Merlot

Matua Valley's 1985 cabernet sauvignon was the first of what are now known as 'new breed' New Zealand reds to be made in commercial quantities, and as such marked a turnaround for the local industry.

CURRENT RELEASE 1991 Merlot's old-leather calling card gives the nose a bit of a dung-like character — think of it as an acquired taste. The palate, however, is all about ripe fruit. Overall, the wine is smooth and classy.

STYLE dry

QUALITY ▼▼▼▼

VALUE ★★★+

GRAPES cabernet sauvignon 65%, merlot 35%

REGION West Auckland

CELLAR ▮ 3

PRICE $15-17

Matua Cabernet Sauvignon Smith-Dartmoor Estate

Careful label-watching is necessary when buying Matua Valley cabernets. This one looks very similar to the home-vineyard version.

CURRENT RELEASE 1991 Chocolate and blackberries do their thing on the nose. The wine is on the bigger side of medium when it comes to weight, and has some nice, ripe, berryfruit characters and a reasonably long finish. Try it with corned beef.

STYLE dry
QUALITY ▼▼▼▼
VALUE ★★★
GRAPES cabernet sauvignon
REGION Hawke's Bay
CELLAR ▬ 2-4
PRICE $19-23

Matua Merlot Smith-Dartmoor Estate

Merlot used to be used solely to blend with cabernet sauvignon, but more and more winemakers are realising it makes a deeply satisfying wine on its own.

CURRENT RELEASE 1991 The bouquet is gamey and boasts lots of typical merlot leatheriness. In the mouth the wine is soft and smooth, thanks to the nicely integrated tannins. It makes a fine companion to casseroled wild duck.

STYLE dry
QUALITY ▼▼▼▼
VALUE ★★★+
GRAPES merlot
REGION Hawke's Bay
CELLAR ▬ 2-4
PRICE $19-23

Millton Te Arai River Cabernet Sauvignon/Cabernet Franc

An unusual blend of two grapes usually seen in the company of merlot, the third member of the classic Bordeaux trio.

CURRENT RELEASE 1991 This conceptually lightish red is soft, spicy and surprisingly rich. All that adds up to make it thoroughly drinkable, and a fine companion to a pink-lamb sandwich.

STYLE dry
QUALITY ▼▼▼
VALUE ★★★
GRAPES cabernet sauvignon 70%, cabernet franc 30%
REGION Gisborne
CELLAR ▮ 2
PRICE $18-23

Mission Cabernet/Merlot

Mission hasn't had a lot of medal success with its reds, but they continue to be good sellers at the winery shop. CURRENT RELEASE 1992 The nose is like cassis-spiked coffee — and that's no bad thing — and the wine is smooth and clean on the palate. Good with braised lamb chops.

STYLE dry

QUALITY ♟♟♟♟

VALUE ★★★★

GRAPES cabernet sauvignon 70%, merlot 30%

REGION Hawke's Bay

CELLAR ▮ 2

PRICE $12-14

Mission Cabernet Sauvignon

Manager Warwick Orchiston and winemaker Paul Mooney style this pleasant red for early drinking. It is very reasonably priced.
CURRENT RELEASE 1992 The wine hasn't had a lot of oak, yet the nose is quite sawdusty at this stage. Once you get over that, however, it is soft and smooth with a light, undemanding finish. One for the mince on toast set.

STYLE dry

QUALITY ♟♟♟

VALUE ★★★+

GRAPES cabernet sauvignon

REGION Hawke's Bay

CELLAR ▮ 1

PRICE $12-14

Mission Estate (Kiri in Concert) Cabernet Franc

Hosting the Kiri Te Kanawa concert was quite a coup for Mission Vineyards, so who can blame them for commemorating the event on a couple of wine labels? CURRENT RELEASE 1991 The colour's good and rich, and there's a healthy amount of Hawke's Bay berryness on the nose. The wine is quite mouth-filling, thanks to the ripe, sweet fruit, but the finish is a bit green.

STYLE dry

QUALITY ♟♟♟♟

VALUE ★★

GRAPES cabernet franc

REGION Hawke's Bay

CELLAR ▮ 2

PRICE $25-28

Montana Estates Fairhall Cabernet Sauvignon

This wine, like its stablemates in the Montana Estates collection, is identified by a large letter on the label — in this case, 'F'.

CURRENT RELEASE 1989 There aren't many Marlborough reds that boast a bouquet as big as this. Coffee, sweet berries and a bit of smokiness all try to grab your attention even before you put the wine into your mouth. Once you do, it is soft, rich and shows no sign of that infamous Marlborough herbaceousness, save for a wee hint right on the finish.

STYLE dry

QUALITY ♟♟♟♟

VALUE ★★

GRAPES cabernet sauvignon 92%, merlot 8%

REGION Marlborough

CELLAR ▭ 3-5

PRICE $33-36

Montana Marlborough Cabernet Sauvignon

Making good reds is difficult in Marlborough, but this line from Montana has done well, particularly in restaurants.

CURRENT RELEASE 1991 The bouquet seems pretty stalky, and there's a good dose of Marlborough herbaceousness, but things get better on the palate. Once you get it into your mouth the wine is round and soft, and finishes with a nice touch of spice.

STYLE dry

QUALITY ♟♟♟

VALUE ★★★

GRAPES cabernet sauvignon

REGION Marlborough

CELLAR ▮ 2

PRICE $11-13

Morton Estate Cabernet/Merlot (White Label)

This mid-range red seldom rises above bronze status in competition, but it is a popular choice at the restaurant adjoining Morton Estate's Katikati cellars.

CURRENT RELEASE 1991 There's something vaguely chemical in the bouquet, but it doesn't carry though onto the palate. The wine is soft and smooth though the finish is a bit lean. A good picnic quaffer.

STYLE dry

QUALITY ♟♟♟

VALUE ★★★

GRAPES cabernet sauvignon 75%, merlot 25%

REGION Hawke's Bay

CELLAR ▮ 2

PRICE $15-17

Morton Estate Cabernet/Merlot (Yellow Label)

Morton Estate's well-priced Yellow Label wines are designed to be enjoyed while they're relatively young. CURRENT RELEASE 1991 This understated red offers sweet berry characters and smooth tannins. It's on the light side, but that's how it was designed. Enjoy it with barbecued chicken.

STYLE dry

QUALITY ♟♟♟

VALUE ★★★

GRAPES cabernet sauvignon 55%, merlot 30%, cabernet franc 15%

REGION Hawke's Bay

CELLAR ▌ 2

PRICE $11-13

Morton Estate Cabernet Sauvignon/Merlot (Black Label)

Morton Estate, founded by New Zealand entrepreneur Morton Brown, is now part of Australia's Mildara-Blass group. When the purchase was made, a company executive described it as 'the most perfect little winery in the world'.

CURRENT RELEASE 1991 Leather, cassis, cigar boxes — you name it, it's there on the nose of this peasant-style red. Ripe fruit dominates the palate, and delivers some mouth-filling berry flavours and a chocolatey finish. Try it with ricotta-cheese-stuffed ravioli.

STYLE dry

QUALITY ♟♟♟♟

VALUE ★★★

GRAPES cabernet sauvignon 87%, merlot 13%

REGION Hawke's Bay

CELLAR ▬ 2-4

PRICE $20-22

Morton Estate Merlot (Black Label)

John Hancock and his winemaker, Steve Bird, have established a better reputation for their whites than their reds, but the current batch of biggies like this flavoursome merlot could change all that.

CURRENT RELEASE 1991 Smelling this is like sniffing just-polished leather, to which I have no objection whatever. The wine tastes sweet, is smooth enough to please anybody's tongue, and finishes with a dash of chocolate. Enjoy it with chicken cooked in red wine.

STYLE dry

QUALITY ♟♟♟♟

VALUE ★★★

GRAPES merlot

REGION Hawke's Bay

CELLAR ▬ 2-4

PRICE $24-27

Nautilus Cabernet Sauvignon/Merlot

Nautilus is an Australian-owned company that for the first couple of years restricted its production to white wines. Now it also makes a classy sparkler and this red, which won a silver medal at the 1992 Air New Zealand Wine Awards.

CURRENT RELEASE 1990 The colour is dark and the bouquet full of spicy blackberry aromas. The wine is richly mouth-filling and boasts a long, sweet finish. Enjoy it with an eggplant casserole, ideally served with wild rice.

STYLE dry
QUALITY ▼▼▼▼
VALUE ★★★+
GRAPES cabernet sauvignon 75%, merlot 25%
REGION Marlborough
CELLAR ▬ 2-4
PRICE $20-23

Neudorf Moutere Cabernet Sauvignon

It's no easier to make big reds in Nelson than it is across the hills in Marlborough, but Neudorf's Tim and Judy Finn are content to produce a series of conceptually lighter but well-flavoured styles.

CURRENT RELEASE 1991 The nose is a wee bit green, but some nice berryfruit characters keep things in reasonable check. On the palate it is warm and sweet, quite mouth-filling, but a bit thin on the finish.

STYLE dry
QUALITY ▼▼▼
VALUE ★★+
GRAPES cabernet sauvignon
REGION Nelson
CELLAR ▌ 2
PRICE $16-19

Ngatarawa Glazebrook Cabernet/Merlot

The top red for this Hastings company, named after the Glazebrook family, which owns a share of the vineyard.
CURRENT RELEASE 1991 Espresso coffee and cassis were the impressions a sniff of this richly coloured red left me with. The wine is solid in the mouth but lacks a little bit of warmth at this stage. Give it time to open out, then partner it with rabbit (or hare, if you're lucky) casseroled in red wine.

STYLE dry
QUALITY ▼▼▼▼
VALUE ★★★
GRAPES cabernet sauvignon 80%, merlot 15%, malbec 5%
REGION Hawke's Bay
CELLAR ▌ 5
PRICE $25-30

Ngatarawa Stables Red Cabernet/Merlot/Franc

The list of three classic grapes on the label gives notice that this formerly basic red has taken a step up for the vintage now on sale.
CURRENT RELEASE 1991 The nose has notes of coffee and cassis, and the taste is rich and mouth-filling. This is quite a big, chunky wine that would go well with a piece of grilled sirloin and garlic-spiked sautéed potatoes.

STYLE dry

QUALITY ▼▼▼▼

VALUE ★★★★

GRAPES cabernet sauvignon 77%, merlot 9%, cabernet franc 14%

REGION Hawke's Bay

CELLAR ▐ 4

PRICE $15-18

Nobilo Cabernet Sauvignon Marlborough

Grapes for this middleweight red came from several vineyards in Marlborough's sun-baked Wairau Valley.
CURRENT RELEASE 1991 The nose is earthy and oaky from the wine's sixteen-month sojourn in oak barrels. In the mouth it is well rounded and doesn't suffer from Marlborough greenness until right at the end. Try it with barbecued pork sausages.

STYLE dry

QUALITY ▼▼▼▼

VALUE ★★+

GRAPES cabernet sauvignon

REGION Marlborough

CELLAR ▐ 2

PRICE $18-22

Nobilo Reserve Hawke's Bay Cabernet Sauvignon

The Nobilo family used to be best known for red wines, but since the late 1970s they've built up more of a reputation here and overseas for whites. Nevertheless, this cabernet is good drinking.
CURRENT RELEASE 1989 The bouquet is so intense it has something of a burned character about it. This is a chunky, European-style wine with lots of earthy characters accompanying the berryfruit tastes on the palate. Try it with beef stew and dumplings.

STYLE dry

QUALITY ▼▼▼▼

VALUE ★★★

GRAPES cabernet sauvignon

REGION Hawke's Bay

CELLAR ▐ 2

PRICE $25-27

Okahu Estate Ninety-Mile Red

Dalmatian gumdiggers used to make wine in the Far North towards the end of last century. Okahu Estate's Monty Knight is carrying on the tradition. Monty lost a consignment of this wine through pilfering, so now it's available only from the winery or by mail order (see list of addresses at the back of the book).
CURRENT RELEASE 1991 There's a hint of stalkiness on the nose but plenty of berry character to hold your interest. The wine is rich, mouth-filling and spicy, and would be a good partner for a casseroled duck.

STYLE dry
QUALITY 🍷🍷🍷🍷
VALUE ★★★★
GRAPES cabernet sauvignon 70%, pinotage 15%, cabernet franc 10%, merlot 5%
REGION Northland
CELLAR ▬ 2-5
PRICE $17-19

C. J. Pask Cabernet/Merlot

The straight cabernet is aged in French and American oak, but only French is used for this blend.
CURRENT RELEASE 1991 Spicy oak and sweet Hawke's Bay berries create a good first impression. The fruit is rich and soft, and the tannins approachable. Nice wine for a rare-beef open sandwich.

STYLE dry
QUALITY 🍷🍷🍷🍷
VALUE ★★★
GRAPES cabernet sauvignon 70%, merlot 30%
REGION Hawke's Bay
CELLAR ▬ 2-4
PRICE $20-24

C. J. Pask Cabernet Sauvignon

The first Pask cabernet startled a few people when it beat a bunch of high-fliers to take first place in a *Cuisine* magazine tasting. Later vintages have been less successful, but the potential is obviously there.
Previous outstanding vintages: '86
CURRENT RELEASE 1991 The colour's good, and the nose has some nice earthy, berryish tones that carry through onto the palate. This wine is smooth, well rounded and makes a fine partner for a grilled T-bone.

STYLE dry
QUALITY 🍷🍷🍷🍷
VALUE ★★★
GRAPES cabernet sauvignon
REGION Hawke's Bay
CELLAR 🍷 2
PRICE $19-22

C. J. Pask Merlot

Plain merlots used to be rare, but now they are all the rage. Winemaker Kate Radburnd has been blending it with cabernet for years. Now she's giving it a go on its own.

CURRENT RELEASE 1991 The colour is pretty dramatic and the bouquet rich and spicy, so that's a good start, and things stay pretty flash on the palate. The wine is well rounded with plenty of sweet berry flavours and firm tannins. Enjoy it with ratatouille or something equally strong-flavoured.

STYLE dry
QUALITY ▼▼▼▼
VALUE ★★★
GRAPES merlot
REGION Hawke's Bay
CELLAR ▬ 2-5
PRICE $22-25

Peninsula Estate Cabernet/Merlot

Peninsula Estate is one of a handful of new wineries on Waiheke Island, in Auckland's Hauraki Gulf. Owner Doug Hamilton's intention is to concentrate on making big, flavoursome reds.

CURRENT RELEASE 1990 The bouquet has developed a certain amount of French-style grubbiness in the twelve months since I reviewed this wine for the last guide, and I'm quite happy about that — it's a character I find very appealing. In the mouth there is plenty of rich fruit to go with the well-integrated tannins. Its food match has to be a thick barbecued steak.

STYLE dry
QUALITY ▼▼▼▼▼
VALUE ★★★
GRAPES cabernet sauvignon 81%, merlot 11%, cabernet franc 8%
REGION Waiheke Island
CELLAR ▮ 2
PRICE $25-38

Riverside Cabernet/Merlot

Winery owners Ian and Rachel Cadwallader planted cabernet sauvignon vines in 1981, and merlot a little later. They designed this blend for early drinking.

CURRENT RELEASE 1991 There's something like espresso coffee in the bouquet and a heap of ripe fruit on the palate, all of which add up to pleasant drinking. Try it alongside a pan-fried lamb leg steak.

STYLE dry
QUALITY ▼▼▼▼
VALUE ★★★★
GRAPES cabernet sauvignon 75%, merlot 25%
REGION Hawke's Bay
CELLAR ▮ 2
PRICE $16-19

Robard & Butler Amberley Cabernet Sauvignon

A new label for R&B, using grapes from the vineyard next door to the source of the company's much-praised Amberley Rhine Riesling. This wine picked up a silver medal in its first outing at last year's Air New Zealand Wine Awards.

CURRENT RELEASE 1990 There's an inevitable touch of South Island herbaceousness on the nose, but plenty of berry character to back it up. In the mouth it is soft, round and squeaky-clean, and the finish is long and warm.

STYLE dry

QUALITY ▼▼▼▽

VALUE ★★★+

GRAPES cabernet sauvignon 90%, merlot 10%

REGION Waipara/ Amberley, Canterbury

CELLAR ▭▬ 3-4

PRICE $17-19

Robard & Butler Hawke's Bay Cabernet/Merlot

It's not mentioned on the label, but this wine also contains a small amount of cabernet franc, so it's a classic Bordeaux blend.

CURRENT RELEASE 1990 The nose is berryish with a nice touch of cabernet's minty chocolate character in there as well. In the mouth the tannins impart a dusty feeling behind the warmth and richness. It's nice wine — partner it with meat-topped pasta.

STYLE dry

QUALITY ▼▼▼▼

VALUE ★★★+

GRAPES cabernet sauvignon 85%, merlot 10%, cabernet franc 5%

REGION Hawke's Bay

CELLAR ▮ 3

PRICE $17-19

Rongopai Te Kauwhata Cabernet Sauvignon/Merlot

Te Kauwhata is a little-known grape-growing area nowadays, but it is the home of the now-wound-down Viticultural Research Station, where many new grape varieties were pioneered.

CURRENT RELEASE 1991 Merlot is the minority grape, but its leathery calling card sure stands out on the nose — cabernet's berry characters are hiding way at the back. The wine is smooth and well rounded in the mouth, and has a lingering finish. It would be great with casseroled venison, but I'd settle for a good old-fashioned beef stew.

STYLE dry

QUALITY ▼▼▼▼

VALUE ★★★+

GRAPES cabernet sauvignon 55%, merlot 45%

REGION Te Kauwhata

CELLAR ▭▬ 1-3

PRICE 16-20

Rongopai Te Kauwhata Merlot

Rongopai's Tom van Dam now has enough merlot to put a higher percentage in the blend reviewed earlier, as well as make a single variety wine from it.

CURRENT RELEASE 1991 The colour is surprisingly light, but there's nothing wimpish about the nose — it's full of merlot's polished-leather aroma. The wine is nicely rounded, quite rich and very smooth on the finish. Try it with Middle Eastern-style spiced lamb.

STYLE dry
QUALITY ▼▼▼▼
VALUE ★★★+
GRAPES merlot
REGION Te Kauwhata
CELLAR 3
PRICE $20-24

St George Estate Cabernet/Merlot

Owner/winemaker Michael Bennett subjects this wine to a minimum of filtration to retain the full flavour of his grapes.

CURRENT RELEASE 1991 The colour's deep and the nose a bit earthy — both characteristics more usually found in Aussie reds. The taste has a bit more style than the 1990 version; it's rich and smooth, and would go well with a rare steak topped with a smear of melting blue cheese.

STYLE dry
QUALITY ▼▼▼▼
VALUE ★★★+
GRAPES cabernet sauvignon 75%, merlot 25%
REGION Hawke's Bay
CELLAR 2-5
PRICE $17-20

St Jerome Cabernet/Merlot

Davorin seems determined to make a name for himself as producer of the biggest reds in New Zealand. The 1988 was gigantic, and attracted much favourable comment from those brought up on a diet of old-style Aussie boomers.

Previous outstanding vintages: '88

CURRENT RELEASE 1990 The inky-black colour's pretty impressive for a start, and it suggests just what you get on the bouquet — lots of earthy, old-leather aromas. The taste is not as primitive as this suggests, in fact it is quite soft and well rounded, despite the presence of some pretty assertive tannins. Partner it with the biggest, meanest sirloin steak you can find.

STYLE dry
QUALITY ▼▼▼▼
VALUE ★★+
GRAPES cabernet sauvignon 65%, merlot 35%
REGION West Auckland
CELLAR 3-6
PRICE $27-34

St Jerome Cabernet Sauvignon

This Henderson-based winery has been making wine for many years under the names of Nova or Ozich. St Jerome has been used only recently, but already it has been associated with some huge, inky-black reds.

CURRENT RELEASE 1990 Not designed to be one of winemaker Davorin Ozich's blockbusters, this straight cabernet has been made for easy drinking. The wine is fruity and reasonably pleasant, but a bit ungiving in the middle. Try it with cheese-topped spaghetti.

STYLE dry

QUALITY ▼▼▼

VALUE ★★★

GRAPES cabernet sauvignon

REGION West Auckland

CELLAR 🍷 1

PRICE $12-13

Seibel Cabernet Franc/Merlot/Cabernet Sauvignon

Norbert Seibel established a good reputation for white wines during his time at Corbans a few years ago, but this warmly welcoming red shows he can change colours quite happily.

CURRENT RELEASE 1989 The nose fairly screams of leather from the merlot component, but it doesn't dominate the taste. The wine is a middleweight, but its softly berryish flavours give it a lot of depth. If you see it in a restaurant, try it with quail.

STYLE dry

QUALITY ▼▼▼▼

VALUE ★★★★

GRAPES cabernet franc 60%, merlot 30%, cabernet sauvignon 10%

REGION Waikato, West Auckland

CELLAR 🍷 1

PRICE $13-15

Seifried Estate Cabernet Sauvignon

I called the 1990 version of this wine a 'lightish red' in last year's guide, but this latest model is considerably gutsier.

CURRENT RELEASE 1991 Blackberries, coffee and cassis are pretty evenly spread in the bouquet. The wine tastes big and chunky, and goes splendidly with casseroled lamb shanks and mashed potatoes.

STYLE dry

QUALITY ▼▼▼▼

VALUE ★★★+

GRAPES cabernet sauvignon

REGION Nelson

CELLAR 🍷 3

PRICE $15-18

Selaks Cabernet Sauvignon

Winemaker Darryl Woolley used to get the grapes for the company's 'standard' cabernet from Gisborne, but now they're sourced from Hawke's Bay and Marlborough.

CURRENT RELEASE 1991 The nose is a bit dungy, a character often found in French reds, but the taste is all about rich, sweet fruit and spicy oak. It goes well with moussaka.

STYLE dry
QUALITY ▼▼▼▼
VALUE ★★★+

GRAPES cabernet sauvignon 75%, merlot 25%

REGION Hawke's Bay, Marlborough

CELLAR 🍷 2

PRICE $12-14

Marino Selak Founder's Selection Cabernet Sauvignon/Merlot

The Selaks have produced a number of big, meaty reds under this label in the past, but recent vintages have been a little more subdued.

CURRENT RELEASE 1989 When I reviewed this wine last year, I found green, leafy characters — a result of the young vines the grapes had come from. It's taken a while for these to soften out, but they're beginning to now. The bouquet is chunky and rich, and there's some nice, soft fruit on the palate. Partner it with spaghetti Bolognese.

STYLE dry
QUALITY ▼▼▼▼
VALUE ★★+

GRAPES cabernet sauvignon 70%, merlot 30%

REGION Hawke's Bay

CELLAR ▬ 1

PRICE $22-25

Shingle Peak Cabernet Sauvignon

The white wines in this Matua Valley-owned collection are better, but this mid-priced red still managed to pick up a bronze medal at the 1992 Air New Zealand Wine Awards.

CURRENT RELEASE 1991 The nose is quite perfumed, with cassis and cedarwood doing their thing. The wine is a middleweight in the mouth, with soft, well-rounded flavours that would suit fettucine with pesto sauce.

STYLE dry
QUALITY ▼▼▼
VALUE ★★★

GRAPES cabernet sauvignon

REGION Marlborough

CELLAR 🍷 2

PRICE $14-16

Soljans Cabernet/Merlot

Many people say Auckland has the wrong sort of climate to grow cabernet sauvignon successfully. Tony Soljan is determined to prove they're wrong.

CURRENT RELEASE 1991 The nose is a bit leafy, but there are good fruit characters and a smack of oak as well. The wine is soft in the mouth, a bit lean but pleasant enough for barbecue duties.

STYLE dry

QUALITY ▼▼▼

VALUE ★★★★

GRAPES cabernet sauvignon 75%, merlot 25%

REGION West Auckland

CELLAR 🍾 2

PRICE $13-15

Solway Cabernet/Merlot

A second label for Bloomfield Vineyards of Masterton, in the Wairarapa. The grapes were sourced from Hawke's Bay, unlike the top-of-the-range red, which used owner David Bloomfield's own fruit.

CURRENT RELEASE 1991 The wine has had minimal oak treatment, so the tastes are all about minty/chocolatey cabernet fruit. The wine tastes broad and pleasant, and would go nicely with a brace of lamb cutlets.

STYLE dry

QUALITY ▼▼▼▼

VALUE ★★★+

GRAPES cabernet sauvignon 88%, merlot 12%

REGION Hawke's Bay

CELLAR 🍾 1

PRICE $13-15

Stafford Brook Cabernet Franc/Merlot

This easy-drinking red is a new line for Vavasour of Marlborough; no doubt designed to get in a bit of quick cash each year.

CURRENT RELEASE (non-vintage) There's some nice smokiness on the nose along with a bit of berry character. The taste is pretty lean and light but there's nothing offensive happening in there. One for grilled beef bangers.

STYLE dry

QUALITY ▼▼▼

VALUE ★★★+

GRAPES cabernet franc 60%, merlot 35%, malbec 5%

REGION Marlborough

CELLAR 🍾 1

PRICE $13-15

Stonecroft Cabernet Sauvignon

Alan Limmer's Stonecroft vineyard is, as the name suggests, dry and stony — an unusual combination for Hawke's Bay. Consequently, his wines are a little different from others in the area.

CURRENT RELEASE 1991 Chocolate, cassis and raspberries form a pleasant introduction to this beautifully made wine. It is richly coloured, soft and chock-full of ripe fruit characters, backed by nicely integrated oak from the barrels in which it lay for twenty-one months. You guessed it — I like it! Partner it with rare roast beef fillet.

STYLE dry

QUALITY ▾▾▾▾▾

VALUE ★★★

GRAPES cabernet sauvignon 85%, merlot 15%

REGION Hawke's Bay

CELLAR ▍4

PRICE $24-28

Stoneleigh Cabernet Sauvignon

The only red wine in the Stoneleigh collection, named after the pebble-strewn Corbans vineyard where the grapes are grown.

CURRENT RELEASE 1991 I haven't been impressed by this wine in the past, but the 1991 vintage is a big improvement on previous models. There's a nice, berryish bouquet that even boasts a hint of cabernet's chocolate character, and a soft, round and welcoming feeling on the palate. Partner it with rare rump steak topped with a knob of blue-cheese butter.

STYLE dry

QUALITY ▾▾▾▾

VALUE ★★★

GRAPES cabernet sauvignon 85%, merlot 15%

REGION Marlborough

CELLAR ▍3

PRICE $17-19

Stonyridge Larose Cabernet Sauvignon/Merlot

Larose, in most years the only wine made at Stephen White's Waiheke Island winery, has established the sort of reputation that only extreme rarity can bring. It is almost impossible to buy off the shelf, so get on the mailing list (see winery addresses at back of book).
Previous outstanding vintages: '87

CURRENT RELEASE 1991 Slightly lighter in colour than the near-legendary '87, this latest vintage nevertheless displays a perfect balance between power and elegance, with rich, deeply flavoursome fruit flavours in perfect harmony with the oak. Good enough for the best piece of beef fillet you can find, cooked rare.

STYLE dry

QUALITY ▾▾▾▾▾

VALUE ★★★★

GRAPES cabernet sauvignon 73%, merlot 18%, cabernet franc 5%, malbec 4%

REGION Waiheke Island

CELLAR ▤ 2-5

PRICE $27-40

Te Kairanga East Plain Cabernet Sauvignon

Wine consultant Raymond Chan has called Te Kairanga the 'sleeping giant' of Martinborough. It is one of the region's biggest wineries, but top medal success has so far eluded it.

CURRENT RELEASE 1991 This wine is a big improvement on the 1990 version. There's a trace of unwelcome leafiness on the nose, but in the mouth it is quite rich and firm, with good berryfruit flavours backed up by vanilla from the oak. Partner it with beef stroganoff.

STYLE dry

QUALITY 🍷🍷🍷🍷

VALUE ★★★+

GRAPES cabernet sauvignon

REGION Martinborough

CELLAR ▬ 2-4

PRICE $24-28

Te Mata Estate Awatea Cabernet/Merlot

Rarity, particularly in the upper half of the North Island, has helped give Te Mata Coleraine near-legendary status, yet Awatea, a similar blend from the same winery, deserves at least equal kudos.

Previous outstanding vintages: '85, '87

CURRENT RELEASE 1991 There's oak spice, sweet earthy loam and plenty of plums all together in the bouquet of this richly coloured wine. That sounds like quite a mixture, but it sure works. In the mouth it is sweet and rich, immensely powerful but still soft and smooth. Try some on its own before you partner it with something hearty like casseroled beef shin on the bone.

STYLE dry

QUALITY 🍷🍷🍷🍷🍷

VALUE ★★★

GRAPES cabernet sauvignon 56%, merlot 34%, cabernet franc 10%

REGION Hawke's Bay

CELLAR ▬ 3-6

PRICE $25-29

Te Mata Estate Cabernet/Merlot

This is the 'baby' wine of the Te Mata red trio, but it is still bigger and more flavoursome than many top-line reds.

CURRENT RELEASE 1991 I get coffee and tobacco on the nose, plus some nice spice at the back. The palate is chock-full of sweet, berryish fruit that lasts for a long time after the wine has been swallowed. It's great with a serious hamburger.

STYLE dry

QUALITY 🍷🍷🍷🍷

VALUE ★★★+

GRAPES cabernet sauvignon 62%, merlot 35%, cabernet franc 3%

REGION Hawke's Bay

CELLAR ▮ 3

PRICE $17-22

Te Mata Coleraine Cabernet/Merlot

Arguably New Zealand's most famous red, Coleraine in '82 and '83 vintage colours often sells for $150 or more at auction, such is its reputation.

Previous outstanding vintages: '82, '85, '90

CURRENT RELEASE 1991 If you can imagine blackcurrants steeped in a cup of espresso coffee, that gives you a rough idea of what's in the bouquet of this powerful but elegant red. The surprising thing is that, despite its power, it is soft and velvet-smooth in the mouth. Winery owner John Buck and winemaker Peter Cowley reckon it could be cellared for fifteen years. I'd certainly give it ten years, but it's tasting so good now I don't think much of it will still be around.

STYLE dry

QUALITY ♟♟♟♟♟

VALUE ★★★

GRAPES cabernet sauvignon 59%, merlot 29%, cabernet franc 12%

REGION Hawke's Bay

CELLAR ▬▬ 3-10

PRICE $32-38

Te Whare Ra Sarah Jennings Cabernet/Merlot/Cabernet Franc

The belief that great red wine will never be made in Marlborough is pretty common, but a few makers are doing their best to prove otherwise. Allen and Joyce Hogan sell their Te Whare Ra wines only by mail order, so this big, richly coloured cabernet-based wine is probably one of the country's best-kept secrets.

Previous outstanding vintages: '86

CURRENT RELEASE 1991 The nose was sweet and earthy and the taste big, chunky and decidedly tannic when I tried this wine a few weeks ago. Things will have evened themselves out a little by now, but cellaring for three or four years will still be a good idea. Then, pour a little into a beef casserole and enjoy the rest alongside it.

STYLE dry

QUALITY ♟♟♟♟

VALUE ★★★+

GRAPES cabernet sauvignon 40%, merlot 35%, cabernet franc 25%

REGION Marlborough

CELLAR ▬▬ 2-5

PRICE $18-22

Totara Winemaker's Reserve Cabernet Sauvignon

It's good to see this Thames-based company back in the medals. This softly stylish red picked up a silver at the 1992 Air New Zealand Wine Awards.

CURRENT RELEASE 1991 Things start out earthy, berryish and invitingly warm on the nose, and the taste doesn't disappoint. There's plenty of depth in the middle, but the finish isn't as long as that would suggest. Try it with spaghetti Bolognese.

STYLE dry

QUALITY ▼▼▼▼

VALUE ★★★

GRAPES cabernet sauvignon

REGION Hawke's Bay

CELLAR 🍷 2-3

PRICE $23-26

Tui Vale Cabernet Sauvignon

This Hawke's Bay vineyard is under the control of Keith Crone, who was once a viticulturalist for Montana. CURRENT RELEASE 1990 The wine has had only a tiny bit of merlot blended into it, yet that variety's distinctive leatheriness is quite strong in the bouquet. The taste is rich and chocolatey, and there's a catchy touch of spice on the finish. Enjoy it with a rare-beef salad.

STYLE dry

QUALITY ▼▼▼▼

VALUE ★★★★+

GRAPES cabernet sauvignon 95%, merlot 5%

REGION Hawke's Bay

CELLAR 🍷 3

PRICE $15-18

Tui Vale Cabernet Sauvignon Reserve

Contrary to normal practice, this Reserve bottle is straight cabernet; its less-expensive brother gets the merlot.

CURRENT RELEASE 1990 Rich cassis and cedarwood characters dominate the bouquet. The wine is soft, ripe and opulent on the palate and would go well with a pot roast of beef.

STYLE dry

QUALITY ▼▼▼▼

VALUE ★★★

GRAPES cabernet sauvignon

REGION Hawke's Bay

CELLAR ▦ 4-6

PRICE $23-26

Vavasour Cabernet Sauvignon Reserve

The team at Vavasour is determined to prove that Marlborough can produce great reds. The weather defeated them for 1991; this wine is straight cabernet sauvignon because the cabernet franc and merlot that usually get blended in with it weren't up to their standards. Even so, if they can make a wine this good with just one variety, I think they've proved their point.

CURRENT RELEASE 1991 Blackberries, blueberries and cedarwood do their thing when you stick your nose into the glass. The wine is a big softy on the palate, with rich cassis-like flavours and a lingering finish. Enjoy it with a whole roast Scotch fillet on the bone.

STYLE dry
QUALITY 🍷🍷🍷🍷🍷
VALUE ★★★
GRAPES cabernet sauvignon
REGION Marlborough
CELLAR 2-6
PRICE $23-27

Vidal Private Bin Hawke's Bay Cabernet Sauvignon/Merlot

The middle-of-the-road Private Bin reds do quite well in the medal stakes for brand-owner Villa Maria.
Previous outstanding vintages: '89

CURRENT RELEASE 1991 There's some nice spice on the nose, but also a bit of unwelcome stalkiness. The wine is soft and reasonably mouth-filling, but the finish is short and hard.

STYLE dry
QUALITY 🍷🍷½
VALUE ★★+
GRAPES cabernet sauvignon 65%, merlot 35%
REGION Hawke's Bay
CELLAR 2
PRICE $14-16

Vidal Reserve Hawke's Bay Cabernet Sauvignon

There are so many Vidal and Villa Maria Hawke's Bay reds that it is easy to get confused. This is the top Vidal straight cabernet version.
Previous outstanding vintages: '90

CURRENT RELEASE 1991 Chocolate and vanilla are the two taste keys on the nose. The wine is smooth, mouth-filling and just plain enjoyable. Sample it with a lamb or beef stew.

STYLE dry
QUALITY 🍷🍷🍷🍷½
VALUE ★★★
GRAPES cabernet sauvignon
REGION Hawke's Bay
CELLAR 3-5
PRICE $26-29

Vidal Reserve Hawke's Bay Cabernet Sauvignon/Merlot

A fistful of awards have been won by various vintages of this wine, both in New Zealand and overseas. Previous outstanding vintages: '87, '89, '90
CURRENT RELEASE 1991 Tobacco from the merlot component and spice from the oak barrels in which the wine spent twenty months stand out in the bouquet. The wine is gloriously smooth and mouth-fillingly rich, and would be a fine companion to a rare beef roast.

STYLE dry
QUALITY ♟♟♟♟♟
VALUE ★★★
GRAPES cabernet sauvignon 82%, merlot 18%
REGION Hawke's Bay
CELLAR ▭ 3-5
PRICE $26-29

Villa Maria Cellar Selection Cabernet/Merlot

The only red in the Cellar Selection series has been a steady seller for Villa.
CURRENT RELEASE 1991 The nose is softly berryish and the taste round, smooth and easy-going. Not a big wine in the Reserve series mould, but hardly less enjoyable for that.

STYLE dry
QUALITY ♟♟♟♟
VALUE ★★★
GRAPES cabernet sauvignon 51%, merlot 49%
REGION Hawke's Bay
CELLAR ▮ 3
PRICE $16-18

Villa Maria Private Bin Cabernet Sauvignon/Franc/Merlot

Last year this mid-range red was a straight cabernet, made from West Auckland grapes, but the Villa is getting so much good Hawke's Bay fruit that this year they could afford to put some aside and make it a classic Bordeaux blend.
CURRENT RELEASE 1991 That minty Hawke's Bay fruit is immediately evident when you sniff the wine. The taste is ripe at first, but turns a bit green in the middle. Overall, though, it's good wine for the money. Enjoy it with beef sausages and mashed potatoes.

STYLE dry
QUALITY ♟♟♟♟
VALUE ★★★
GRAPES cabernet sauvignon 51%, cabernet franc 28%, merlot 21%
REGION Hawke's Bay
CELLAR ▭ 2-3
PRICE $13-16

Villa Maria Reserve Hawke's Bay Cabernet Sauvignon

The sister wine to the highly rated Vidal version, and equally successful in the medal stakes.

Previous outstanding vintages: '87

CURRENT RELEASE 1991 The bouquet is rich and chocolatey, and the taste is so smooth it's unctuous, but also very, very powerful. Wine this good should sit alongside something baronial, like a venison roast.

STYLE dry
QUALITY ♟♟♟♟♟
VALUE ★★★
GRAPES cabernet sauvignon
REGION Hawke's Bay
CELLAR ▬ 3-5
PRICE $26-29

Villa Maria Reserve Hawke's Bay Cabernet Sauvignon/Merlot

There have been some astonishingly good wines made under this label over the years. This latest model continues the tradition.

CURRENT RELEASE 1991 Berries, chocolate and leather combine to start things off well on the bouquet. The wine is big, but smooth, and boasts a long, lingering finish.

STYLE dry
QUALITY ♟♟♟♟♟
VALUE ★★★
GRAPES cabernet sauvignon 78%, merlot 22%
REGION Hawke's Bay
CELLAR ▬ 2-4
PRICE $26-29

Villa Maria Reserve Marlborough/Hawke's Bay Cabernet Sauvignon/Merlot

It's hard to make good red in Marlborough, but that's where the cabernet component of this blend came from. Colin Fletcher's vineyard is on stony soil in an old riverbed, and the grapes ripen before any others in the area. That means they get super-ripe.

CURRENT RELEASE 1990 This is very classy wine. The nose is quite understated at first, but develops a bit of enthusiasm when the bottle has been open for an hour or so. The taste is smooth, velvety and full of class. Partner it with a whole roast fillet of beef, if you can afford it; or a really good hamburger, if you can't.

STYLE dry
QUALITY ♟♟♟♟♟
VALUE ★★★
GRAPES cabernet sauvignon 85%, merlot 15%
REGION Marlborough and Hawke's Bay
CELLAR ▬ 2-5
PRICE $24-28

Voss Estate Merlot

There's very little merlot grown in Martinborough, but Gary Voss has done well with this one — it won a silver medal in the 1992 Air New Zealand Wine Awards.
CURRENT RELEASE 1992 The grapes were obviously very ripe, judging by the strong fruit-led character of this stylish wine. Nicely rounded and vaguely cherry-like, it sits well with Italian food like pasta topped with herbed tomato sauce.

STYLE dry
QUALITY ▼▼▼▼▼
VALUE ★★★★
GRAPES merlot
REGION Martinborough
CELLAR ▆▬ 2-4
PRICE $16-19

Waimarama Estate Cabernet Sauvignon

John Loughlin credits contract winemaker Nick Sage with the impressive success of his first vintage. Nick was born in Hawke's Bay, but returned there only recently after an absence of twenty-three years.
CURRENT RELEASE 1991 I thought the merlot in the blended version might have been responsible for its dark colour, but this straight cabernet is just as intense. The wine is full of cassis, ripe berry and spicy oak characters, is wonderfully full on the palate but doesn't quite have the complexity of its stablemate on the finish.

STYLE dry
QUALITY ▼▼▼▼▼
VALUE ★★★
GRAPES cabernet sauvignon
REGION Hawke's Bay
CELLAR ▆▬ 2-4
PRICE $25-32

Waimarama Estate Cabernet/Merlot

Eye surgeon Dr John Loughlin's Hawke's Bay vineyard came from nowhere to take a gold and silver medal with the only two wines it makes at the 1992 Air New Zealand Wine Awards. This blend was awarded the gold.
CURRENT RELEASE 1991 The colour is near black and the bouquet full of cassis and leather — both good signs. The palate doesn't disappoint. It is rich, full and chunky, but it also boasts a good measure of elegance. Great wine for the best eye-fillet steak you can find.

STYLE dry
QUALITY ▼▼▼▼▼
VALUE ★★★
GRAPES cabernet sauvignon 85%, merlot 15%
REGION Hawke's Bay
CELLAR ▆▬ 2-5
PRICE $25-32

Waitakere Road Harrier Rise Cabernet Sauvignon

Tim Harris has been a wine critic for several years. Now he's fulfilling a long-held ambition by making his own wine.

CURRENT RELEASE 1991 The rich colour suggests good things to come, and the bouquet speaks of well-thought-out oak treatment. In the mouth Harrier Rise has medium depth and enough rich berry character to give it a long finish.

STYLE dry

QUALITY ▼▼▼▼

VALUE ★★★+

GRAPES cabernet sauvignon

REGION West Auckland

CELLAR ▭ 1-3

PRICE $18-22

Waitakere Uppercase Merlot/Cabernet Sauvignon

Tim designed this wine as an earlier-drinking alternative to Harrier Rise.

CURRENT RELEASE 1991 Merlot's leathery calling card is obvious on the nose. In the mouth the wine is soft and pleasant, but a little ungiving. Partner it with barbecued lamb chops.

STYLE dry

QUALITY ▼▼▼▼

VALUE ★★★★

GRAPES merlot 95%, cabernet sauvignon 5%

REGION West Auckland

CELLAR ▌ 1

PRICE $12-14

West Brook Henderson Merlot

West Brook's Tony Ivicevich makes chunky, flavoursome wines that appeal to the peasant side of my palate.

CURRENT RELEASE 1991 The nose is pure merlot leather, and there's a nice belt of sweet fruit at the front. The wine is soft but quite mouth-filling, and would do good service alongside a stew of beef shin and baby onions.

STYLE dry

QUALITY ▼▼▼▼

VALUE ★★★★

GRAPES merlot 95%, cabernet sauvignon 5%

REGION West Auckland

CELLAR ▌ 3

PRICE $9-11

Winslow Cabernet Sauvignon/Franc

Another new name from Martinborough, one of the fastest-growing winemaking regions in the country. The vineyard owners borrowed the winery equipment of the area's senior statesman, Stan Chifney, to make this red.

CURRENT RELEASE 1991 I swear there's a trace of Worcestershire sauce in the bouquet, which is something I've never smelled in a wine before. You live and learn! Things are more normal on the palate; there's a tonne of rich, sweet fruit and a long-lasting finish. Good enough for a roasted fillet of beef.

STYLE dry

QUALITY ♟♟♟♟

VALUE ★★★

GRAPES cabernet sauvignon 83.5%, cabernet franc 11%, merlot 5.5%

REGION Martinborough

CELLAR ▬▬ 2-5

PRICE $25-29

Yelas Estate Cabernet Sauvignon

Pleasant Valley Wines, the company that makes the Yelas Estate collection, has one of the oldest vineyards in Auckland's Henderson Valley. It is a popular tasting spot for tourists.

CURRENT RELEASE 1989 The bouquet is nicely spicy with some good fruit in evidence at the back. On the palate the berry characters fill the mouth and give the wine a friendly finish. Good with barbecued rump steak.

STYLE dry

QUALITY ♟♟♟

VALUE ★★★

GRAPES cabernet sauvignon

REGION West Auckland

CELLAR ▮ 2

PRICE $14-16

Pinot Noir

Cabernet sauvignon, the great grape of France's Bordeaux region, makes wines that have a strong family resemblance wherever in the world they are produced. Things are not so straightforward, however, with France's other famous red grape, pinot noir. This is the variety used for the great burgundies, but wines made from it elsewhere in the world develop their own characteristics.

Early New Zealand pinot noir wines attempted to duplicate the style of Burgundy and almost invariably failed, but in the last couple of years winemakers have abandoned this copy-cat attitude and started producing pinot noirs that owe nothing to those of other countries, but stand instead as fine wines in their own right. This is where the future must lie for this temperamental superstar; we can look forward to tasting a greater number of world-class New Zealand pinot noir wines in the years to come.

Ata Rangi Pinot Noir

This soft, flavoursome pinot has taken the Rangitoto Beefsteak and Burgundy Club's top pinot noir trophy for two years in a row at the Air New Zealand Wine Awards.

CURRENT RELEASE 1991 The nose reminds me of sweet loam, so well integrated are the grape and oak characters. In the mouth it starts with a burst of chocolate/coffee sweetness before rounding out and grouping its flavours for a long finish. Give it two or three years then partner it with a roast leg of lamb studded with garlic and rosemary.

STYLE dry
QUALITY ▼▼▼▼▼
VALUE ★★★
GRAPES pinot noir
REGION Martinborough
CELLAR ▬ 2-5
PRICE $25-32

Blue Rock Pinot Noir

There's a bit of a trick involved when you buy this wine. Blue Rock produced two 1991 pinot noirs: one made by Jenny Clark, the other by Ata Rangi's Clive Paton. The Clive Paton version is more widely available, so that's the one reviewed here.

CURRENT RELEASE 1991 There's an intense cherry-like nose and a reasonable amount of warm richness on the palate. Good wine for grilled lamb chops.

STYLE dry
QUALITY ▼▼▼▼
VALUE ★★★
GRAPES pinot noir
REGION Martinborough
CELLAR ▬ 2
PRICE $20-24

Collards Marlborough Pinot Noir

Marlborough isn't well known for pinot noir, but when the grapes are put in the hands of a skilled winemaker, the results are often very good. This is a new label for the Collard family, and it will be worth watching.

CURRENT RELEASE 1992 I've been told many times that pinot noir should smell like boiled lollies, but this is the first time I've found them. They're there in abundance, along with cherry and strawberry characters, and even a hint of chocolate. The wine is rich, full and very stylish. Some first effort!

STYLE dry
QUALITY ▼▼▼▼▼
VALUE ★★★
GRAPES pinot noir
REGION Marlborough
CELLAR ▬ 3-5
PRICE $24-27

Crab Farm Pinot Noir

Hawke's Bay is not known as a great pinot noir area, but Crab Farm's Hamish Jardine is keen on the variety. Besides, it sells well at the winery restaurant.

CURRENT RELEASE 1991 I get chocolate in with the strawberries on the nose of this unassuming wine. There are no hard edges on the palate, just lots of soft, smooth fruit. The overall impression is pleasant but unexciting. Hamish reckons it needs five years. I think he's being a bit optimistic, but you never know.

STYLE dry
QUALITY ▼▼▼
VALUE ★★+
GRAPES pinot noir
REGION Hawke's Bay
CELLAR ▮ 5
PRICE $17-22

Dry River Pinot Noir

Dry River's Neil and Dawn McCallum first made a name for their tiny vineyard with a brilliant pinot gris and a couple of superb dessert wines, but lately other varieties have come to the fore. Their pinot noir is lighter than many, but chock-full of flavour.

CURRENT RELEASE 1991 The colour is light and the nose reminiscent of strawberries, and the taste is a bit like spicy lollies. It's nice wine — partner it with rabbit in a red-wine-based sauce.

STYLE dry
QUALITY ▼▼▼▼
VALUE ★★★
GRAPES pinot noir
REGION Martinborough
CELLAR ▬ 2-4
PRICE $23-28

Gibbston Valley Pinot Noir

Rippon has grabbed the early attention when it comes to Central Otago pinot noir, but Gibbston's Alan Brady is keen to establish a similar reputation.

CURRENT RELEASE 1991 The bouquet is steely but perfumed, and the taste smooth and well rounded. It's nice wine, but is a little light to win top honours. Enjoy it with olives, salami and similar snacks.

STYLE dry

QUALITY ▼▼▼▽

VALUE ★★

GRAPES pinot noir

REGION Central Otago

CELLAR ▮ 3

PRICE $25-31

Landfall Pinot Noir

Winery founder Ross Revington reports that he and his team thinned the fruit out by half to get more character in the remainder before the crop was hand-picked. That sort of care and attention usually adds up to an expensive wine, but this one is quite reasonable at the winery. CURRENT RELEASE 1991 There's an earthy, plummy (Black Dorises, I fancy) character on the nose, and soft, smooth tannins in the mouth. The wine is pleasant but a bit light. Partner it with barbecued pork sausages.

STYLE dry

QUALITY ▼▼▼

VALUE ★★★

GRAPES pinot noir

REGION Gisborne

CELLAR ▮ 2

PRICE $15-18

Lintz Estate Pinot Noir

Chris Lintz is one of the newer players on the Martinborough wine scene, but his wines are rapidly catching up with the established names when it comes to recognition.

CURRENT RELEASE 1991 Chris gets good colour into his pinot, and the bouquet has classic cherry characters along with a touch of sweet loam. The taste is round, warm and quite rich, but the finish is just a bit short.

STYLE dry

QUALITY ▼▼▼▽

VALUE ★★★

GRAPES pinot noir

REGION Martinborough

CELLAR ▬▶ 2-4

PRICE $20-23

Martinborough Vineyards Pinot Noir

Martinborough has been the early leader in the 'top pinot noir region' stakes, and Martinborough Vineyards has been the leading producer. Larry McKenna concentrates every effort on this most difficult of varieties. His dedication has paid off with a fistful of medals. Previous outstanding vintages: '88, '89, '90

CURRENT RELEASE 1991 The earthiness that caused this wine to miss out on export certification (the panel found it 'malodorous', but their decision was later reversed) is much in evidence on the nose, along with sweet, cinnamon characters. The taste is what it's all about, however, and that is full, rich and memorable. Stick slivers of garlic and sprigs of rosemary into a leg of lamb, roast it medium-rare and enjoy it with this stylish wine. That's living!

STYLE dry
QUALITY ▼▼▼▼▼
VALUE ★★★
GRAPES pinot noir
REGION Martinborough
CELLAR ▬ 2-5
PRICE $26-30

Mark Rattray Vineyard Pinot Noir

Mark Rattray established Waipara Springs a few years ago, but has now sold his interest to set up what he promises will be his last stop. He made his name with chardonnay, but he's no slouch with pinot noir.

CURRENT RELEASE 1992 There are mushroom aromas in the bouquet and sweet, ripe fruit on the palate. The wine is soft and mouth-filling but gets a bit angular on the finish.

STYLE dry
QUALITY ▼▼▼▼
VALUE ★★+
GRAPES pinot noir
REGION Canterbury
CELLAR ▬ 2-4
PRICE $25-28

Matua Pinot Noir

The Matua Valley winery is at Waimauku in West Auckland, but the grapes for this pinot noir were picked in Canterbury.

CURRENT RELEASE 1990 The bouquet has some delightful sweet strawberry characters, and the same ripe fruit is evident on the palate. Only the leafy finish lets the wine down. Try it with pickled pork.

STYLE dry
QUALITY ▼▼▼
VALUE ★★★★
GRAPES pinot noir
REGION Canterbury
CELLAR ▮ 2
PRICE $11-13

Muirlea Rise Pinot Noir

Made by Willy Brown, who used to be in the liquor trade in Auckland, and named for his wife, Lea. Willy says good pinot should have a 'Monet' character — it should be reminiscent of daffodils and other spring flowers.
CURRENT RELEASE 1991 I don't know about daffodils, but I reckon I get cherry pips on the nose of this soft-centred red. The fruit is clean, spicy and beautifully balanced with the oak. Enjoy it with a garlic-studded leg of lamb.

STYLE dry
QUALITY ▼▼▼▼
VALUE ★★+
GRAPES pinot noir
REGION Martinborough
CELLAR ▬ 3-5
PRICE $27-33

Neudorf Pinot Noir

Winemaker Tim Finn has done well with the notoriously difficult pinot noir at his Nelson winery, although top medal success has so far eluded him.
CURRENT RELEASE 1991 The nose seems a bit leafy, but there is no sign of that character on the palate. Rather, the wine is rich, fruity and moreish. Enjoy it alongside a lamb stew with plenty of rich gravy.

STYLE dry
QUALITY ▼▼▼▼
VALUE ★★★
GRAPES pinot noir
REGION Nelson
CELLAR ▮ 4
PRICE $20-23

Okahu Estate Te Hana Pinot Noir

Monty Knight is fiercely proud of his vineyard, which is so far north it overlooks the sand dunes of Ninety Mile Beach. This pinot is made from grapes picked at Te Hana (still well north of Auckland, but quite a few kilometres south of the winery), chilled overnight and delivered to Monty the next day.
CURRENT RELEASE 1991 Carbonic maceration — the process that subjects whole bunches of grapes to a tumultuous fermentation — has been used to produce a wine with a heap of upfront flavour. Sweet strawberry stands out, but there are lots of other characters. It's fun now, but it won't be a keeper. Enjoy it with minted lamb rissoles.

STYLE dry
QUALITY ▼▼▼▼
VALUE ★★★
GRAPES pinot noir
REGION Northland
CELLAR ▮ 1
PRICE $14-17

Palliser Estate Pinot Noir

Although it is one of the newer players on the Martinborough winemaking scene, Palliser aims to be one of the biggest with planned production of 15,000 cases. This stylish pinot won a silver medal at the 1992 Air New Zealand Wine Awards.

CURRENT RELEASE 1991 Mushrooms and cherries are much in evidence on the nose, and the same flavours carry through onto the palate, but there's a nice bit of earthiness in there as well. A good partner for roast duckling with cherry sauce.

STYLE dry
QUALITY ▼▼▼▼
VALUE ★★★
GRAPES pinot noir
REGION Martinborough
CELLAR ▬ 2-3
PRICE $26-30

C. J. Pask Pinot Noir

Winemaker Kate Marris doesn't believe in overpowering her pinot fruit with too many oak characters, so she uses mostly puncheons for ageing. They're bigger than the more common barriques, which means the wine absorbs less oak.

Previous outstanding vintages: '87

CURRENT RELEASE 1991 Chocolate and plums share the honours on the bouquet, while in the mouth the wine starts sweet, fills out pleasantly with ripe fruit characters and finishes with a nicely rounded flourish. Try it with pesto-topped pasta.

STYLE dry
QUALITY ▼▼▼
VALUE ★★+
GRAPES pinot noir
REGION Hawke's Bay
CELLAR ▮ 3
PRICE $18-23

Rippon Pinot Noir

Martinborough has so far shown itself as the natural home of pinot noir in New Zealand, despite a strong challenge from Canterbury. If Rippon's Rolfe and Lois Mills have anything to do with it, however, Central Otago will be the region to watch in the future.

CURRENT RELEASE 1991 The bouquet covers the gamut of pinot characteristics—cherries, strawberries and mushrooms are all in there having a great old time. The taste starts with lovely sweet fruit, cuts in with a touch of spice and finishes firmly. Great wine for pink-roasted racks of lamb.

STYLE dry
QUALITY ▼▼▼▼▼
VALUE ★★+
GRAPES pinot noir
REGION Central Otago
CELLAR ▮ 5
PRICE $28-33

Robard & Butler Marlborough Pinot Noir

A new label for Corbans-owned Robard & Butler, this wine has won immediate medal success — a silver at last year's Air New Zealand Wine Awards.

CURRENT RELEASE 1991 The bouquet is classic pinot — all strawberries and cherries with a hint of chocolate — and the taste is full of delightfully sweet fruit. This very stylish wine deserves to sit alongside a pile of nicely pink lamb rump slices.

STYLE dry
QUALITY ♟♟♟♟
VALUE ★★★★
GRAPES pinot noir
REGION Marlborough
CELLAR ▮ 3
PRICE $16-18

Rongopai Pinot Noir

You can't miss the grey label with the splash of blue across the top. Rongopai is best known for sweet dessert wines, but the team has made a pretty good job of this pinot.

CURRENT RELEASE 1991 The nose is earthy and mushroomy, with a touch of the plums that often stand out on more southern examples. The taste is rich and welcoming, and has a reasonably long finish. Try it with barbecued lamb chops.

STYLE dry
QUALITY ♟♟♟
VALUE ★★+
GRAPES pinot noir
REGION Te Kauwhata
CELLAR ▬- 3-4
PRICE $24-28

St Helena Pinot Noir

St Helena wines from the 1991 and 1992 vintages boast a new set of colourful labels, which should help them to stand out on the shelf.

CURRENT RELEASE 1991 The nose is highly perfumed, with cherries standing out in front. The wine starts sweet and gets stuck in with a lovely burst of flavour in the middle, but then finishes a bit suddenly. Try it with medium-spicy salami.

STYLE dry
QUALITY ♟♟♟
VALUE ★★★
GRAPES pinot noir
REGION Canterbury
CELLAR ▮ 3
PRICE $16-19

Silverstream Pinot Noir 1992

Expect big things of this new Canterbury vineyard. Consultant winemaker is Mark Rattray, ex-Waipara Springs, whose pinot noirs have been enthusiastically reviewed in British wine magazines.

CURRENT RELEASE 1992 There's an earthy note about the bouquet and some good, ripe fruit on the palate. The wine is bigger than many of its competitors and has an intriguingly smoky aftertaste. Enjoy it with mushrooms on toast.

STYLE dry
QUALITY ▼▼▼▼
VALUE ★★+
GRAPES pinot noir
REGION Canterbury
CELLAR ■■► 3-4
PRICE $25-28

Te Kairanga Reserve Pinot Noir

It surprises me that Te Kairanga puts out two pinots. There's not much difference in price, but I believe this is superior wine — an opinion not shared by the judges at the Air New Zealand Wine Awards.

CURRENT RELEASE 1991 The bouquet is shy, but there are cherry tones in there somewhere. On the palate it tastes riper than the standard version (see *Overflow*) and boasts a considerably longer finish.

STYLE dry
QUALITY ▼▼▼
VALUE ★★+
GRAPES pinot noir
REGION Martinborough
CELLAR ▮ 2
PRICE $27-29

Villa Maria Pinot Noir

Villa sales supremo Angela Lewis reports that the company has had more phone calls about this wine than any other recent release.

CURRENT RELEASE 1991 Mushrooms are one of pinot noir's calling cards, and this wine's bouquet has them in spades. The taste starts sweet, but there's a cutting edge of acid in there and the finish is faintly earthy. Try it with (what else?) mushrooms on toast.

STYLE dry
QUALITY ▼▼▼▼
VALUE ★★★★
GRAPES pinot noir
REGION Auckland
CELLAR ■■► 1-2
PRICE $11-13

Unusual and Unspecified Red Varieties and Blends

Just as white wines labelled 'Chablis' or 'White Burgundy' are far rarer than they were a decade ago, so reds with names like 'Claret' and 'Burgundy' are disappearing. Most of the wines in this section are at the lower end of the price scale, but also included are a couple of high-fliers whose makers choose not to mention the grape varieties on the label. Several of the wines are based on pinotage, an unusual variety grown only in New Zealand and South Africa.

Ata Rangi Célèbre

Ata Rangi's Phyl Pattie and Clive Paton don't put the varieties that go into this flavoursome red on the label because they believe as long as people enjoy the wine, it doesn't matter what it's made from.

Previous outstanding vintages: '86, '90

CURRENT RELEASE 1991 The nose is earthy, and I fancy I could find a touch of steel in there as well. On the palate it is firm, flavoursome but not quite as warm as previous examples. Try it with barbecued lamb chops.

STYLE dry
QUALITY ▼▼▼▼
VALUE ★★+
GRAPES cabernet sauvignon 55%, merlot 30%, shiraz 15%
REGION Martinborough
CELLAR ▋ 1-3
PRICE $25-32

Babich Dry Red

Makers of wines simply labelled 'Dry Red' are often a bit cagey about the varieties within, but this Babich version specifies pinotage, so you know where you stand.

CURRENT RELEASE (non-vintage) The bouquet is a bit stalky and just faintly peppery but the taste boasts nicely integrated tannins and at least a touch of class. Partner it with barbecued sausages.

STYLE dry
QUALITY ▼▼▼
VALUE ★★★
GRAPES pinotage
REGION West Auckland
CELLAR ▋ 1
PRICE $7-9

Babich Pinotage/Cabernet

This big-selling wine for the family-owned Babich winery in West Auckland is light but invariably well made.

CURRENT RELEASE 1991 There's a hint of pepper on the nose, a characteristic of the pinotage grape. The palate boasts some pleasingly sweet fruit and just a hint of cabernet's chocolate character. The only flaw is a slightly herbaceous finish. Good with mild salami.

STYLE dry

QUALITY ▼▼▼

VALUE ★★★+

GRAPES pinotage 70%, cabernet sauvignon 30%

REGION West Auckland

CELLAR ▌ 2

PRICE $8-10

Blackhawk

This wine is a bit of fun for the maker, Alastair Pain of The Grape Republic winery at Te Horo, Horowhenua. Even he describes the price as 'esoteric'.

CURRENT RELEASE 1991 The nose is smoky and earthy, partly the result of the used barrels in which the wine was aged. It's bone dry, but starts with a burst of grape sweetness that fills the mouth. This is a big, rich wine that deserves to sit alongside something medieval like a haunch of venison.

STYLE dry

QUALITY ▼▼▼▼

VALUE ★★

GRAPES cabernet sauvignon 65%, merlot 30%, malbec, cabernet franc, zinfandel

REGION Horowhenua

CELLAR ▬ 3-6

PRICE $38-44

Coopers Creek Coopers Red

Last year, this wine was made from pinot noir, but for the 1992 vintage the Creek's winemaker, Kim Crawford, blended cabernet sauvignon and pinotage together.

CURRENT RELEASE 1992 The nose has soft berry characters, but there's little evidence of pinotage's typical pepper aromas. The wine is light and simple but clean, with a refreshing finish. A good one to sit around sipping before the barbecue.

STYLE dry

QUALITY ▼▼▼

VALUE ★★★

GRAPES cabernet sauvignon 60%, pinotage 40%

REGION West Auckland

CELLAR ▌ 1

PRICE $11-13

Crab Farm Petane Red

It doesn't say so on the label, but this light, soft red is made from 100 per cent Hawke's Bay cabernet sauvignon.

CURRENT RELEASE 1992 There's an attractive spicy, earthy, warm feeling about the bouquet, and a reasonable amount of Hawke's Bay berryishness on the palate, but the finish is a bit lean. Take it to a party.

STYLE dry

QUALITY ▼▼▼▾

VALUE ★★★+

GRAPES cabernet sauvignon

REGION Hawke's Bay

CELLAR ▮ 2

PRICE $10-12

Forrest Estate Gibson Creek

Last year this wine was called Gibson Creek Claret, but the Forrests are exporting it to Britain, where the term Claret has been banned by the European Community.

CURRENT RELEASE 1991 There's some lovely spice on the nose, backed up by cherry and plum characters. The wine is big, rich and chunky, and would suit a leg of lamb rubbed with rosemary and garlic and roasted.

STYLE dry

QUALITY ▼▼▼▼

VALUE ★★★

GRAPES cabernet sauvignon 40%, merlot 40%, cabernet franc 20%

REGION Marlborough

CELLAR ▮ 4

PRICE $18-22

Gibbston Valley Ryecroft Red

Winery owner Alan Brady describes this unassuming wine as a good picnic red, which pretty well sums it up.

CURRENT RELEASE 1992 I fancied I could detect a touch of smokiness on the nose, along with a light plummy character. In the mouth it has very upfront acids for a red, a reasonable amount of softness in the middle but a leafy finish.

STYLE dry

QUALITY ▼▼▼

VALUE ★★+

GRAPES pinot noir

REGION Marlborough

CELLAR ▮ 1

PRICE $12-14

Matawhero Bridge Estate

Good to see this big chunky red in the Matawhero range. The company was long associated with a series of brilliant gewürztraminers, but its recent direction has been unfocused.

CURRENT RELEASE 1990 The nose is earthy and the taste rich, warm and welcoming. This is a red that would go well with lamb shanks stewed in good stock with plenty of chopped onions and tomato pulp.

STYLE dry

QUALITY ▼▼▼▼

VALUE ★★+

GRAPES merlot 40.5%, malbec 31%, cabernet sauvignon 20%, cabernet franc 8.5%

REGION Gisborne

CELLAR ▬ 2-5

PRICE $25-30

Matawhero Syrah

Syrah, a grape believed to have come from ancient Persia, is the same grape as shiraz, Australia's most widely grown variety. Denis Irwin at Matawhero is one of the few people in the country to grow it.

CURRENT RELEASE 1990 Wow! Coffee and toffee combine on the nose of this deeply coloured red. The taste is big, burned and impressive, but drinking it now is committing infanticide. Give it at least two years then partner it with a wild venison casserole.

STYLE dry

QUALITY ▼▼▼▼

VALUE ★★★

GRAPES syrah

REGION Gisborne

CELLAR ▬ 2-5

PRICE $20-24

Matua Valley Claret

The top Matua cabernet-based reds have done well on the show circuit. This relatively inexpensive blend is also based on cabernet, and it outsells its more exalted cellarmates despite its lack of medals.

CURRENT RELEASE 1990 The nose is interestingly earthy, and there's a healthy amount of cheek-gripping tannin once you get it into your mouth. The wine has some depth but is a bit angular. Still, they tell me it's a winner with baked beans.

STYLE dry

QUALITY ▼▼▼

VALUE ★★★

GRAPES cabernet sauvignon 60%, pinotage 25%, pinot noir 15%

REGION Gisborne, Hawke's Bay, West Auckland

CELLAR ▐ 2

PRICE $11-13

Mission Claret

Selling for not much more than $8 in most outlets, this is the most inexpensive red in the Mission collection. The 1992 version boasts rather more warmth than the '91, which makes it very good value.

CURRENT RELEASE 1992 There can't be too many under-$10 cabernet/merlot blends around, and this one offers a touch of style for '92. The nose is warm and faintly toasty, and the palate is light but nicely smooth with a touch of spice on the end. Try it with spicy sausages and mashed potatoes.

STYLE dry

QUALITY ▼▼▼

VALUE ★★★★+

GRAPES cabernet sauvignon 80%, merlot 20%

REGION Hawke's Bay

CELLAR 🍷 2

PRICE $8-10

Mount Riley Marlborough Classic Red

The Mount Riley name hasn't been seen for a few years. Now Alan Scott has resurrected it as a second label to his eponymously named wines.

CURRENT RELEASE 1992 Leather and sweet vanilla can be found on the nose. The wine is light in the mouth but has some nice sweet fruit that makes it a pleasant summer lunchtime quaffer.

STYLE dry

QUALITY ▼▼▼▾

VALUE ★★★

GRAPES cabernet sauvignon 34%, merlot 34%, cabernet franc 32%

REGION Marlborough

CELLAR 🍷 2

PRICE $14-16

Nobilo Pinotage

The Nobilo name has been put on a number of pinotage and cabernet/pinotage blends over the years. This straight version is a good argument for continuing with this much-maligned variety.

CURRENT RELEASE 1990 The bouquet has a bit of leafiness but also some nice green-pepper characters The wine is spicy, a bit lean but boasts a touch of pepper that lingers on the finish. A good partner for lamb racks.

STYLE dry

QUALITY ▼▼▼

VALUE ★★★

GRAPES pinotage

REGION West Auckland

CELLAR 🍷 2

PRICE $15-17

Ohinemuri Estate Gisborne Pinotage (Primeur)

Gisborne reds are generally pretty light, and pinotage is regarded as very much a second-tier grape. So much for preconceived notions — this wine scored a bronze medal at the 1992 Air New Zealand Wine Awards.
CURRENT RELEASE 1992 There's a tonne of cracked pepper on the nose — yep, that's pinotage all right! The wine is soft, fresh, sweetish and clean. Just right for a light summer lunch.

STYLE off-dry
QUALITY ???
VALUE ★★★
GRAPES pinotage
REGION Gisborne
CELLAR ▮
PRICE $12-14

C. J. Pask Roy's Hill Red

This blended red is consistently the biggest-selling wine from Chris Pask's Hawke's Bay winery. The blend varies from year to year, but for '92 a bigger percentage of cabernet sauvignon has added extra warmth.
CURRENT RELEASE 1992 There's some nice, sweet fruit on the nose, along with a touch of oaky spice. The wine tastes warm and welcoming, and is quite generously flavoured. Partner it with beef olives.

STYLE dry
QUALITY ????
VALUE ★★★
GRAPES cabernet sauvignon 60%, cabernet franc 20%, merlot 20%
REGION Hawke's Bay
CELLAR ▮ 3
PRICE $14-17

Rongopai Te Kauwhata Syrah

Auckland talkback king Leighton Smith is a great fan of Aussie shiraz. I thought I'd fool him by serving this wine blind, but he picked it straight away as a New Zealand interpretation of the same grape. Maker Tom van Dam has great hopes for the variety in his region.
CURRENT RELEASE 1990 There's a musty, earthy nose more reminiscent of shiraz from the Rhone Valley in France than Australia. The taste is soft, voluptuous and seemingly sweet, although the wine is bone dry. Partner it with rabbit casseroled in red wine, preferably this one — darn the price!

STYLE dry
QUALITY ????
VALUE ★★+
GRAPES syrah (shiraz)
REGION Te Kauwhata
CELLAR ▮ 3
PRICE $28-33

St George Petite Syrah

Not to be confused with shiraz, this wine is actually made from a grape more commonly known as durif. It has a loyal local following.

CURRENT RELEASE 1992 The colour is almost black, and the nose is more like coffee liqueur than wine. This is a love-it-or-hate-it style — it's big, but it certainly isn't elegant!

STYLE dry
QUALITY ♈♈♈
VALUE ★★+
GRAPES durif
REGION Hawke's Bay
CELLAR ▬ 4-6
PRICE $12-15

St Jerome Dry Red

There used to be dozens of wines simply labelled 'Dry Red' on the New Zealand market, but nowadays they're few and far between.

CURRENT RELEASE 1991 This wine has softened a bit since I tried it for last year's *Penguin Guide*, so I've whacked it up half a point — mind you, the price has gone up since last year as well. It's got a smoky, earthy bouquet and some chunky but enjoyable flavours once you get it into your mouth. Put some in a beef casserole and drink the rest as an accompaniment.

STYLE dry
QUALITY ♈♈♈
VALUE ★★+
GRAPES seibel, pinotage
REGION West Auckland
CELLAR ▮ 1
PRICE $15-17

Seifried Estate Refosca

Refosca is an Italian grape variety, and to the best of my knowledge Hermann and Agnes Seifried's Nelson winery is the only one in New Zealand to make a wine from it.

CURRENT RELEASE 1992 The nose is very berryish, with strawberries the major aroma. In the mouth it reminds me of boiled lollies. It's softly sweet, and I can't imagine a suitable food for it, but it's pleasant enough drinking and certainly different.

STYLE off-dry
QUALITY ♈♈♈
VALUE ★★★
GRAPES refosca
REGION Nelson
CELLAR ▮ 1
PRICE $8-10

Soljans Pinotage

Pinotage used to be a common red variety in New Zealand. Now there is very little of it grown, but a few makers continue to champion the variety.
CURRENT RELEASE 1991 Pinotage is said to have a peppery smell, and there is a tiny bit of that on the nose. The wine is quite rich and spicy on the palate and has a clean, satisfying finish. Try it with casseroled lamb shanks, and add a bit to the pot as well.

STYLE dry
QUALITY ▼▼▼▼
VALUE ★★★★
GRAPES pinotage
REGION West Auckland
CELLAR ▌3
PRICE $11-13

Stonecroft Syrah

Syrah is an unusual variety for New Zealand, and it was this wine that first brought the Stonecroft name to public attention. The wine is very rare but worth searching for.
CURRENT RELEASE 1990 Syrah usually has a peppery nose, but this wine speaks more of Hawke's Bay berryishness. Both the bouquet and palate boast beautifully ripe fruit, and a lingering aftertaste finishes things off nicely. If you have access to game, try it with casseroled hare.

STYLE dry
QUALITY ▼▼▼▼▼
VALUE ★★★
GRAPES syrah
REGION Hawke's Bay
CELLAR ▬ 2-5
PRICE $27-32

Te Kairanga Durif

Durif is a richly coloured grape that is known as petite syrah in California. Just to confuse you, it is not related to the other syrah, known as shiraz in Australia.
CURRENT RELEASE 1991 The bouquet reminded me of home-made plum jam. It's certainly a blockbuster of a wine, but it lacks finesse. If you were brought up on old-style Aussie teeth-blackeners, you'll love it.

STYLE dry
QUALITY ▼▼▼
VALUE ★★+
GRAPES durif
REGION Martinborough
CELLAR ▬ 2-5
PRICE $25-27

Te Kairanga East Plain Nouveau Rouge

Durif is obviously a versatile grape. Not only does winemaker Chris Buring use it for the inky-black red reviewed earlier, he also adds a bit to this much lighter little number.

CURRENT RELEASE 1992 The nose suggests something quite sweet, but in fact the wine is off-dry. It's fresh, fruity and fun — just what you want for the barbecue season.

STYLE off-dry
QUALITY ♟♟♟♟
VALUE ★★+

GRAPES cabernet sauvignon 50%, pinot noir 45%, durif 5%

REGION Martinborough

CELLAR 🍾 1

PRICE $15-17

Waitakere Road SBV

Wine writer and solicitor Tim Harris is nostalgic for the West Auckland reds he enjoyed in his early twenties, when the dominant grape variety was a lowly regarded hybrid called seibel. SBV stands for 'seibel-based vino'.

CURRENT RELEASE (non-vintage) The colour is considerably richer than anything I remember from my early twenties, but I guess the slight stalkiness in the bouquet is a blast from the past. The wine starts sweet in the mouth and has good, chunky tannins backed up by an appealing warmth. Try it alongside a lamb and baby potato casserole.

STYLE dry
QUALITY ♟♟♟
VALUE ★★+

GRAPES seibel 55%, cabernet sauvignon 45%, cabernet franc 5%

REGION West Auckland

CELLAR 🍾 1

PRICE $14-16

Vavasour Syrah

I first tasted this wine out of a barrel during a visit to Vavasour's Marlborough winery. I knew then it had tremendous potential — future vintages will be worth watching out for.

CURRENT RELEASE 1991 There's a dollop of Aussie-style eucalyptus on the nose, which wasn't there in the barrel, but the palate is full of soft, rich flavours backed up by attractive earthiness. Good wine for marinated lamb steaks, cooked rare on the barbecue.

STYLE dry
QUALITY ♟♟♟♟
VALUE ★★★

GRAPES shiraz

REGION Marlborough

CELLAR 🍾 3

PRICE $25-27

Sparkling Wines

First rule: don't call them champagne. That name is reserved by law in New Zealand and most other countries for sparkling wines from the French province where the product was first created.

Wines made using the full champagne technique, and often from the same grapes (predominantly pinot noir and chardonnay) are usually labelled *méthode champenoise* or *méthode traditionelle*. This term describes the system that legend attributes to the blind monk Dom Perignon, whereby the wine is forced to undergo a second fermentation in the actual bottle in which it is sold. The trick then is to get rid of the resultant sludge of dead yeast cells. Traditionally, this is done by turning the bottle a little each day (riddling) until it is upside down, then freezing the neck of the bottle and ejecting the wad of gunk sitting on the cork. That takes two or three weeks, so some makers cheat a little by transferring the finished wine under pressure, through a set of filters, to another bottle. They swear it makes no difference to the taste, but strictly speaking they are no longer using the full *méthode champenoise*.

Sparkling wines that don't carry the words *méthode champenoise*, 'bottle fermented' or something similar are almost certainly made either by the simple addition of gas or by the Charmat method, which induces a second fermentation in a pressurised tank rather than in a bottle.

Corbans Amadeus

This *méthode champenoise* began life in 1987 colours as 100 per cent chardonnay, but the latest model is a more traditional blend of pinot noir and chardonnay.
CURRENT RELEASE 1989 Pinot noir seems to dominate the bouquet, backed up by a hint of yeast character. The taste is fresh, frisky and fun. The wine leans to the light side of the spectrum but finishes cleanly with a touch of class.

STYLE dry

QUALITY ▼▼▼

VALUE ★★★

GRAPES pinot noir, chardonnay

REGION Hawke's Bay

CELLAR ▊ 3

PRICE $18-20

Corbans Italiano Spumante

A new sweet sparkler that Corbans' marketing boffins presumably hope will give Montana's big-selling Bernadino a bit of a shake-up.

CURRENT RELEASE (non-vintage) Good muscat flavours in a clean, sweet but not cloying style. Enjoy it, well chilled, on a hot Sunday afternoon.

STYLE sweet
QUALITY ♟♟♟♟
VALUE ★★★★
GRAPES muscat
REGION Hawke's Bay
CELLAR 🍾
PRICE $5-7

Daniel Le Brun Blanc de Blancs

The most successful wine the Le Bruns have produced, with a brace of gold and silver medals and a trophy under its belt. An all-chardonnay version (blanc de blancs means white wine from white grapes) with a considerable dose of style.

CURRENT RELEASE 1990 The nose carries a combination of flint and bread characters, and the palate is clean, firm and long-lasting.

STYLE dry
QUALITY ♟♟♟♟♟
VALUE ★★★
GRAPES chardonnay
REGION Marlborough
CELLAR 🍾 2
PRICE $43-45

Daniel Le Brun Blanc de Noirs

This all-pinot variation on the theme was one of the few Le Brun wines to miss out on a medal at the 1992 Air New Zealand Wine Awards.

CURRENT RELEASE 1989 This is a much chunkier, gutsier wine than the stylish blanc de blancs, which means it could be served with food as strong as curry.

STYLE dry
QUALITY ♟♟♟♟
VALUE ★★
GRAPES pinot noir
REGION Marlborough
CELLAR 🍾 2
PRICE $43-47

Daniel Le Brun Brut

Méthode champenoise made by a genuine Frenchman from a genuine Champagne family. Daniel and his New Zealand-born wife, Adele, had a hard time of it at first, but since they've perfected their act, they have been cleaning up in the medal stakes.

CURRENT RELEASE (non-vintage) A mouth-filling style that still manages to retain a touch of Marlborough fruitiness. So beefy it wouldn't look silly alongside a steak, but probably best, well chilled, on its own.

STYLE dry

QUALITY ▼▼▼▼

VALUE ★★★+

GRAPES pinot noir 60%, chardonnay 30%, pinot meunier 10%

REGION Marlborough

CELLAR ▮ 2

PRICE $25-30

Daniel Le Brun Rosé

The huge world-wide success of pink and frothy Mateus has given all rosés a reputation as flippant little numbers to be treated as little more than liquid candyfloss. That's a shame; let it be known right now that there are some quite serious rosés out there, and this is one of them.

CURRENT RELEASE (non-vintage) Clean, fresh and crisp, with hints of strawberries and cherries lurking in there somewhere, the wine is quite full-flavoured, tastes faintly fruity on the palate but finishes pleasantly dry. A good partner for similarly coloured pork.

STYLE dry

QUALITY ▼▼▼▼

VALUE ★★★

GRAPES pinot noir

REGION Marlborough

CELLAR ▮ 2

PRICE $28-32

Daniel Le Brun Cuvée Adele

Daniel made this wine to honour his wife, Adele, and launched it with much fanfare at a spectacular winery ball.

CURRENT RELEASE 1989 The nose is the nearest thing to genuine Champagne I have yet encountered in New Zealand, but on the palate things are more obviously Marlborough, with strong fruit tastes. It's good wine, but at this stage of its life it finishes a bit short.

STYLE dry

QUALITY ▼▼▼▼

VALUE ★+

GRAPES pinot noir 60%, chardonnay 40%

REGION Marlborough

CELLAR ▮ 2

PRICE $ 49-52

Daniel Le Brun Vintage

Daniel and Adele follow the French practice of making a vintage wine only in years they consider exceptional. CURRENT RELEASE 1989 The bouquet is yeasty and has a sort of 'old cellar' aroma that adds a bit of extra interest. In the mouth it is richly textured and flavoured but has a refreshingly crisp finish.

STYLE dry
QUALITY ▼▼▼▼▼
VALUE ★★★
GRAPES pinot noir, chardonnay
REGION Marlborough
CELLAR 🍾 3
PRICE $38-42

Deutz Marlborough Cuvée

The first New Zealand *méthode champenoise* wine made in co-operation with a French Champagne house — quite a coup for Montana, and if sales are any guide, a thoroughly sensible decision for Champagne Deutz. CURRENT RELEASE (non-vintage) The bouquet is fruity and elegant, and the same suggestion of fruitiness can be found on the palate. The wine is made in a clean style that is frighteningly easy to drink.

STYLE dry
QUALITY ▼▼▼▼▼
VALUE ★★★+
GRAPES pinot noir, chardonnay
REGION Marlborough
CELLAR 🍾 2
PRICE $29-32

Deutz Marlborough Cuvée Blanc de Blancs

Montana doesn't enter Deutz in wine shows. That's a pity; it would be interesting to see how this new release rates against the multi-award-winning Daniel Le Brun equivalent. CURRENT RELEASE (non-vintage) The bouquet speaks more of steel than yeast. In the mouth the wine is crisp and clean. Imagine the sort of chardonnay that doesn't make a big thing of oak, then add bubbles, and you've got the picture.

STYLE dry
QUALITY ▼▼▼▼▼
VALUE ★★★
GRAPES chardonnay 90%, pinot noir 10%
REGION Marlborough
CELLAR 🍾 3
PRICE $35-38

Hunter's Brut

A sparkling wine from from Hunter's is always a much-talked-about event, partly because Tony Jordan, from Domaine Chandon in Australia, is a consultant to the local winery.

CURRENT RELEASE 1989 The nose is yeasty, and the tastes are big, chunky and attention-grabbing. A full-bodied style that will win many friends.

STYLE dry

QUALITY ▼▼▼▼

VALUE ★★★+

GRAPES chardonnay 50%, pinot noir 50%

REGION Marlborough

CELLAR ▮ 3

PRICE $23-26

Mills Reef Chardonnay

This new release from Tauranga-based Mills Reef has already drawn a lot of praise.

CURRENT RELEASE 1990 There's a gentle amount of yeast on the nose, but mostly this wine is about good, well-rounded fruit. Good wine for hot-afternoon sipping.

STYLE dry

QUALITY ▼▼▼▼

VALUE ★★★

GRAPES chardonnay

REGION Hawke's Bay

CELLAR ▮ 1

PRICE $30-33

Montana Bernadino

Montana's big-selling Asti-style sweet sparkler is often dismissed as 'just a party wine', but it's actually a lot better than many Italian Astis and has won a brace of medals to prove it.

CURRENT RELEASE (non-vintage) Fruity, fresh and full of flavour, Bernadino is a fun wine for summer. Pour a little over fresh strawberries and finish it as an accompaniment.

STYLE dry

QUALITY ▼▼▼▼

VALUE ★★★★★

GRAPES Dr Hogg muscat

REGION Gisborne

CELLAR ▮

PRICE $5-8

Montana Fricante

The fun-shaped bottle says it all — this is party wine! Given that obvious aim, it is surprising to discover it is made by the full Champagne method.

CURRENT RELEASE (non-vintage) The nose is honeyed and the palate frisky and fun. The wine is refreshing, clean and very drinkable. Best on its own.

STYLE medium

QUALITY ♟♟♟♟

VALUE ★★★

GRAPES muscat, riesling, chenin blanc

REGION Hawke's Bay and Gisborne

CELLAR ▉

PRICE $14-16

Montana Lindauer Méthode Champenoise Brut

A big seller for Montana, and a wine that has won critical acclaim in the UK — it recently shared an award for 'Sparkling Wine of the Year'.

CURRENT RELEASE (non-vintage) Lindauer Brut starts crisp but broadens out on the palate to leave an overall impression of softness. A pleasant, undemanding wine that works well as a pre-dinner palate stimulant.

STYLE dry

QUALITY ♟♟♟♟

VALUE ★★★★

GRAPES chardonnay, pinot noir

REGION Marlborough and Gisborne

CELLAR ▉ 1

PRICE $10-12

Montana Lindauer Méthode Champenoise Rosé

For many people, pink bubbly is the ultimate party wine; the Montana Lindauer version is the right colour, and it's well priced.

CURRENT RELEASE (non-vintage) There's a steely character in the bouquet and a tiny hint of yeast, if you search for it. The taste is fruity, clean and well rounded.

STYLE dry

QUALITY ♟♟♟

VALUE ★★★

GRAPES pinot noir, chardonnay

REGION Marlborough and Gisborne

CELLAR ▉ 1

PRICE $10-12

Montana Lindauer Special Reserve Brut de Brut

Touted as a higher-class version of standard Lindauer, mainly because it has spent more time sitting on the dead yeast cells that are a by-product of the fermentation process.

CURRENT RELEASE (non-vintage) A little drier than the standard version, boasting more flavour and an extra touch of elegance.

STYLE dry

QUALITY ▼▼▼▼

VALUE ★★★+

GRAPES chardonnay, pinot noir

REGION Marlborough and Gisborne

CELLAR ▋ 2

PRICE $13–15

Morton Estate Méthode Champenoise Brut

Morton manager and chief winemaker John Hancock says he started making this classy sparkler because he was bored and needed a new challenge. He did well — the wine took a gold medal on its first show outing.

CURRENT RELEASE 1990 John and his winemaker, Steve Bird, have managed to get a strong yeast character into the wine for this vintage — the bouquet is like fresh-baked bread. On the palate it is round, smooth and clean enough to ensure a crisp finish.

STYLE dry

QUALITY ▼▼▼▼▼

VALUE ★★★+

GRAPES chardonnay 80%, pinot noir 20%

REGION Gisborne (chardonnay) and Hawke's Bay

CELLAR ▋ 2

PRICE $23-27

Morton Méthode Champenoise

This new line for the Morton team is designed to sell for under $20, but its classy packaging makes it look like a much more expensive proposition.

CURRENT RELEASE (non-vintage) The bouquet carries a hint of yeast, but overall the wine has been made in a soft, broad style that will find wide appeal. Good enough for a high-class party.

STYLE dry

QUALITY ▼▼▼

VALUE ★★★+

GRAPES chardonnay 75%, pinot noir 25%

REGION Gisborne (chardonnay) and Hawke's Bay

CELLAR ▋ 1

PRICE $17-21

Nautilus Cuvée Marlborough

Australian-owned Nautilus has been planning to make a sparkling wine from Marlborough fruit for some years. This first release is designed to be clean, relatively simple and easy to drink.

CURRENT RELEASE (non-vintage) The nose is clean, fresh and steely, and the taste is on the light side but thoroughly enjoyable. With this as a first effort, future vintages will be worth watching.

STYLE dry
QUALITY ▼▼▼▼
VALUE ★★+
GRAPES chardonnay 75%, pinot noir 25%
REGION Marlborough
CELLAR ▮ 1
PRICE $30-33

Parker Méthode Champenoise Classical Brut

Phil Parker lectures on winemaking and marketing at Tarawhaiti Technical Institute in Poverty Bay. He makes wine — mostly sparkling — in his spare time.

CURRENT RELEASE 1989 There's a steely feel about the bouquet of this stylish sparkler, which suggests chardonnay is the major grape in the blend, but according to the label it is pinot noir that predominates. The taste is firm and yeasty, with an impressive amount of depth.

STYLE dry
QUALITY ▼▼▼▼
VALUE ★★★
GRAPES pinot noir 75%, chardonnay 25%
REGION Gisborne
CELLAR ▮ 1
PRICE $26-34

Pelorus

Last year this wine, in debut colours, was my top sparkler. It didn't quite make it this year, but it was very close.

CURRENT RELEASE 1988 The nose has more yeast than I remember in the previous model, but the same faintly fruity, clean and stylish tastes are on the palate. It's still top stuff.

STYLE dry
QUALITY ▼▼▼▼▼
VALUE ★★★
GRAPES pinot noir 60%, chardonnay 40%
REGION Marlborough
CELLAR ▮ 2
PRICE $39-43

Penfolds Hyland

Producing a *méthode champenoise* that sells for well under $10 is quite a feat, and Hyland is consistently flavoursome and pleasant.

CURRENT RELEASE (non-vintage) There's a wee bit of nuttiness from yeast contact on both the nose and the front of the palate, but mostly this wine is about undemanding, clean fruit characters with a dash of sweetness. Perfect for parties and passable as an aperitif.

STYLE dry
QUALITY ▼▼▼
VALUE ★★★★+
GRAPES pinot noir, chardonnay
REGION Gisborne and Marlborough
CELLAR ▯
PRICE $7–9

Selaks Méthode Champenoise Brut

This wine was a labour of love for Mate Selak, who died a couple of years ago. Rumour has it that he was so proud of his first vintage, he gave it all away before it could be marketed.

CURRENT RELEASE 1990 There's some light yeast character in with the fruit on the nose. The wine is in the full-flavoured mould, but remains fresh and clean to the end.

STYLE dry
QUALITY ▼▼▼▼
VALUE ★★★+
GRAPES pinot noir, chardonnay
REGION West Auckland
CELLAR ▯ 2
PRICE $22-25

Selaks Méthode Champenoise Extra Dry

Made with the same three-year yeast contact as the brut bottling, the extra dry version has no added sugar and is therefore more austere.

CURRENT RELEASE 1990 The nose is steely, and there's a sort of gunmetal character in the taste that I like a lot. The wine is quite austere but very clean, and makes a great aperitif.

STYLE dry
QUALITY ▼▼▼▼
VALUE ★★★+
GRAPES pinot noir, chardonnay
REGION West Auckland
CELLAR ▯ 2
PRICE $22-25

Vidal Méthode Champenoise Brut

Not a high-profile sparkler, but consistently well made and with more character than most.

CURRENT RELEASE (non-vintage) Quite an earthy style, which you will either love or hate — very different from run-of-the-mill sparklers.

STYLE dry

QUALITY ▼▼▼

VALUE ★★★

GRAPES pinot noir 70%, chardonnay 30%

REGION Hawke's Bay

CELLAR ▮

PRICE $21-25

West Brook Bakchos Brut

Sparkling wines are best made from high-acid grapes, so the chenin blanc used for this new line was a logical choice.

CURRENT RELEASE (non-vintage) The bouquet is steely and crisp, with fruit just coming through at the back. In the mouth the wine is lighter than the bouquet suggests and has quite an austere finish.

STYLE dry

QUALITY ▼▼▼

VALUE ★★★+

GRAPES chenin blanc

REGION West Auckland

CELLAR ▮

PRICE $9-11

Rosé and Blush Wines

English wine-writer Hugh Johnson once said that the producer of a rosé wine owed as much to the art of the confectioner as to traditional winemaking skills. He was alluding, I presume, to the importance of achieving an appealing colour — not too dark, not too watery. Pink wines aren't big sellers in New Zealand, which is a pity. Slightly chilled, they are as fine a companion to a spring or summer lunch as has yet been devised.

Clearview Estate Dave's Blush

The Dave referred to is David Ward, a partner in this seaside winery at Te Awanga, Hawke's Bay. This blush contains a portion of a grape called chambourcin, and is almost certainly the only New Zealand wine to do so. CURRENT RELEASE 1992 The colour is so pale it could be described as off-white. On the palate there are good, crisp acids and a nice touch of steel and spice on the finish. Try it with a Mediterranean-style salad of barbecued vegetables.

STYLE dry

QUALITY ♀♀♀♀

VALUE ★★★

GRAPES chambourcin 50%, sauvignon blanc 50%

REGION Hawke's Bay

CELLAR ▮ 1

PRICE $12-14

Collards Franc

Designed as a cheap and cheerful summer wine, this latest style from Collards has a dashing label wearing the name 'Franc' in bold script-style lettering. CURRENT RELEASE 1991 Clean, refreshing and loads of fun, this charming little wine smells of blueberries and tastes of sunshine. Enjoy it with a bowl of strawberries.

STYLE off-dry

QUALITY ♀♀♀♀

VALUE ★★★★

GRAPES cabernet franc

REGION West Auckland

CELLAR ▮

PRICE $8-10

Forest Flower Collection Gisborne Blush

This wine's pink colour was obtained by leaving the skins in contact with the juice for no more than five hours, with the result that it has a very gentle hue indeed.

CURRENT RELEASE 1992 Upping the percentage of pinotage and swapping the pinot noir in last year's wine for cabernet sauvignon has given this latest model a nice cracked-pepper bouquet. It starts fruity but dries out in the middle and finishes with a touch of spice. Good with a bowl of not-too-salty mixed nuts.

STYLE off-dry

QUALITY ▼▼▼

VALUE ★★★+

GRAPES pinotage 80%, cabernet sauvignon 20%

REGION Gisborne

CELLAR ▮

PRICE $7-9

Forrest Estate Cabernet Rosé

John and Brigid Forrest scored a gold medal with the 1990 vintage of this pretty wine, but since then have managed only bronzes. The latest was at the 1992 Air New Zealand Wine Awards.

CURRENT RELEASE 1992 The nose is pretty serious stuff, with the sort of cabernet berryishness you would expect to find in full-coloured versions. In the mouth it starts fruity, but dries out for a crisp, clean finish. Try it with a roast-pork sandwich.

STYLE medium-dry

QUALITY ▼▼▼▼

VALUE ★★+

GRAPES cabernet sauvignon 90%, merlot 10%

REGION Marlborough

CELLAR ▮ 2

PRICE $13-16

French Farm Rosé

The winery is at Banks Peninsula, but the grapes for this crisp rosé come from Waipara, a couple of hours away.
CURRENT RELEASE 1992 The nose is steely, and the taste is firm and zingy, thanks to some positive acids. It would work well with grilled fresh sardines, which a few restaurants are now able to get their hands on.

STYLE medium-dry

QUALITY ▼▼▼▼

VALUE ★★★

GRAPES sauvignon blanc 80%, cabernet sauvignon 20%

REGION Waipara, Canterbury

CELLAR ▮ 2

PRICE $13-16

Grove Mill Le Clairet

Love the label! Grove Mill winemaker David Pearce
has often said he makes only serious wines. It could
probably be argued that this is more serious than most
rosés, but the fun, party-style label suggests a different
philosophy.

CURRENT RELEASE 1991 The berryish bouquet does suggest a certain amount of seriousness about the wine,
but the taste is all fruity, flippant fun. Great wine for
summer, and probably best on its own.

STYLE off-dry

QUALITY ▼▼▼▼

VALUE ★★★

GRAPES cabernet
sauvignon 66%,
pinotage 34%

REGION Marlborough

CELLAR 🍷

PRICE $12-14

Matawhero Rosé

Matawhero's Denis Irwin holds most of his wine back
until he feels it is ready to drink, but the rosé is being
released now while it's relatively young and fresh.

CURRENT RELEASE 1991 Cherries dominate the bouquet,
while the taste is pleasant and fresh. Best, lightly chilled,
on its own.

STYLE off-dry

QUALITY ▼▼▼▼

VALUE ★★★+

GRAPES pinot noir,
malbec

REGION Gisborne

CELLAR 🍷 1

PRICE $10-12

Millton Cabernet Rosé

There used to be several rosé wines made from cabernet
sauvignon grapes, but lately pinot noir has taken over as
the most popular choice. James and Annie Millton
pursue a different route and use organically grown
cabernet franc.

CURRENT RELEASE 1992 There are nice, soft berry characters in the bouquet that carry through onto the palate.
The wine is nicely balanced and refreshing, and would
be a fine companion to a piece of grilled snapper topped
with a light tomato-based sauce.

STYLE off-dry

QUALITY ▼▼▼

VALUE ★★+

GRAPES cabernet
franc

REGION Gisborne

CELLAR 🍷 1

PRICE $15-17

Mission Crackling Rosé

To make a wine 'crackle', a little bit of gas is injected to give it a spritzig feel on the tongue. It works well with this style.

CURRENT RELEASE 1992 I didn't get as much 'crackle' out of the test bottle as I found in the '91 vintage, but the wine was a refreshing mouthful nonetheless. It has a berryish nose and is fruity on the palate, but with enough acid crispness to give it a clean finish. Best on its own.

STYLE medium
QUALITY 🍷🍷🍷🍷
VALUE ★★★+
GRAPES a winery secret (!)
REGION Hawke's Bay
CELLAR 🍷
PRICE $9-11

Morton Estate Blush (White Label)

In the past, Morton's pinkie has been labelled 'Pinot Noir Blush', but now it's being made from cabernet sauvignon and cabernet franc.

CURRENT RELEASE 1992 The nose is pretty shy, but there are some crisp, berryish notes on the palate and enough acids to ensure a crisp finish. Good picnic wine.

STYLE off-dry
QUALITY 🍷🍷🍷
VALUE ★★★
GRAPES cabernet sauvignon 50%, cabernet franc 50%
REGION Hawke's Bay
CELLAR 🍷 1
PRICE $10-13

Montana Wohnsiedler Rosé

Wohnsiedler has been around for years as a simple, medium-sweet white wine, and no doubt it has introduced many people to the wonders of the grape. Now it has been joined by a sweeter Sauterne and this medium rosé.

CURRENT RELEASE (non-vintage) Sniff it or sip it — the fruity sensations are much the same either way. The wine is clean, a bit flabby in the middle but pleasant enough. Save it for barbecue duties.

STYLE medium
QUALITY 🍷🍷🍷
VALUE ★★★
GRAPES müller-thurgau 85%, pinotage 15%
REGION Gisborne
CELLAR 🍷
PRICE $6-8

Nobilo Rosé

The Nobilos produced a sparkling rosé a few years back called Lily the Pink. This one is more plainly labelled, and it doesn't sparkle.

CURRENT RELEASE (non-vintage) The bouquet is berryish and particularly reminiscent of strawberries. The taste is clean, quite full and crisp thanks to some nicely integrated acids.

STYLE dry

QUALITY ▼▼▼

VALUE ★★★+

GRAPES müller-thurgau 45%, sauvignon blanc 45%, cabernet sauvignon 10%

REGION Gisborne and Marlborough

CELLAR ▮ 1

PRICE $9-10

Okahu Estate Pinot Blush

Monty Knight says he prefers the pale blush style to the near-red rosés favoured by many of his contemporaries. He achieves the colour by leaving the skins in contact with the juice for just twenty-four hours.

CURRENT RELEASE 1992 The aroma on this little charmer is like crushed cherries. On the palate it is fruity, fresh and delicate. A wine to suit any sort of picnic occasion.

STYLE off-dry

QUALITY ▼▼▼

VALUE ★★★

GRAPES pinot noir

REGION Northland

CELLAR ▮ 1

PRICE $12-14

Riverside Cabernet Rosé

The pretty pink colour of this wine was obtained by leaving the skins in contact with the cabernet juice for twenty-four hours, then filtering them off.

CURRENT RELEASE 1992 Hey — this is fun! There are some lovely, crisp acids and pleasant fruitiness, although the wine is almost bone dry. Enjoy it with a smoked-salmon salad.

STYLE dry

QUALITY ▼▼▼▼

VALUE ★★★+

GRAPES cabernet sauvignon

REGION Hawke's Bay

CELLAR ▮ 1

PRICE $10-12

St George Estate Rosé

The bulk of St George's wine is sold at the pleasant winery restaurant, where this rosé is a popular summer choice.

CURRENT RELEASE 1991 Sauvignon's celebrated crispness jumps out of the glass, but the malbec makes its presence felt on the palate with a bit of spicy backbone. Great with tuna salad, or any similar light lunch dish.

STYLE dry

QUALITY ♟♟♟♟

VALUE ★★★+

GRAPES sauvignon blanc 90%, malbec 10%

REGION Hawke's Bay

CELLAR █ 1

PRICE $9-11

Seibel Henderson Cabernet Sauvignon Blanc de Noir

Norbert Seibel makes this wine entirely from free-run juice; in other words, the juice given off by the grapes purely from their own weight, without pressing.

CURRENT RELEASE 1990 Unusually for a rosé, this wine is virtually bone dry. There's a hint of cabernet chocolate on the nose, and some full, berryish flavours on the palate. Not just for fun, this is serious wine that would look good alongside a roast of pork.

STYLE dry

QUALITY ♟♟♟♟

VALUE ★★★+

GRAPES cabernet sauvignon

REGION West Auckland

CELLAR █ 2

PRICE $10-12

Te Mata Estate Rosé

A rosé from Te Mata? That's a common reaction when people hear that the makers of a couple of the country's meatiest reds also produce this pretty little number. Nevertheless, it's a big seller, particularly at the cellar door.

CURRENT RELEASE 1992 There's more of sauvignon's herbaceousness on the nose than in last year's model, along with a bit of appealing earthiness. The taste, however, is all about ripe fruit, right through to the slightly spicy finish. Enjoy it with well-peppered smoked salmon folded into a length of buttered French bread.

STYLE dry

QUALITY ♟♟♟♟

VALUE ★★★+

GRAPES cabernet sauvignon 35%, cabernet franc 35%, sauvignon blanc 30%

REGION Hawke's Bay

CELLAR █ 1

PRICE $11-13

Torlesse Southern Blush (Dry)

Winemaker Kym Rayner makes this delicately pink wine from white grapes, and gets the colour by steeping cabernet sauvignon skins in the blend for a while. The result was good enough to win him a bronze medal at the 1992 Air New Zealand Wine Awards.

CURRENT RELEASE 1992 The wine is dry, as the label denotes, but there are some pleasantly fruity tones on the palate. It is refreshingly clean and finishes with a dash of spice. Try it with a chicken salad.

STYLE dry

QUALITY ⚊⚊⚊⚊

VALUE ★★★

GRAPES gewürztraminer 40%, breidecker 35%, chardonnay 25%

CELLAR 🍶 1

PRICE $13-16

West Brook Cabernet Rosé

There was a bit of a spate of cabernet rosés about five years ago; nowadays this is one of the few on the market.

CURRENT RELEASE 1992 The nose is quite berryish, and the taste is soft, ripe and just sweet enough to be refreshing. Enjoy it, slightly chilled, on its own.

STYLE medium

QUALITY ⚊⚊⚊

VALUE ★★★

GRAPES cabernet sauvignon

REGION West Auckland

CELLAR 🍶 1

PRICE $8-10

Dessert Wines

A lusciously sweet dessert wine can make a lovely finish to a meal, either on its own or as an accompaniment to a sweet course. These opulent examples of bottled passion are designed to be enjoyed in small doses, which is why they're usually sold in half-bottles or offered by the glass in restaurants. One recommendation: try them with blue cheese for a match made in heaven.

There are several ways to make super-sweet wine. The grapes can be left hanging on the vine for long after the normal harvest time, so they turn into neo-raisins. Sometimes, they will become infected with a mould called botrytis (see *Glossary*). Or the winemaker can make wine sweeter by freezing the tank of juice and pouring off the non-frozen grape essence, or by stopping the fermentation process before the yeasts have eaten all the sugar.

Cooks Winemaker's Reserve Late Harvest

The grapes were left to hang on the vine until they'd shrivelled up like raisins to make this wine, which is why the label carries the description 'Late Harvest'.
CURRENT RELEASE 1989 The herbaceousness of the semillon and sauvignon blanc in the blend tend to override the sweetness on the nose. The wine is clean and nicely flavoured but finishes a bit short.

STYLE medium-sweet

QUALITY ▼▼▼

VALUE ★★★

GRAPES semillon 66%, sauvignon blanc 34%

REGION Marlborough

CELLAR ▮ 2

PRICE $12-15 (375 ml)

Corbans Private Bin Rhine Riesling

This luscious wine has won a couple of silver medals and, most recently, a bronze, but has never quite made it to gold status.
CURRENT RELEASE 1989 The nose is delightfully sweet but toasty — like honey on Vogel's. The taste is clean, luscious and nicely balanced with a refreshingly crisp finish. Great with a bowl of fruit salad.

STYLE sweet
QUALITY ▼▼▼▼▼
VALUE ★★★+
GRAPES riesling
REGION Marlborough
CELLAR ▮ 3
PRICE $12-15 (375 ml)

Collards Late Harvest Semillon

The Collards don't make a song and dance about dessert wines, but when they decide to create one, they do it well.
CURRENT RELEASE 1990 The crystallised-ginger nose suggests a big, overblown style, but in fact the wine is clean, middleweight and beautifully balanced. Try it with a bowl of crystallised ginger.

STYLE sweet
QUALITY ▼▼▼▼
VALUE ★★★★
GRAPES semillon
REGION West Auckland
CELLAR ▮ 3
PRICE $12-15 (375 ml)

Coopers Creek Riesling Late Harvest

This stylish wine won a gold medal at the 1992 Air New Zealand Wine Awards.
CURRENT RELEASE 1990 The nose is like cinnamon-baked apples. This is not an over-the-top style, but it's clean and refreshing, and makes a great late-afternoon sipper.

STYLE sweet
QUALITY ▼▼▼▼▼
VALUE ★★★★
GRAPES riesling
REGION Hawke's Bay
CELLAR ▮ 2
PRICE $13-15 (375 ml)

Forrest Estate Sauvignon Blanc Select Late Harvest

Sauvignon blanc is used, along with semillon, to create the great sweet wines of Sauternes, in France, yet few people here use it for dessert wines. John and Brigid Forrest are happy they did.

CURRENT RELEASE 1992 The nose is citric and still definably sauvignon blanc. On the palate, it is a cleanly made middleweight that boasts good acid and a crisp finish.

STYLE sweet

QUALITY ▼▼▼▼

VALUE ★★★+

GRAPES sauvignon blanc

REGION Marlborough

CELLAR ▮ 3

PRICE $12-16 (375 ml)

Giesen Canterbury Burnham Main Road Riesling Late Harvest

The Giesens have made some of the sweetest dessert wines this country has seen, but this one is in the middle of the scale.

CURRENT RELEASE 1990 The nose is nicely honeyed, but the wine is nowhere near as sweet as the first impression suggests. It has been made in quite a light style that uses sweetness to highlight riesling's best qualities. Chill it well and enjoy it one hot day at the beach.

STYLE medium-sweet

QUALITY ▼▼▼▼▼

VALUE ★★★+

GRAPES riesling

REGION Burnham, Canterbury

CELLAR ▮ 5

PRICE $23-26 (750 ml)

Grape Republic Rhine Riesling

You have to look hard to realise this one, like the chardonnay reviewed later, is a dessert wine. The words 'Late Harvest' are part of the tiny print on the back label.

CURRENT RELEASE 1992 This lighter style of dessert wine is the sort of thing that's enjoyable on its own on a hot afternoon. It's got a delicate floral bouquet and just a bit of honey on the palate, but mostly it's about clean, fresh grapes.

STYLE sweet

QUALITY ▼▼▼▼

VALUE ★★★+

GRAPES riesling

REGION Hawke's Bay and Horowhenua

CELLAR ▮ 2

PRICE $12-16 (375 ml)

Grape Republic Waterfall Bay Chardonnay

My palate got quite a shock when I tried this wine. Only the back label gives any idea that it is a dessert wine, so I had it lined up with the dry chardonnays.

CURRENT RELEASE 1990 Dried figs, butterscotch and honey make for a pretty exciting introduction. In the mouth the wine is grainy, honeyed and luscious, but it could do with a touch more acid to keep things in balance.

STYLE sweet
QUALITY ▼▼▼▽
VALUE ★★★+
GRAPES chardonnay
REGION Horowhenua
CELLAR 🍾 4
PRICE $13-18 (375 ml)

Grove Mill Botrytised Sauvignon Blanc

Few wineries make a sweet wine from sauvignon blanc, which is surprising because it works well.

CURRENT RELEASE 1991 The wine has been barrel-fermented and oak-aged, so there are all sorts of things happening on the nose — it reminded me vaguely of Chinese sweet and sour sauce. In the mouth there is a jigsaw of flavours, with nectarines and lychees in there somewhere. The finish is a highlight — luscious and clean, it goes on forever.

STYLE very sweet
QUALITY ▼▼▼▼▽
VALUE ★★★+
GRAPES sauvignon blanc
REGION Marlborough
CELLAR 🍾 5
PRICE $15-17 (375 ml)

Highfield Estate Marlborough Noble Late Harvest

It's not mentioned on the label, but this wine is made entirely from müller-thurgau grapes, a large percentage of which were botrytised.

CURRENT RELEASE 1990 The nose has a burned quality about it, which gives evidence of the amount of botrytised fruit present. In the mouth it is luscious, opulent and boasts a delightful spiced-honey finish.

STYLE sweet
QUALITY ▼▼▼▼▽
VALUE ★★★
GRAPES müller-thurgau
REGION Marlborough
CELLAR 🍾 4
PRICE $15-18 (375ml)

Jackson Estate Botrytised Riesling

The first dessert wine from this relatively new Marlborough company, and a silver-medal winner at the 1992 Air New Zealand Wine Awards.

CURRENT RELEASE 1991 The nose smells to me like a combination of ginger and super-intense roses. In the mouth things are luscious, rich and intense, but also impressively clean and fresh.

STYLE sweet
QUALITY ♟♟♟♟♟
VALUE ★★
GRAPES riesling
REGION Marlborough
CELLAR ▮ 5
PRICE $35-39 (375 ml)

Lincoln Ice Wine Hawke's Bay Gewürztraminer

True ice wine is made in Germany when the grapes freeze over in the vineyard. It's tricky stuff — the grapes must be picked as soon as they freeze, even if it's the middle of the night. There are no such problems at Lincoln. Winemaker Nick Chan simply freezes the tank of juice and drains off the concentrated grape essence, leaving the frozen water content behind.

CURRENT RELEASE 1990 The wine is charmingly golden in colour, and the distinctive gewürz aromas of cloves and overripe pineapple are exacerbated by the sugar level. On the palate the wine is clean, spicy and reminiscent of a tropical fruit salad.

STYLE very sweet
QUALITY ♟♟♟♟
VALUE ★★★
GRAPES gewürztraminer
REGION Hawke's Bay
CELLAR ▮ 2
PRICE
$13-15 (375 ml),
$18-20 (750 ml)

Lintz Martinborough Noble Selection Optima

Making this wine is a labour of love for Chris Lintz, because the style is a personal favourite. His price is almost as over the top as the wine. but it's the only optima-based wine in the country, so I guess it allows for rarity value.

CURRENT RELEASE 1992 The colour is delightfully golden, and there is plenty of botrytis's trade-mark burned-rubber aroma on the nose. The wine is very luscious, but good acids keep it crisp at the back and help ensure a long finish.

STYLE sweet
QUALITY ♟♟♟♟
VALUE ★+
GRAPES Optima
REGION Martinborough
CELLAR ▮ 6
PRICE $37 (375 ml)

Martinborough Müller-Thurgau Late Harvest

Winemaker Larry McKenna reports that 1992 was a great year for müller in Martinborough, which is partly why he chose to make this dessert wine from the variety, rather than the riesling he used in 1991. Sadly, it'll be the last — the vines have been pulled out.

CURRENT RELEASE 1992 The bouquet is a little shy, but there are some nice floral hints in there, backed by honey. In the mouth the wine is clean, luscious and moreish. Partner it with crème brulée.

STYLE sweet
QUALITY ♛♛♛♛♛
VALUE ★★★★
GRAPES müller-thurgau
REGION Martinborough
CELLAR ▐ 5
PRICE $11-13 (375 ml)
$19-23 (750 ml)

Matua Late Harvest Gewürztraminer

Only a handful of makers use gewürztraminer for their dessert wines, which is a pity because the grape suits the style well.

CURRENT RELEASE 1990 There's plenty of gewürz's trademark spice on the nose, but there's something faintly medicinal in there as well. The taste has flattened out a little in the last year or so, and the wine is now a middleweight — albeit a thoroughly pleasant one.

STYLE sweet
QUALITY ♛♛♛
VALUE ★★★+
GRAPES gewürztraminer
REGION Hawke's Bay
CELLAR ▐ 1
PRICE $9-11 (375 ml)

Millton Gisborne Semillon Tête de Cuvée

James and Annie Millton have produced some excellent dessert wines over the years, from a variety of grapes.

CURRENT RELEASE 1990 The nose is like honey and dried apricots, but I get spicy ginger on the palate. Whatever, it's lovely wine that is wonderful alongside Kapiti Kikorangi blue cheese.

STYLE sweet
QUALITY ♛♛♛♛♛
VALUE ★★+
GRAPES semillon
REGION Gisborne
CELLAR ▐ 6
PRICE $40-43 (750 ml)

Mission Estella

A time-honoured name for Mission, but made very differently today from when it first appeared a couple of decades ago. For 1992, winemaker Paul Mooney used riesling grapes, a good percentage of which were botrytised.

CURRENT RELEASE 1992 The bouquet is shy and suggests lightness, but on the palate there are some pleasant floral and spicy tones that give the wine broad appeal. Enjoy it with fresh pineapple.

STYLE sweet

QUALITY ▼▼▼▼

VALUE ★★★★

GRAPES riesling

REGION Hawke's Bay

CELLAR ▮ 3

PRICE $8-10 (750 ml)

Montana Late Harvest Riesling

A bit naughty, this one. The wine is clearly labelled as riesling, but in fact it's made from müller-thurgau.

CURRENT RELEASE 1984 When I tasted this vintage last year, I thought it was getting a bit past it. Either it's had a second wind, or there's a bit of bottle variation, because the sample I was sent this year was still quite lively. The wine has a great golden colour and a good dose of spicy honey on the nose, and is still rich and pleasant on the palate. It is beginning to fade, but there's life in there for a good couple of years yet.

STYLE sweet

QUALITY ▼▼▼

VALUE ★★★+

GRAPES müller-thurgau

REGION Marlborough

CELLAR ▮ 2

PRICE $12-14 (375 ml)

Morton Estate Late Harvest Sauvignon Blanc (Black Label)

Morton's John Hancock and Steve Bird have made a couple of dessert wines from sauvignon blanc, and they promise there will be more in the future.

CURRENT RELEASE 1992 The nose is all about dried fruit, and there's a good measure of botrytis's faintly burned character in there as well. The wine tastes wonderfully rich and full, but has a counterbalancing measure of crisp acidity. The back label suggests partnering it with fresh fruit, which sounds like a good idea.

STYLE sweet

QUALITY ▼▼▼▼▼

VALUE ★★★★+

GRAPES sauvignon blanc

REGION Hawke's Bay

CELLAR ▮ 6

PRICE $12 (375 ml)

Ngatarawa Penny Noble Harvest (Riesling)

Winemaker Alwyn Corban named this wine for Penny Glazebrook, the daughter of his partner in the winery business. She must be a very sweet person indeed!
CURRENT RELEASE 1992 Ginger, flowers and a bit of spice start things nicely on the nose, and the taste is equally sensuous. The wine is rich and luscious, but nicely balanced acids mean it stays clean and refreshing. It's great on its own, but if you want an over-the-top experience, partner it with soft blue cheese.

STYLE very sweet
QUALITY ♛♛♛♛♛
VALUE ★★★
GRAPES riesling
REGION Hawke's Bay
CELLAR ▯ 5
PRICE
$27-32 (375 ml)

Ngatarawa Stables Late Harvest Riesling

Alwyn Corban has made some wonderful dessert wines over the years. This is his second-tier wine, but it was still good enough to take a silver medal at the 1992 Air New Zealand Wine Awards.
CURRENT RELEASE 1991 The nose is sweet and spicy, like cinnamon sprinkled over dried fruit. The taste is light, clean and frisky, but still has enough lusciousness to make it a fine companion to a creamy blue cheese.

STYLE sweet
QUALITY ♛♛♛♛
VALUE ★★★
GRAPES riesling
REGION Hawke's Bay
CELLAR ▯ 3
PRICE $11-13 (375 ml)

Penfolds Ne Plus Ultra Late Pick Rhine Riesling

One of the better buys of the dessert wine world, and the good news is there's heaps of it.
CURRENT RELEASE 1989 A bouquet like glazed honey promises good things, and the palate is in no way a disappointment. Luscious, moreish and richly delicious. Partner it with a wedge of strong blue cheese.

STYLE very sweet
QUALITY ♛♛♛♛
VALUE ★★★+
GRAPES riesling
REGION Marlborough
CELLAR ▯ 2
PRICE $12-14 (375 ml)

Robard & Butler As Good as Gold

The unique label, designed by New Zealand/New York artist Billy Apple, has the writing on the inside, so you have to read it through the wine by turning the bottle round.
CURRENT RELEASE 1990 The bouquet is just great — it reeks of dried apricots, ginger and figs. The taste is right up there, too. There's plenty of crispness to balance the sweetness, and a nice dash of spice as well. Partner it with a fresh fruit salad.

STYLE sweet
QUALITY ♀♀♀♀
VALUE ★★★
GRAPES müller-thurgau
REGION Marlborough
CELLAR ▮ 3-4
PRICE $15-18 (375 ml)

Robard & Butler Noble Late Harvest

The 'noble' in the title means the grapes were infected with botrytis — 'noble rot' is an alternative name for this sometimes-beneficial mould.
CURRENT RELEASE 1990 There's plenty of spicy honey on the nose, along with a dash of dried apricots from the botrytis. The wine is sweet but with enough acid to keep things in balance, and finishes cleanly. Try it with a pineapple-based dessert.

STYLE sweet
QUALITY ♀♀♀♀
VALUE ★★★+
GRAPES müller-thurgau
REGION Marlborough
CELLAR ▮ 3
PRICE $14-15 (375 ml)

Rongopai Te Kauwhata Botrytised Riesling

This small Waikato vineyard has made quite a name for itself with sweet wines, attracting the attention of such luminaries as English wine-writer Jancis Robinson.
CURRENT RELEASE 1991 A year ago the bouquet was quite shy. Now, it's busting out all over with honey, muscat and ginger notes. In the mouth the wine is opulent and rich, but good acids keep everything under control.

STYLE sweet
QUALITY ♀♀♀♀♀
VALUE ★★★
GRAPES riesling
REGION Te Kauwhata
CELLAR ▬ 2-6
PRICE $21-25 (375 ml)

Rongopai Te Kauwhata Botrytised Selection

The 'Selection' wine is a blend of two obscure German varieties, scheurebe and würzer.
CURRENT RELEASE 1992 Dried apricots and pears stand out on the nose. The wine is rich and luscious, which is par for the course, but also refreshingly clean.

STYLE sweet

QUALITY ♟♟♟♟

VALUE ★★★

GRAPES scheurebe, würzer

REGION Te Kauwhata

CELLAR ▋ 3

PRICE
$20-25 (375 ml)

Seibel Wines Hawke's Bay White Riesling Late Harvest

Norbert Seibel makes very few dessert wines, yet with his German training, he does them well.
CURRENT RELEASE 1990 Peaches and dried pears form a pleasant introduction in the bouquet. The wine is just sweet enough to be moreish, and nicely controlled, thanks to the refreshingly crisp acids.

STYLE medium-sweet

QUALITY ♟♟♟♟

VALUE ★★★★

GRAPES riesling

REGION Hawke's Bay

CELLAR ▋ 2

PRICE $13 (750 ml)

Seifried Estate Nelson Gewürztraminer Ice Wine

Hermann Seifried and Saralinda MacMillan attempt to duplicate the grape-freezing frosts that spawn genuine German ice wine by snap-freezing the fruit on trays.
CURRENT RELEASE 1991 Using artificial means to achieve results means the wine is a little simpler than its European role model, but it is delightfully fresh, clean and lusciously sweet. The gewürztraminer spiciness suits the treatment well. Try it with caramelised pineapple and French vanilla ice cream.

STYLE very sweet

QUALITY ♟♟♟♟

VALUE ★★★

GRAPES gewürztraminer

REGION Nelson

CELLAR ▋ 2

PRICE
$15-17 (375 ml),
$25-27 (750 ml)

Seifried Estate Nelson Rhine Riesling Beerenauslese-Style

Hermann Seifried uses German terminology to describe his sweet wines. In that country, beerenauslese is one step below the super-sweet trockenbeerenauslese style.

CURRENT RELEASE 1991 Dried apples are the key character in the bouquet, but on the palate the wine is luscious but with enough spicy friskiness to make it refreshing rather than cloying. Great wine for a fruit brulée.

STYLE sweet
QUALITY ♟♟♟♟♟
VALUE ★★★★
GRAPES riesling
REGION Nelson
CELLAR ▯ 6
PRICE $15-17 (375 ml)

Seifried Estate Nelson Riesling Late Harvest

Another medium-sweet model, but showing a lot more class than the simple sauterne (see *Overflow*).
CURRENT RELEASE 1991 The nose is floral and clean, and the same crisp cleanness is much in evidence on the palate. Try it with a semi-soft cheese like gouda.

STYLE medium-sweet
QUALITY ♟♟♟♟
VALUE ★★★+
GRAPES riesling
REGION Nelson
CELLAR ▯ 2
PRICE $14-16 (750 ml)

Selaks Ice Wine

Winemaker Darryl Woolley uses the technique of freezing the water content of his grape juice, then siphoning off the remaining syrup for fermentation. It beats waiting for the grapes to freeze on the vine.
CURRENT RELEASE 1992 The spice is light on the nose and combines with a hint of riesling's floral character. The flavours in the mouth are rich, but also crisp and clean — not easy attributes to achieve with this style.

STYLE sweet
QUALITY ♟♟♟♟
VALUE ★★★★
GRAPES gewürztraminer 60%, riesling 40%
REGION Marlborough and Hawke's Bay
CELLAR ▯ 3
PRICE $9-12 (375 ml)
$16-18 (750 ml)

Te Whare Ra Botrytis Bunch Selection

The words 'bunch selection' mean the bunches were hand-sorted to eliminate any that weren't sufficiently infected with botrytis.

CURRENT RELEASE 1990 Spicy pears and lychees dominate the bouquet of this extravagantly flavoured wine. On the palate it is luscious, as would be expected, but with enough frisky acid to stop it being cloying. Partner it with a well-chilled Golden Queen peach.

STYLE sweet

QUALITY ☗☗☗☗☗

VALUE ★★★

GRAPES sauvignon blanc

REGION Marlborough

CELLAR ▬▬▶ 3-5

PRICE $18 (375ml)

Villa Maria Noble Riesling

Villa Maria has been winning medals with sweet wines as far back as the mid-1970s. This latest version took a gold medal at the 1992 Air New Zealand Wine Awards.
CURRENT RELEASE 1992 The nose is so intense it smells burned, which is not unusual with botrytis-affected wines. In the mouth it is wonderfully opulent but has enough acid to give it a squeaky clean finish. Great with Ferndale Bleu de Montagne cheese.

STYLE sweet

QUALITY ☗☗☗☗☗

VALUE ★★★+

GRAPES riesling

REGION Marlborough

CELLAR ▮ 6

PRICE
$18-20 (375 ml)

Overflow

So many wines were submitted for assessment this year, that we couldn't fit them all into the main text. The 'overflow' wines below are rated for quality and value.

WHITE	QUALITY	VALUE	PRICE
Akarangi Chardonnay 1992	♟♟♟	★★★	$15-17
Clearview Estate Chardonnay 1992	♟♟♟	★★	$21-24
Dry River Chardonnay 1991	♟♟♟♟♟	★★★	$23-26
Endeavour Chardonnay 1991	♟♟♟	★★+	$10-12
Forrest Chardonnay 1992	♟♟♟♟	★★★+	$15-18
Longridge Chardonnay 1992	♟♟♟	★★+	$14-16
Matawhero Chardonnay 1987	♟♟♟	★	$24-26
Montana Estates Ormond Estate Chardonnay 1990	♟♟♟♟♟	★★+	$29-33
Ohinemuri Estate Chardonnay 1989	♟♟♟	★+	$18-21
Penfolds Buchanan Point Chardonnay 1991	♟♟♟	★★+	$11-13
Penfolds Clive River Chardonnay 1991	♟♟♟	★★★	$6-8
Phoenix Chardonnay 1990	♟♟♟	★★+	$13-15
Riverside Chardonnay 1992	♟♟♟♟	★★★★	$15-19
Soljans Hawke's Bay Chardonnay 1991	♟♟♟♟	★★★★	$13-15
Timara Chardonnay Semillon 1991	♟♟♟	★★★	$7-9
West Brook Barrique-Fermented Chardonnay 1990	♟♟♟	★★	$12-14
Chifney Chenin Blanc 1992	♟♟♟	★★+	$14-16

WHITE	QUALITY	VALUE	PRICE
Matua Valley Chenin Blanc/Chardonnay 1991	🍷🍷🍷	★★+	$8-10
Villa Maria Private Bin Chenin Blanc/Chardonnay 1992	🍷🍷🍷	★★★	$10-13
Babich Gewürztraminer 1992	🍷🍷🍷🍷	★★★★★	$9-11
Crab Farm Gewürztraminer Medium 1992	🍷🍷🍷	★★+	$12-14
Longridge Gewürztraminer 1992	🍷🍷🍷	★★+	$12-14
Ohinemuri Estate Gewürztraminer 1990	🍷🍷🍷🍷	★★★+	$13-15
Penfolds Gewürztraminer Winemakers' Reserve 1991	🍷🍷🍷	★★+	$14-16
Revington Vineyard Gewürztraminer 1991	🍷🍷🍷	★★	$13-18
Te Whare Ra Gewürztraminer 1991	🍷🍷🍷🍷	★★★★	$12-13
Whitecliff Gewürztraminer 1992	🍷🍷🍷	★★+	$16-18
Akarangi Dry Müller-Thurgau 1992	🍷🍷🍷	★★+	$9-11
Corbans White Label Marlborough Müller-Thurgau 1992	🍷🍷🍷	★★★	$6-8
Merlen Müller-Thurgau Dry 1992	🍷🍷🍷	★★★	$9-11
Mission Müller-Thurgau 1992	🍷🍷🍷	★★+	$7-9
Penfolds Clive River Müller-Thurgau 1991	🍷🍷🍷	★★★	$6-8
Pleasant Valley Müller-Thurgau	🍷🍷🍷	★★★	$6-8
Totara Müller-Thurgau	🍷🍷🍷	★★+	$8-10
Chard Farm Riesling 1991	🍷🍷🍷🍷	★★★	$15-18
Blue Rock Riesling 1992	🍷🍷	★+	$15-18
Vidal Private Bin Müller-Thurgau 1992	🍷🍷🍷	★★★	$6-8
Akarangi Sauvignon Blanc	🍷🍷🍷	★★+	$11-13
Blue Rock Sauvignon Blanc 1992	🍷🍷🍷🍷	★★★+	$15-19
Brajkovich Sauvignon 1991	🍷🍷🍷	★★★+	$11-15

WHITE	QUALITY	VALUE	PRICE
Clearview Fumé Blanc 1992	🍷🍷🍷	★★	$20-22
Crab Farm Sauvignon Blanc 1992	🍷🍷	★★	$13-16
Forest Flower Collection Sauvignon Blanc 1992	🍷🍷🍷	★★★	$9-11
Goldwater Sauvignon Blanc Fumé 1991	🍷🍷🍷	★★	$17-22
Lawson's Dry Hills Sauvignon Blanc 1992	🍷🍷🍷	★★★	$17-19
Linden Estate Sauvignon Blanc 1992	🍷🍷🍷	★★+	$13-15
Longridge Fumé Blanc 1992	🍷🍷🍷	★★★	$12-14
Matawhero Sauvignon Blanc Semillon 1987	🍷🍷🍷	★★	$16-19
Mission Semillon/Sauvignon Blanc 1992	🍷🍷🍷	★★★	$9-11
Mission Sugar Loaf Semillon 1990	🍷🍷🍷	★★★	$9-11
Ngatarawa Stables Sauvignon Blanc 1991	🍷🍷🍷🍷	★★★+	$13-15
Nobilo Hawke's Bay Sauvignon Blanc 1990	🍷🍷🍷	★★★★	$11-15
Phoenix Sauvignon Blanc 1990	🍷🍷🍷	★★★	$12-14
Rippon Vineyards Fumé Blanc 1991	🍷🍷🍷	★★+	$17-20
Rongopai Te Kauwhata Sauvignon Blanc 1991	🍷🍷	★★	$13-15
St George Estate Sauvignon Blanc 1992	🍷🍷🍷	★★★	$11-13
Wairau River Sauvignon Blanc 1992	🍷🍷🍷	★★★	$17-21
West Brook Henderson Semillon 1990	🍷🍷🍷	★★★	$11-13
Cooks Chasseur Dry	🍷🍷🍷	★★★	$4-5
Cooks Chasseur Medium	🍷🍷🍷	★★★	$4-5
Corbans Liebestraum	🍷🍷	★★★	$4-6
Corbans Cresta Dore	🍷🍷	★★★	$4-6
Corbans St Amand Chablis	🍷🍷🍷	★★★	$5-7

WHITE	QUALITY	VALUE	PRICE
Gibbston Valley Waitiri White 1992	🍷🍷🍷	★★+	$12-14
Lintz Estate Dry White 1991	🍷🍷	★★	$12-14
Matua Valley Chablis	🍷🍷🍷	★★★	$6-10
Mission White Meritage 1991	🍷🍷🍷	★★★	$8-12
Montana Blenheim Dry Chablisse	🍷🍷	★★★	$6-8
Nobilo White Cloud	🍷🍷🍷	★★★	$9-11
Rippon Vineyard Dry White	🍷🍷🍷	★★+	$12-14
St George Estate July Muscat 1992	🍷🍷🍷	★★+	$12-14
Soljans Breidecker 1992	🍷🍷🍷	★★★	$7-9

RED	QUALITY	VALUE	PRICE
Akarangi Cabernet Sauvignon 1991	🍷🍷	★★	$15-18
Babich Cabernet/Merlot 1990	🍷🍷🍷	★★★+	$11-14
Benfield & Delamare Cabernet Sauvignon/ Merlot/Cabernet Franc 1991	🍷🍷🍷🍷🍷	★★★	$28-33
Chifney Cabernet Sauvignon 1991	🍷🍷🍷🍷	★★★	$25-28
Collards Cabernet/Merlot 1991	🍷🍷🍷	★★★	$13-16
Corbans White Label Gisborne Cabernet Sauvignon 1991	🍷🍷🍷	★★★	$9-10
Jackman Ridge Cabernet Sauvignon 1991	🍷🍷🍷	★★+	$10-13
Limeburners Bay Cabernet/Merlot 1990	🍷🍷🍷	★★+	$16-19
Linden Estate Franc/Merlot/Cabernet 1991	🍷🍷🍷	★★★	$13-15
Ohinemuri Estate Cabernet Franc/Merlot 1991	🍷🍷🍷	★★+	$14-16
Penfolds Clive River Cabernet Sauvignon/Pinotage 1991	🍷🍷	★★★	$6-9
Penfolds Cabernet Sauvignon Winemaker's Reserve 1991	🍷🍷🍷	★★★	$15-18

RED cont	QUALITY	VALUE	PRICE
Resolution Cabernet Sauvignon 1991	♉♉♉	★★+	$9-10
St Aubyns Cabernet Sauvignon/Pinotage 1992	♉♉♉	★★+	$8-10
St Nesbit Cabernet Sauvignon & Franc/Merlot 1988	♉♉♉♉♉	★★★+	$22-27
Timara Cabernet Sauvignon/Merlot	♉♉♉	★★★	$7-9
Babich Pinot Noir 1991	♉♉♉	★★★	$10-12
Black Ridge Pinot Noir 1992	♉♉♉	★★	$22-26
Chateau deRedcliffe Pinot Noir 1989	♉♉♉	★★	$13-16
Daniel Le Brun Marlborough Terrace Pinot Noir 1991	♉♉	★★	$15-17
Morton Estate Pinot Noir 1991	♉♉♉	★★+	$15-18
Daniel Schuster Pinot Noir 1991	♉♉♉	★★	$24-27
Seifried Estate Pinot Noir 1992	♉♉	★★+	$13-15
Te Kairanga Pinot Noir 1991	♉♉♉	★+	$25-28
Blue Rock Magenta 1991	♉♉♉♉	★★★	$18-22
Chifney Garden of Eden Red 1991	♉♉♉	★★+	$14-16
Corbans Velutto Rosso	♉♉	★★★	$6-8
deRedcliffe Simply Red 1989	♉♉♉	★★+	$11-14
Fairhall River Claret	♉♉♉	★★+	$6-8
Grove Mill Pinotage 1989	♉♉♉♉♉	★★★★	$16-19
Henderson Valley Estate Pinotage	♉♉♉	★★★	$9-11
Hunters Estate Red 1991	♉♉♉	★★★	$10-14
Yelas Estate Pinotage 1991	♉♉♉	★★+	$11-13
SPARKLING	QUALITY	VALUE	PRICE
Matua Valley 'M' Méthode Champenoise	♉♉♉	★★★+	$17-19

SPARKLING	QUALITY	VALUE	PRICE
Montana Lindauer Méthode Champenoise Sec	🍷🍷🍷	★★★	$10-12
Parker Rosé Brut Méthode Champenoise	🍷🍷🍷	★★+	$18-20
Penfolds Chardon (White)	🍷🍷🍷	★★★	$5-6
Penfolds Chardon (Pink)	🍷🍷🍷	★★★	$5-6
Seifred Estate Chamé Brut	🍷🍷🍷	★★★	$10-12
Seifred Estate Sekt	🍷🍷🍷	★★★	$8-12

ROSÉ	QUALITY	VALUE	PRICE
Corbans Pink Flamingo	🍷🍷🍷	★★★	$6-8
Landfall Pinot Noir Blush 1991	🍷🍷🍷🍷	★★★	$11-13
Lincoln Pinot Noir Blush 1991	🍷🍷🍷	★★★	$8-10
Martinborough Vineyards Pinot Noir Blanc 1991	🍷🍷🍷🍷	★★+	$15-17
Matua Valley Pinot Noir Blanc 1991	🍷🍷🍷🍷	★★★+	$10-12

DESSERT	QUALITY	VALUE	PRICE
Clearview Estate Sea Red 1991	🍷🍷🍷	★★	$25-29
Corbans Montel Sauterne	🍷🍷	★★★	$6-8
Lincoln Auslese Hawke's Bay Rhine Riesling 1992	🍷🍷🍷	★★	$13-15
Limeburners Bay Cabernet Sauvignon Dessert Wine	🍷🍷🍷	★★★	$11-13
Montana Wohnsiedler Sauterne	🍷🍷🍷	★★★	$6-7
Alan Scott Autumn Riesling 1991	🍷🍷🍷🍷	★★★★	$13
Seifred Estate Moutere Sauterne	🍷🍷🍷	★★★	$7-9

Glossary

The handful of technical terms used in the wine descriptions will be found in this section, but also included are explanations for a large number of words we didn't use, but which you may come across in other publications.

Acid   More obvious in white wine than red, acid is the upfront crispness that gives a wine 'zing' in the mouth. Think of it as like biting into a chilled Splendour apple.

Aftertaste   The flavour and taste sensation that lingers in the mouth after the wine has been swallowed. Also referred to as 'finish'.

Alcohol   A by-product of the fermentation process. High-alcohol wines feel warm in the mouth.

Alcohol by volume   The amount of alcohol as a percentage of the contents. The figure is supposed to be printed on every bottle of wine sold in New Zealand, but imports often manage to escape the net.

Aperitif   A drink taken before a meal with the purpose of stimulating the appetite. It should not, therefore, be too heavy.

Aroma   A grapey odour most often detected in young wine. Not the same as *bouquet*.

Aromatic   A quality that makes a wine's flavours seem to jump out of the glass into your nostrils. Most Marlborough sauvignon blancs, for example, have it in abundance.

Astringent   Extremely dry and tannic, causing puckering of the mouth. Can be an indication that the wine will age well.

Auslese   German term, used in New Zealand to describe a sweet dessert wine.

Autolysis   Usually called yeast autolysis, and used to describe the fresh-baked-bread character found in some sparkling wines.

Back-blending   The process of adding unfermented grape juice to finished wine to add viscosity, body and sweetness. Common for New Zealand müller-thurgau.

Balance   Harmony between the wine's various flavour components. Think of it as an orchestra in which no one instrument dominates.

Barnyard   A not-unpleasant character often found in French wines and those that have had a minimum of filtration. Earthy and basic.

Barrel   An oak container in which some wines are stored and aged. Oak's porosity allows just enough air into the wine to help the ageing process, but not so much that it is ruined by *oxidation*.

Barrel fermentation The process of fermenting the infant wine in oak barrels rather than stainless-steel tanks. It can often be detected through a mealy, nutty taste.

Barrique The most common size of small barrel, containing 225 litres. Small barrels give more oak character to the wine because there is more wood in proportion to liquid.

Bead The bubbles in sparkling wine, usually referring to their individual size.

Beerenauslese German term, used occasionally in New Zealand to describe a sweet dessert wine.

Bitterness Desirable in some beer, but not in wine. Usually detected at the back of the tongue, and caused by crushing too many stalks with the grapes, or by bacterial spoilage.

Blend A mixture of two or more grape types in the same bottle.

Body Substance — the opposite of thin and reedy.

Botrytis A mould (*Botrytis cinerea*) that insinuates itself over the surface of each grape and sends probing fingers through the pores to suck out all the water content. Grapes thus infected are not always desirable, but they can add complexity to dry wine and also make the greatest sweet dessert wines in the world. Known as 'edelfaule' or noble rot in Germany, and 'pourriture noble' in France.

Bouquet The jigsaw of interesting and, one hopes, pleasing odours given off by wine. Some come from the grapes, forming part of the *aroma*, but most are created during the winemaking process. Far more important than the taste when it comes to determining quality and origin, but no substitute when it comes to plain enjoyment!

Breathing The process of allowing air into the wine by removing the cork and (sometimes) decanting. To some extent, it compresses the ageing process, and is therefore useful in allowing fiercely tannic young red wines to be enjoyed long before their prime.

Broad A wine that is soft and often flabby.

Brut The lowest level of sweetness in sparkling wine. Only 'brut natur' or similarly labelled wines are drier, containing no sweet components whatever.

Carbonic maceration The technique of fermenting whole, uncrushed bunches of grapes. It makes red wines that are chock-full of flavour when they are young but that fade within a couple of years.

Cassis A flavour often found in cabernet sauvignon, named after a blackcurrant liqueur originally from Dijon, in France.

Chalky A dry, dusty character sometimes found in very young wine.

Cheesey A sour-milk character that suggests carelessness with the wine's *malolactic fermentation*.

Cigar box The smell of wood and tobacco often found in young cabernet sauvignon and merlot wines.

Cloudy Tiny particles suspended in the wine, causing it to lose its sheen. Usually a cause for concern.

Cloying Sweet and out of balance, so that the palate is overpowered by sugar.

Corked Tainted by a faulty cork. Often detected by a smell like old wet sawdust. Corked bottles should always be rejected in restaurants or returned to retail suppliers.

Creamy Smooth and viscous — a textural term usually applied to white wine.

Crisp As refreshing as biting into a chilled, tree-ripened apple. Usually used for white wine.

Cuvée French term for a blend of several varieties.

Depth Richness and generosity of flavour.

Doughnut A wine that starts and finishes well but lacks flavour in the middle.

Dry A wine with no apparent sweetness.

Dull Unexciting. Can be used to describe the colour, the bouquet or the taste.

Dumb Lacking bouquet and, to some extent, taste. May be caused by excessive youth or overchilling.

Dusty A mouth feel caused by the presence of oak components in the wine, particularly obvious in hot-climate reds.

Earthy A loamy, *barnyard* character, often adding character and interest.

Esters Volatile compounds that sometimes occur during maturation. They can be detected by a medicinal character in the bouquet.

Extractive A very tannic wine that has spent considerable time fermenting on the grape skins, extracting maximum flavour. Acceptable if it's not overdone.

Finesse Delicacy and elegance.

Fining The process of floating a substance (classically, beaten egg whites) on top of unfiltered wine to force solid particles to the bottom of the tank or barrel. The wine is then siphoned into another container.

Finish See *aftertaste*.

Firm The opposite of flabby. Wine that seems complete and well controlled in the mouth.

Flabby Lacking acid 'zing'.

Fleshy A grapey character often found in young wines.

Flinty A dry, stony odour like a newly struck flint.

Flowery (floral) Aromatic and highly perfumed.

Fortified Wine strengthened by the addition of brandy or grape spirit, e.g., port and sherry.

Freeze concentration The process of freezing the water content of grape juice to allow the remaining syrup to be pumped off. Used to make sweet wine.

Fresh Full of youthful exuberance.

Furry A tooth-coating sensation caused by tannin.

Garlic A highly undesirable odour that indicates the presence of sorbic acid.

Generic In this country, usually meaning a wine labelled as simply 'New Zealand', rather than after the actual region where the grapes were grown.

Grassy A herbaceous character often found in young sauvignon blanc, particularly from Marlborough.

Grip The feeling that the wine has got hold of the inside of your mouth. The opposite of flabby.

Hard Ungiving, lacking warmth.

Hollow A wine with no middle. See *doughnut*.

Hot A warm sensation in the mouth usually caused by a high alcohol level.

Implicit sweetness The sensation of sweetness in a dry wine, usually caused by glycerol or a high alcohol level, and sometimes simply by very ripe fruit.

Inky Once used to describe a metallic taste caused by contact with iron fittings. Since most iron in wineries has been replaced by stainless steel, the term is used to describe a red wine so dark it is opaque.

Integrated The marriage of wine's various components. See *balance*.

Jammy Obvious, unsubtle. Sometimes found in young red wines.

Late harvest Wine made from grapes left to hang on the vine for days or weeks after the normal harvest time, in which time they shrivel like raisins and concentrate their sugar levels. Used to make sweet wines.

Leathery An earthy aroma often found in merlot.

Lifted Desirable volatility that helps give the wine a distinctive bouquet.

Limpid Very clear and bright. Used to describe the colour.

Long A lingering finish. Sign of a very good wine.

Malic acid The sharp, fruit acid found in grapes. Think of a Granny Smith apple.

Malolactic fermentation An additional fermentation that converts malic (fruit) acids into lactic (milk) acids and consequently softens the wine. Occurs naturally in red wines but often has to be induced in whites. Commonly used in chardonnay and sauvignon blanc for 20 or 30 per cent of the final blend, but a few makers put all white juice through the process.

Meaty Commonly, a wine with considerable body. Occasionally used to describe an unpleasant raw-beef character.

Mercaptans Unpleasant odours variously reminiscent of stale cabbage, burned rubber, garlic or dirty socks.

Méthode Champenoise The process of putting wine through a second fermentation in the actual bottle in which it will eventually be sold. Used to create the world's best sparkling wines.

Mouldy An unpleasant smell that can come from a faulty cork or the use of old barrels.

Mousse The bubbly head on sparkling wine.

Mousey A grubby taste caused by bacterial spoilage.

Mouth feel The feeling in the mouth, such as viscosity, as opposed to the flavour.

Must The mixture of skins, pips and odd leaves and stalks left after the juice has been extracted from the grapes.

Musty A stale odour, caused by a faulty cork or old barrels.

Nose The wine's smell or bouquet.

Nutty A pleasant odour and taste sometimes found in oak-aged white wines.

Oxidation Excessive exposure to air, causing a browned colour and flat taste.

Peppery A flavour usually found in Australian shiraz, but also associated with New Zealand pinotage.

Phenolics Resin-like substances produced by the presence of solids in the fermenting wine.

Preservative Substance, usually sulphur, added to wine in minute quantities to guard against spoilage.

Pressings The mixture of skins and pips left after the weight of grapes has extracted the first ('free run') lot of juice. Sometimes added back to increase the intake of colour and flavour.

Pricked A smell like glue or floor polish. Betrays the undesirable presence of ethyl acetate.

Prickly Slightly effervescent. Often found in very young whites, sometimes by design.

Puncheon A barrel holding 500 litres of wine. Less desirable than a *barrique* because there is a greater wine-to-wood ratio.

Pungent A wine with a glass-leaping bouquet.

Rancio A nutty character often found in old fortified wines.

Residual sugar Unfermented naturally occurring fructose and/or glucose remaining in the wine after fermentation is complete.

Rough Out of balance; unrefined.

Round Smooth, velvety and generous in the mouth.

Rubbery Betrays the presence of *mercaptans*. A fault.

Sappy A stalky character sometimes found in wines made from unripe grapes. Early Marlborough reds often suffered from it.

Sec French for dry, but in the case of Montana's Lindauer sparkler, meaning less dry than the *brut* version.

Soft A wine with a smooth, unctuous finish.

Solera A series of barrels containing wine from various vintages. The newest is topped up from the next in line, and so on until the oldest wine is used. Common for sherry.

Solids Suspended particles of skin and flesh in grape juice. Removed by filtration, cold settling or *fining*.

Spicy Spice-like character, most often associated with gewürztraminer but also found on the finish of some oak-aged white wines.

Stalky Green, bitter character caused by having too many stalks in with the grape juice.

Tannin A character most often associated with wood, but also found in the skins, pips and stalks of grapes. Gives the wine *grip* and helps it age with character.

Tart Suggests a temporary excess of acid; should soften with age.

Toasty A desirable well-done toast character usually caused by using barrels with heavily charred interiors.

Trockenbeerenauslese Used in Germany and occasionally New Zealand to describe super-sweet dessert wine.

Vanillan A vanilla-bean character that suggests the use of oak, often American. French oak is less obvious.

Varietal Wine that strongly reflects the character of the grape variety used to make it.

Vintage The year the grapes for the wine were picked.

Volatile Spoiled by an excess of undesirable components such as acetic and formic acids.

Volatile acidity (VA) See *volatile*.

Wood ageing The process of ageing wine in oak barrels, to add complexity and flavour.

Yeast autolysis See *autolysis*.

New Zealand Wineries

Akarangi Wines
P.O. Box 8539
Havelock North

Alexander Vineyard
PO Box 87
Martinborough

Amberley Estate Vineyards
P.O. Box 81
Amberley

Antipodean Farm
P.O. Box 14-614
Auckland

Aspen Ridge Wines
Waerenga Rd, RD 1
Te Kauwhata

Ata Rangi Vineyard
P.O. Box 43
Martinborough

Awaiti Vineyard
Awaiti South Rd, RD 2
Paeroa

Babich Wines Ltd
Babich Rd
Henderson

Benfield & Delamare
Vineyards
35 New York St
Martinborough

Black Ridge Winery
P.O. Box 54
Alexandra

Bloomfield Vineyards
119 Solway Crescent
P.O. Box 280
Masterton

Blue Rock Vineyard
P.O. Box 55
Martinborough

Brookfield   Vineyards
(1977) Ltd
P.O. Box 7174, Taradale
Hawkes Bay

Brownlie Brothers
6 Franklin Rd
Bayview
Hawkes Bay

Campagna Wines
PO Box 11 308
Auckland

Cedar Wines Ltd
P.O. Box 77
Kumeu

Cellier Le Brun
P.O. Box 33
Renwick
Blenheim

Chard Farm Vineyard
Gibbston, RD 2
Queenstown

Chifney Wines
Huangarua Rd
Martinborough

Clearview Estate
Clifton Rd, RD 2
Hastings

Cloudy Bay Vineyards Ltd
P.O. Box 376
Blenheim

Collard Bros. Ltd
303 Lincoln Rd
Henderson

Conders Bend
23 Birdling Close
Richmond
Nelson

Continental Wines
P.O. Box 6041
Raumanga
Whangarei

Coopers Creek Vineyard
P.O. Box 140
Kumeu

Corbans Wines Ltd
(incorporating Cooks NZ
Wine Co. Ltd,
McWilliams Wines (NZ)
Ltd & Robard & Butler
Ltd)
P.O. Box 21-183
Henderson

Crab Farm Vineyards
125 Main Rd
Bayview

Cross Roads of Hawkes Bay
P.O. Box 1184
Napier

Dartmoor Vineyards Ltd
Trading as Sacred Hill
Winery
Dartmoor Rd, RD 6
Napier

Delegat's Wine Estate Ltd
Hepburn Rd
Henderson

de Redcliffe Estates Ltd
P.O. Box 6306
Auckland

Dry River Wines Ltd
P.O. Box 72
Martinborough

Eskdale Winegrowers Ltd
P.O. Box 77, Bayview
Hawkes Bay

Esk Valley Estate Ltd
P.O. Box 111, Bayview
Napier

Fino Valley Wines Ltd
283 Henderson Valley Rd
Henderson

Forrest Estate
Blicks Rd
Renwick
Blenheim

French Farm Vineyards Ltd
French Farm Valley Rd,
RD 2
Akaroa

Fullers Vineyard
86 Candia Rd
Henderson

Gatehouse Wines Ltd
Jowers Rd, RD 6
West Melton
Christchurch

Gibbston Valley Wines
P.O. Box 489
Queenstown

Giesen Wine Estate Canterbury Ltd
Burnham School Rd, RD 5
Christchurch

Gladstone Vineyard
P.O. Box 2, Gladstone
Wairarapa

Glenmark Wines
RD 3
Amberley

Glover's Vineyard
Gardner Valley Rd
RD 1, Upper Moutere
Nelson

Goldwater Estate
18 Causeway Rd
Putiki Bay
Waiheke Island

Grandview Wines
172A Don Bucks Rd
Henderson 8

Grape Republic Vineyard
Main South Road
Te Horo
Otaki

Grove Mill Wine Co. Ltd
P.O. Box 37
Blenheim

Harvest Wine Company
Bell Road, RD 1
Gisborne

Hawkesbridge Wines &
Estates
PO Box 9
Renwick
Blenheim

Heron's Flight Vineyard
Sharp Road, RD 2
Warkworth

Highfield Estate Ltd
Brookby Rd, RD 2
Blenheim

Holly Lodge Estate Winery
Ltd
PO Box 5008
Wanganui

Hunters Wines (NZ) Ltd
P.O. Box 839
Blenheim

Huthlee Estate Vineyard
Montana Rd, RD 5
Hastings

Jackson Estate Ltd
P.O. Box 30-863
Lower Hutt

Karaka Wineyards
118 Beach Rd
Papakura

Karamea Vineyards
Tuhikaramea Road, RD 10
Frankton

John Kemble Winery Ltd
Aorangi Road, RD 1
Hastings

Kindale Wines
Omaka Valley, RD 2
Blenheim

Kumeu River Wines Ltd
P.O. Box 24
Kumeu

K.V. Wines
Riverhead Rd
Kumeu

Landfall Wines
P.O. Box 162
Manutuke
Gisborne

Langdale Wine Estate
PO Box 13 638
Christchurch

Larcomb Wines
Larcombs Rd, RD 5
Christchurch

Lawson's Dry Hills
Alabama Road, RD 4
Blenheim

Limeburners Bay
112 Hobsonville Rd
Hobsonville

Lincoln Vineyards Ltd
130 Lincoln Rd
Henderson

Linden Estate Ltd
PO Box 177
Martinborough

Lintz Estate Ltd
P.O. Box 177
Martinborough

Lombardi Wines Ltd
P.O. Box 8201
Havelock North

Markovina Vineyards Ltd
P.O. Box 86
Kumeu

Martinborough Vineyard
P.O. Box 85,
Martinborough

Matawhero Wines
P.O. Box 147
Gisborne

Matua Valley Wines Ltd
P.O. Box 100
Kumeu

Mazurans Vineyard
255 Lincoln Rd
Henderson

Merlen Wines
P.O. Box 8, Renwick
Marlborough

Mills Reef Winery Ltd
RD 1
Tauranga

The Millton Vineyard
P.O. Box 66, Manutuke
Gisborne

Mission Trust Board
P.O. Box 7043, Taradale
Hawkes Bay

Misty Valley Wines Ltd
P.O. Box 21-294
Henderson

Montana Wines Ltd
(incorporating Penfolds
Wines)
P.O. Box 18-293
Auckland 6

Morton Estate Winery
RD 2, State Highway 2
Katikati

Moteo Vineyard
RD 3
Napier

Mothers Cellar Ltd
329 Lincoln Rd
Henderson

Mt Riley Vineyard Ltd
PO Box 1243
Gisborne

Muirlea Rise
50 Princess Street
Martinborough

Negoçiants NZ Ltd
Box 4494
Auckland

Neudorf Vineyards
RD 2, Upper Moutere
Nelson

Ngatarawa Wines Ltd
Ngatarawa Rd
RD 5, Hastings

Nobilo Vintners Ltd
Station Rd
Huapai

Ohinemuri Estate
P.O. Box 2
Karangahake

Okahu Estate
P.O. Box 388
Kaitaia

Omihi Hills Vineyard
5 Paulus Terrace
Christchurch

Pacific Vineyards Ltd
90 McLeod Rd
Henderson

Palliser Estate
P.O. Box 110, Kitchener St
Martinborough

Parker Méthode
Champenoise Ltd
P.O. Box 572
Gisborne

C.J. Pask Winery Ltd
P.O. Box 849
Hastings

Pegasus Bay
112 Heaton Street
Merivale
Christchurch

Pelorus Vineyard
Patons Rd, RD, Hope,
Richmond
Nelson

Peninsula Estate
52A Korora Rd, Oneroa
Waiheke Island

Pleasant Valley Wines Ltd
RD 1, Henderson
322 Henderson Valley Rd

Pomona Wines
Pomona Road, RD 1
Upper Moutere
Nelson

Public Vineyards Ltd
132 Bruce McLaren Rd
Henderson

Rippon Vineyard
P.O. Box 175, Wanaka
Central Otago

Riverside Wines
PO Box 2465
Stortford Lodge
Hastings

Robard & Butler Ltd
P.O. Box 21-080
Henderson

Rongopai Wines Ltd
P.O. Box 35
Te Kauwhata

Ruby Bay Wines
Korepo Rd, RD 1
Ruby Bay
Upper Moutere
Nelson

St George Estate
Winery Ltd
P.O. Box 8167
Havelock North

St Helena Wine Estate
P.O. Box 1, Belfast
Christchurch

St Jerome Wines
219 Metcalf Rd
Henderson

St Nesbit Winery
PO Box 2647
Auckland

Sandihurst Wines
23A Snowdon Road
Christchurch

Sapich Bros. Ltd
152 Forest Hill Rd
Henderson

Savidge Estates Ltd
P.O. Box 1247
Gisborne

Alan Scott Wines
Jacksons Rd, RD 3
Blenheim

Seaview Wines
Simpsons Rd
Henderson

Seibel Wines
24 Kakariki Ave
Mt Eden

Seifried Estate
P.O. Box 18
Upper Moutere, 7152
Nelson

Selaks Wines
(Kumeu) Ltd
P.O. Box 34
Kumeu

Sherwood Estate Wines
Weedons Ross Rd, RD 5
Christchurch

Silverstream Vineyard Ltd
Giles Rd, Clarkville, RD 2
Kaiapoi

Solaris Wines
P.O. Box 60-199
Titirangi

Soljan Wines
263 Lincoln Rd
Henderson

Stonecroft Wines
Mere Rd, RD 5
Hastings

Stonyridge Vineyard
P.O. Box 265, Ostend
Waiheke Island

Taramea Wines
Speargrass Flat Rd, RD 1
Queenstown

Te Kairanga Wines
P.O. Box 52
Martinborough

Te Mata Estate Winery
P.O. Box 8335
Havelock North

Te Whare Ra Wines
Anglesea St, Renwick
Blenheim

Torlesse Wines Ltd
P.O. Box 8237
Christchurch

Totara Vineyards SYC Ltd
Main Road, RD 1
Thames

Tutton, Sienko & Hill
Ram Paddock Road
Amberley, RD 2
Christchrch

Vavasour Wines
P.O. Box 72, Seddon
Nelson

Victory Grape Wines
774 Main Rd South, Stoke
Nelson

Vidal of Hawkes Bay
P.O. Box 48
Hastings

Vilagrad Wines
RD
Ohaupo

Villa Maria Estate Ltd
(incorporating Esk Valley
Ltd and Vidals of Hawkes
Bay)
P.O. Box 43-046
Mangere

Vintech Marlborough Ltd
47 Grove Rd
Blenheim

Vodanovich: T.A.
229 Lincoln Rd
Henderson

Voss Estate Vineyards
P.O. Box 78
Martinborough

Waimarama Estate
P.O. Box 8213
Havelock North

Waipara Springs Wine Co.
P.O. Box 17
Waipara
Canterbury

Wairau River Wines
Giffords Rd, RD 3
Blenheim

Waitakere   Vineyard
Kumeu
Waitakere Rd, RD 1
Kumeu

West Brook Winery
P.O. Box 21-443
Henderson

William Hill Vineyard
Dunstan Rd, RD 1
Alexandra

Windy Hill Winery
92 Simpson Rd
Henderson

Wines Polytechnique
(Tairawhiti Polytechnic)
P.O. Box 640
Gisborne

Winslow Estate
81 Dublin Street
Martinborough

Woodhouse Wines Ltd
Trigg Rd, RD 1
Huapai

Acknowledgements

I would like to thank New Zealand's wine companies for their enthusiastic assistance not only with this book, but with the various other projects with which I am involved. Tasting and collecting details on every wine made in New Zealand is a logistical nightmare, and there is no way it could be done without the continued support of the industry.

I am indebted to my fellow wine writers, whose convivial and stimulating company at endless wine-oriented functions makes them all the more pleasurable.

As always, I am grateful to my wife, Shirley, for her honesty and understanding, and her tolerance in living with a man whose every waking moment is, for a couple of months each year, taken up with sniffing, slurping and spitting wine into the kitchen sink.

And finally, my thanks go to the many friends who helped ensure that endless numbers of half-used bottles of wine weren't wasted.